Wartime Sexual Violence Against Men

MEN AND MASCULINITIES IN A TRANSNATIONAL WORLD

Series Editors:
Simona Sharoni (SUNY Plattsburgh) and Henri Myrttinen (International Alert)

In the past two decades, the field of men and masculinities studies has been steadily growing in both breadth and depth. As a result, working with men and masculinities has gained increased interest not only among scholars in the academy but also among policy-makers and practitioners. This is reflected in a steady increase in research on masculinities but also in the growth of the global MenEngage movement. In the political arena, the recent UN Security Council Resolution 2242 on gender, peace and security also specifically mentioned working with men and boys. At the same time, however, critical men and masculinities studies remain under-represented in research and policy debates as well as in academic publications and curricula. The book series aims to advance interdisciplinary/multidisciplinary/transdisciplinary scholarship on men and masculinities

Titles in the Series
Wartime Sexual Violence Against Men: Masculinities and Power in Conflict Zones
Élise Féron

Wartime Sexual Violence Against Men

Masculinities and Power in Conflict Zones

Élise Féron

ROWMAN &
LITTLEFIELD
───── INTERNATIONAL
Lanham • Boulder • New York • London

Parts of this book build upon previously published work. I am grateful to the *European Review of International Studies* (Budrich) and to Springer for permission to reproduce parts of the following publications:

Féron, Élise. "Wartime Sexual Violence Against Men: Why So Oblivious?" *European Review of International Studies* 4, no. 1 (2017): 60–74.
Féron, Élise. "Suffering in Silence? The Silencing of Sexual Violence Against Men in War Torn Countries." In *World Suffering and Quality of Life*, edited by Ron Anderson, 31–44. New York: Springer, 2015.
Féron, Élise. "Support Programs for Male Survivors of Conflict-Related Sexual Violence." In *Alleviating World Suffering, The Challenge of Negative Quality of Life*, edited by Ron Anderson, 339–47. New York: Springer, 2017.

Published by Rowman & Littlefield International Ltd
6 Tinworth Street, London SE11 5AL, United Kingdom
www.rowmaninternational.com

Rowman & Littlefield International Ltd.is an affiliate of Rowman & Littlefield
4501 Forbes Boulevard, Suite 200, Lanham, Maryland 20706, USA
With additional offices in Boulder, New York, Toronto (Canada), and Plymouth (UK)
www.rowman.com

Copyright © 2018, Élise Féron

All rights reserved. No part of this book may be reproduced in any form or by any electronic or mechanical means, including information storage and retrieval systems, without written permission from the publisher, except by a reviewer who may quote passages in a review.

British Library Cataloguing in Publication Data
A catalogue record for this book is available from the British Library

ISBN: HB 978-1-7866-0929-8
       PB: 978-1-7866-0930-4

Library of Congress Cataloging-in-Publication Data
ISBN 978-1-78660-929-8 (cloth : alk. paper)
ISBN 978-1-78660-930-4 (paperback : alk. paper)
ISBN 978-1-78660-931-1 (electronic)

∞™ The paper used in this publication meets the minimum requirements of American National Standard for Information Sciences—Permanence of Paper for Printed Library Materials, ANSI/NISO Z39.48-1992.

Printed in the United States of America

Contents

Acknowledgements		vii
Introduction		1
1	Conflict-Related Sexual Violence Against Men: An Overview	17
2	Making Sense of Wartime Sexual Violence Against Men	35
3	Perpetrators and Bystanders	61
4	Surviving Wartime Sexual Violence	91
5	The Elusiveness of Narratives on Wartime Sexual Violence Against Men	115
6	Conceptualizing and Implementing Care and Support Programs for Male Survivors	131
7	Prosecuting Wartime Sexual Violence Against Men	153
Conclusion		171
Notes		177
Bibliography		183
Index		201
About the Author		209

Acknowledgements

I am forever indebted to those in Eastern DRC, Burundi, Rwanda, and Northern Ireland who agreed to share their stories with me, however painful and daunting. I am also grateful to all my colleagues and MA students in the Great Lakes region of Africa who encouraged me to write this book and who helped me to identify and meet relevant interlocutors for this research. All mistakes or misinterpretations remain my own, and I apologize if I have misrepresented or misinterpreted anything that I witnessed or was told.

A heartfelt thank you goes to Dr. Emanuela Mangiarotti for having read and commented on an earlier version of the manuscript and for the numerous stimulating discussions we have had, many of which are reflected in this book.

My sincere thanks also go to my colleagues at the Tampere Peace Research Institute in Finland, who have been highly supportive of this research.

Writing this book would have been impossible without my friends' encouragement, and in particular without Marie-Cécile's constant support.

May the road rise to meet you.

Introduction

Scholarship has long established the multiple intersections between gender and conflicts, and recognizes gender as a fundamental dimension of politico-cultural mobilization in nationalist politics, conflict and war (Byrne 1996; Cockburn 2004b; Giles and Hyndman 2004; Mayer 2000; Nagel 1998). Literature has, for instance, explored how gender and ethnicity are used in narratives and political discourses, how gender roles, militarism and war are tightly interrelated, how conflict is likely to have a different impact on women and on men, and how the meanings of conflict and security might diverge for women and men. One particularly interesting and fruitful line of inquiry explores how masculinities and femininities are constructed in times of conflict and war, and how conflict actors aspire to build a masculine Self by disempowering/feminizing a threatening Other such that a new, strong masculinity is affirmed (Weeks 1985, 190). So, as the gender hierarchy becomes a signifier of a domination/subordination paradigm, male and female spheres of action and their mutual relations inform conflicts between political, social or cultural communities. Such analysis is particularly relevant for understanding how conflict-related sexual violence participates in enforcing relations of power, weaving together gender with other institutionalized dimensions of social power, for instance, nationalism, religious identity, caste, ethnicity, sexuality and politics.

Yet, despite a widespread recognition of the relational and intersectional character of gender, much of the existing literature has shown a tendency to treat gender as a women's issue, especially when it comes to wartime sexual violence. It is, however, increasingly difficult to ignore the fact that wartime sexual violence targets men too, a fact that a few researchers and NGOs have been describing and analyzing since the mid-1990s, if not in a systematic fashion. As explained by Don Sabo, "Whereas researchers and public health advocates began to recognize the sexual victimization of women in Western countries during the late 1960s, it was not until the latter 1990s that the sexual abuse of men began to receive systematic scrutiny from human service professionals and gender researchers" (2005, 338). In the wake of research on sexual torture of male prisoners during civil wars in Chile, El Salvador or Greece, reports initially focused on the suffering of women have begun to unveil how widespread sexual violence against boys and men in military settings and conflict zones is, for instance, in regions like Eastern Democratic Republic of Congo (DRC) (Johnson et al. 2010), and that it has been a constant feature of most conflicts and wars, though most of the time silenced by political and military authorities, if not by victims themselves (Nizich 1994; Schwartz 1994; Carlson 1997; Oosterhoff et al. 2004; Carpenter 2006; Sivakumaran 2007). These publications have begun to shed light on the extent, features and consequences of this phenomenon, exploring the destructive power of such violence on individuals, but also on communities as a whole. It has, for instance, been shown that wartime sexual violence against men and boys is, like that committed against girls and women, mostly perpetrated by men in arms, belonging either to armed groups or to conventional armies. The combination of rape and sexual mutilation has also been described as the most prevalent form of sexual violence against men, especially in detention, alongside other forms of torture (Carpenter 2006, 94). Further, the public character of this violence, often inflicted in front of an audience, has been pointed at, even if that publicity never guarantees any kind of open debate afterwards, such as shown by Oosterhoff et al. in the case of Croatia (2004, 68).

To this date, however, monographs or articles addressing wartime sexual violence in general rarely dedicate more than a paragraph or a section to wartime sexual violence against men, and never mainstream it in the analysis (see, for instance, Eriksson Baaz and Stern 2013; Heineman 2011; Leatherman 2011; Meger 2016). As a review of policy-oriented as well as academic publications quickly reveals, research on sexual violence during conflicts focuses mainly on girls and women, to the extent that "rape as a weapon of war"[1] has almost become synonymous with sexual violence against girls and women during conflicts. Without a doubt, women make up the majority of victims of such types of violence. However, as we will see, there is good empirical evidence that in some settings like in Eastern DRC, around a third of all conflict-related sexual violence victims are male. Such percentages are hardly anecdotal, so why such an obliviousness? Even the media, with few exceptions, tend to treat wartime sexual violence and rape of women as synonymous, and ignore or gloss over male survivors, as Zarkov (2001) and Houge (2008) have shown in the case of the conflicts in former Yugoslavia. Many factors account for this silence, in particular the fact that systematic or detailed empirical evidence on wartime sexual violence against men is still hard to come by, mostly because more stress is usually put on other types of violence affecting civilian and combatant men, such as killing, maiming or imprisonment. And even if war historians have long been well aware of the practice, low levels of reporting on the ground mean that there is still no way to know exactly if this phenomenon is declining, stable or on the rise.

WHY WE NEED TO PAY ATTENTION TO WARTIME SEXUAL VIOLENCE AGAINST MEN

In the scholarship of gender and conflicts, the failure to systematically address and analyse wartime sexual violence against men eschews the relation between gender norms, sexual violence and the wider social order, and has important theoretical and practical implications. The tendency to associate victims of sexual violence exclusively with women essentializes women as victims and as vulnerable persons in need of protection. In parallel, it participates in the maintenance of stereotypes about men's invulnerability and strength, and reinforces the essentialist equation that is often made between men, masculinity and violence, at the expense of other models of masculinity. In other words, far from helping to improve women's situation, the silencing of male sexual victimization is highly detrimental to feminists' objectives, because it reinforces the link between men, masculinity, power and invulnerability that is at the very core of patriarchal discourses: "Perceiving men only and always as offender and never as victims of rape and other forms of sexual violence is a very specific, gendered narrative of war. In that narrative, dominant notions of masculinity merge with norms of heterosexuality and definitions of ethnicity and ultimately designate who can or cannot be named a victim of sexual violence" (Zarkov 2001, 69).

In discourses about wartime (sexual) violence, gender-based violence, trauma and vulnerability are feminized, paradoxically resulting in a heightened vulnerability of women, and in a reluctance on the part of male survivors to seek physical and mental health help. Such representations also affect our capacity to see and include survivors of sexual violence who do not fit the stereotype of the helpless woman victim. Yet if, as argued by Detraz (2012, 11), "feminist security studies concentrate on the ways world politics can contribute to the insecurity of individuals, especially individuals who are marginalized and disempowered", then specific attention should also be paid to wartime sexual violence against men. Failing to do so results in a dearth of information, and in incomplete data and analyses on wartime sexual violence, which reinforce its impact on survivors, the community and the wider social order. In brief, our politics of analysis and intervention with regard to wartime sexual violence seem imbued with the very gendered ideology that makes it a widespread phenomenon in conflicts and wars.

Further, these myopic representations of wartime sexual violence impede our understanding of the phenomenon itself, in particular with regard to its articulation with wider societal power relations. As advocated by Vojdik (2014, 924), "the growing recognition of the sexual violation of men during war provides the opportunity to broaden our understanding of the relationship between sexual violence, constructions of gender, and the negotiation of power during armed conflict". Overlooking male sexual victimization leads to analyses of sexual violence as directed against women because of their gender, inadvertently masking other dimensions of power that might also come into play, such as social, economic, ethnic, caste or political positioning, to quote but a few. If (wartime) sexual violence is indeed, as generations of feminists have argued, first and foremost about power, it is not only the gender positioning of the victim that explains that s/he is targeted, but also the intersection of various structures of super/subordination, such as ethnicity, race, socioeconomic relations, and so on. That women are more likely than men to be located at the intersection of several of these structures of subordination undoubtedly plays a role in the fact that they are also much more likely to be victims of sexual violence.

, therefore, broadening the analysis by accounting for wartime sexual violence against men is a way to unveil the underlying structures of power that play a key role in conflict and violence patterns—as well as in societal relations during peace time., for instance, it is likely to help us to shed light on endogamic types of structural and physical violence, as well as on internal power struggles, which are often obscured by broader divisions between conflict factions. Temporarily shifting the gaze away from female sexual victimization paradoxically allows us to better understand not only wartime sexual violence as a whole, but also other types of violence perpetrated during conflicts, and to which it is tightly connected. It also enhances our understanding of how the specific social, gender, political, economic and so on positioning of individuals has an impact on the types of violence that they are more likely to be victims of, and what resources they might convey to cope with it. In short, paying more attention to conflict-related male sexual victimization dramatically increases our awareness of conflict patterns, and our ability to come up with appropriate responses.

WARTIME SEXUAL VIOLENCE AGAINST MEN, MASCULINITIES AND THE SOCIAL ORDER

The analysis of wartime sexual violence against men developed in this book is located at the intersection of feminist and masculinity studies, and attempts to "bridge the gap" (Beasley 2013) between postmodern and poststructuralist feminism, and modern and structuralist masculinities studies. Building on Judith Butler's concept of gender performativity and on the debate around masculinities and especially around Raewyn Connell's concept of hegemonic masculinity, I show that wartime sexual violence against men can be understood as a phenomenon embedded in the gendered ideology of conflict and the wider social order. According to Butler, gender is a performative dimension of social differences based on established and socially recognized norms of super/subordination (Butler 1990). Gender is not a quality of the female body, as many approaches to sexual violence in conflict seem to suggest. Instead, bodies become gendered through the repetition of acts and practices that relate to known social norms. In Butler's words, "Gender is an identity tenuously constituted in time, instituted in an exterior space through a stylized repetition of acts" (Butler 1990, 140–41).

If gender has often been conflated with women, so have masculinity and men. Yet, Connell and Messerschmidt state that "masculinities are configurations of practice that are accomplished in social action and, therefore, can differ according to the gender relations in a particular social setting" (Connell and Messerschmidt 2005, 837). Thus, masculinities are not attached to the male body but are played out in the process of configuring the social positioning of individuals and groups in the ensuing power structure. This fluidity allows models of masculinity to adapt to social tensions, stabilizing patriarchal power or reconstituting it in new conditions. Gender has its own historicity so that forms of masculinity and femininity are negotiated in the tensions over relations of power in society. They are subject to change and to constant adaptation, in connection to the structuring of the social hierarchy. Thus, gender differentiations reflect a relation of masculinity/femininity whereby "feminizing processes simultaneously produce and justify profound inequalities" as they are grounded on naturalized hierarchies of dominance and subordination (Hawkesworth 2006, 132). This means that men as well as communities can be feminized by attacking the foundations of their masculinity.

Within this frame of analysis, this book proposes to explore how wartime sexual violence, and in particular wartime sexual violence against men, impacts on gender identities, and on power relations, between individuals, but also between and within the groups they belong to. Because of the association that is usually made between masculinity and power, and between femininity and vulnerability, sexual violence, as a way to subjugate and feminize the victim while empowering the perpetrator, has a strong impact on intersecting gender, ethnic, racial, political and socio-economic hierarchies. Through sexual violence, the victim is simultaneously feminized and subjugated; in parallel, the perpetrator's masculinization and domination are enforced. And because gendered hierarchies play a central ordering and disciplining function in societies, sexual violence against both men and women has notable consequences for the relative positioning of individuals, but also of groups, be they defined in ethnic, cultural, religious, socio-economic or political terms. In other words, the perpetration of wartime sexual violence entails both individual and collective consequences, and is thereby likely to heavily influence, and be influenced by, power relations between conflict actors.

Analyzing the relation between wartime sexual violence, gender identity, and social positioning, therefore, demands to deconstruct common understandings of masculinity, which associate it to strength and physical invulnerability, and which displace that vulnerability into the feminine (Thomas 2002, 62–63). It requires to explore how male survivors try to cope with sexual victimization, how it affects their gender identity as well as the perpetrator's and how communities to which survivors belong react to this attack on those who are traditionally supposed to embody collective strength. The meanings attached to male sexual victimization, be it by survivors, by perpetrators or by the wider community, are paramount for understanding its impact on societal relations of power, and on conflict patterns. In particular, examining the motivations of perpetrators, and the role played by militarized models of masculinity, sheds light on how some individuals can use sexual violence, among other types of violence and coercion, in order to increase their own power over other individuals, armed groups or communities. What is at stake in the perpetration of wartime sexual violence (against men) is, therefore, not just the enactment of powerful and highly violent models of masculinity but also the enforcement or maintenance of a control over economic, social, sexual and political resources.

The book is thus built around the idea that through wartime sexual violence, and wartime sexual violence against men in particular, social hierarchies are imposed, maintained or contested. It explores how conflict-related sexual violence against men builds on the significance of gender norms and values in relation to other dimensions of social, economic, cultural and political power and thereby tries to strengthen or challenge the existing order. This theoretical standpoint allows to understand variations in intensity and types of sexual violence against men in extremely diverse settings, from ethnic conflicts to "anti-terrorism", counter-insurgencies and to international interventions. In that perspective, it obviously requires a careful examination of the context, since gender models, as well as wider societal norms that also play a role in sexual violence, only make sense in specific historical, political and cultural contexts.

From an empirical standpoint, this book builds upon the definition of sexual violence provided by the World Health Organization: "Sexual violence is defined as: any sexual act, attempt to obtain a sexual act, unwanted sexual comments or advances, or acts to traffic, or otherwise directed, against a person's sexuality using coercion, by any person regardless of their relationship to the victim, in any setting" (Krug et al. 2002, 149). It is important to underscore that for the purposes of this book, sexual violence includes, but is not limited to, rape, sexual torture, sexual mutilation, sexual humiliation and sexual slavery, committed by armed actors on- or off-duty, but also sometimes by non-combatant strangers. Instances of domestic/intimate partner sexual violence have been considered and included when survivors or perpetrators connected them to the wider conflict context. Adopting a wide enough definition of sexual violence is particularly important because, as we will see, during conflicts men and boys are less likely than women and girls to be raped, but are more likely to be victims, for instance, of beatings or other forms of torture of the genitals. So in contrast with existing monographs on wartime sexual violence that focus on female sexual victimization and thus mostly on cases of rape and sexual slavery, the data collected for this book includes a broad range of acts, from rape and sexual slavery, to torture of the genitals and to mutilation and castration, among many others.

It is also worth mentioning that throughout this book, the expression "sexual violence against men" will be used, rather than "sexual violence against men and boys". This is not to imply that boys are not targeted for wartime sexual violence, as many such cases have been documented, especially against male child soldiers who are likely to be used as sex slaves by older combatants (Betancourt et al. 2011) and in asylum countries (UNHCR 2017b). However, most evidenced cases of male sexual brutalization in conflict areas refer first and foremost to adult civilians and combatants, as well as to adolescent, rather than pre-adolescent boys (UN 2013, 14–15), a trend that clearly sets apart sexual violence against males in conflict zones from cases of sexual abuse committed in peacetime[2]. In other words, this type of violence is primarily exerted on individuals who are considered, socially, culturally and sexually, as grown men, even though they might not have reached adulthood in the Western legal sense. The choice to refer to "sexual violence against men" thus does not mean to exclude boys, but to underscore the intended meaning of wartime sexual violence against males, that is to attack those who are old enough to embody masculinity and to hold cultural, social, economic, sexual, political and military power.

RESEARCHING WARTIME SEXUAL VIOLENCE AGAINST MEN

Exploring wartime sexual violence against men entails disrupting conventional frames of understanding of wartime (sexual) violence. It requires questioning established narratives that posit women and girls if not as the only victims of sexual violence, at least as making up the "immense majority" of victims, and that often designate men as perpetrators by default. It also demands to critically review common assumptions about combatants, as ruthless, powerful and seemingly invulnerable men preying on what Cynthia Enloe calls defenceless women and children.

Nobody who has set foot in Eastern DRC during the past decade can have missed the plethora of international and local NGOs and programs whose main focus is to provide support to female victims of rape and of other types of sexual violence. Cities like Bukavu in Southern Kivu or Goma in Northern Kivu, host hundreds of such initiatives. And indeed, when I first visited places like the Panzi hospital in Bukavu, which specializes in the treatment of survivors of sexual violence, I was overwhelmed by the number of women and sometimes very young girls admitted every day, by their physical and psychological suffering, but also by their sometimes incredible resilience and strength of will. Some of the (male and female) combatants' stories I had started collecting around the same time, many of which included gruesome episodes of rape and sexual torture, only confirmed that sexual violence has been a crucial characteristic of conflicts in the Great Lakes region and not just one of their side-effects. But as some of the (mostly female) combatants I spoke with started to draw my attention to the fact that men too were targeted by sexual violence, I began to wonder why so few humanitarian organizations or policy-makers, not to mention academics, seemed to be interested in the fate of male survivors of sexual violence, in the Great Lakes region of Africa or in other conflict settings.

I decided at that time to begin what would prove to be a sometimes painfully slow and complicated work for compiling existing empirical information on conflict-related sexual violence against men in various conflict settings, and for gathering male survivors' and perpetrators' stories, as well as others' testimonies, such as medical and humanitarian staff. This book builds on such empirical data, collected mostly in the Great Lakes region of Africa, where I have been spending between three weeks and a month per year between 2009 and 2014. More specifically, I have collected data in the North and South Kivu provinces of the DRC, which appear to be one of the regions in the world where (conflict-related) sexual violence against both males and females is the most widespread. I have also conducted interviews and field observation in Burundi (mostly in the provinces of Bujumbura Mairie and Bubanza) where the use of sexual violence is said to have been one of the main features of the conflict that tore the country apart between 1993 and 2005. I have also collected data in Rwanda, and spoke with Rwandan refugees settled elsewhere, on the issue of sexual violence during the 1994 genocide. The choice to focus a large part of the process of data collection on the Great Lakes region of Africa reflects the role the Congo and the rest of the region play in structuring and framing our current understanding of sexual violence in conflict zones, just like Bosnia-Herzegovina did in the 1990s. Named "rape capital of the world"[3], the Congo and more specifically the wars raging in its Eastern provinces, indeed often convey images of war savagery and of human rights abuses. But the perpetration of sexual violence during conflicts is certainly not limited to that region of the world, and the use of sexual torture against male prisoners has, for instance, been already documented in very different settings, as the well-known cases of Guantánamo and Abu Ghraib illustrate. As I reflected that the type of conflict setting was likely to heavily influence the characteristics of sexual violence that could be observed, the idea of using data collected during interviews that I had also been conducting since 2005 with (former) male members of paramilitary groups in Belfast and in (London)Derry took hold. The use of sexual torture in Northern Ireland, by members of security forces as well as by paramilitary groups, has been if not common, at least recurrent throughout the period called "the Troubles", which spanned from the late 1960s to the signing of the Belfast/Good Friday Peace Agreement in 1998. Unsurprisingly, most of the Northern Irish combatants I have met, many of whom had been imprisoned at some point in their lives, had stories of sexual abuse to share too. I have completed this process of empirical data collection by interviewing medical staff, and in particular mental health professionals, specialized in providing support to asylum seekers and refugees from conflict zones recently settled in Europe. All of them have had to deal on a regular basis with male refugees who have been sexually tortured in their countries of origin, in neighboring countries or in transit countries, notably in Syria, Iraq and Libya.

I do not claim that the cases covered in this book are perfectly representative of all instances of wartime sexual violence against men. Rather, my purpose is to use them to initiate a reflection on what triggers that type of violence, on what its effects on survivors are, on how to support them and on why such violence has so far remained largely neglected in both international discourses and policies. Overall, and though all interviews are quoted in this book, my data on conflict-related sexual violence against men includes more than eighty in-depth, semi-structured as well as life-history interviews with mostly male, but also a few female combatants (former and still active) in Northern Ireland, Burundi and the DRC, with refugees (both male and female) in Burundi and the DRC, and around thirty semi-structured interviews with various local NGO leaders, doctors, surgeons and psychiatrists in the Great Lakes region of Africa as well as in Europe. Some representatives of international organizations have also been interviewed[4]. In addition, this book builds on existing data available on a series of cases of conflict where NGOs and academics have documented episodes of sexual violence against men, such as Sri Lanka, Bosnia-Herzegovina, Croatia, Uganda and El Salvador, as well as some others on which evidence exists but is more scattered, like Afghanistan, Syria and Sudan.

Collecting empirical data on the topic of wartime sexual violence is far from easy. Survivors will rather talk about suffering inflicted upon others than upon themselves, and of course it is paramount to avoid re-traumatizing them (Ford et al. 2009, 5). Similarly, perpetrators seldom acknowledge their direct participation and responsibility in these acts. Both perpetrators and survivors frequently use metaphors to speak about sexual violence, which is a good indication of the weight of the stigma surrounding these acts, but which also represents an obvious challenge when analysing interviews. Considering these obstacles, I decided against the idea of conducting interviews that would primarily focus on sexual violence and opted instead for in-depth interviews on the issue of everyday violence faced, perpetrated or witnessed by my research participants. I assumed that the topic of sexual violence would probably often come up even if I did not mention it myself—which almost always proved true. The interviews thus often took the form of open conversations about experiences of conflict and of violence, rather than of well-structured interactions. I took care during each interview to explain and discuss with my research participants the general purposes of my research project, as well as the potential risks that they ran by participating, such as the risk of being identified with one conflict party or the other[5]. I also informed the people I spoke with about the fact that their anonymity would be preserved and about the notes I intended to take during the process, and I of course underscored the fact that they had the possibility to withdraw at any time if they so wished (Hugman, Pittaway and Bartolomei 2011). I do not claim that my being a white, Western and female researcher puts me in a good position to interpret and understand what I have seen, witnessed and been told. I am well aware of the risk of misunderstanding and misinterpretation carried by conducting research on a phenomenon taking place in a frame of reference that I cannot fully comprehend, despite being reasonably familiar with both the Great Lakes region of Africa and Northern Ireland, where I have been conducting fieldwork for many years. I am also aware that by choosing to adopt a "narrative ethnographic" approach (Björkdahl and Mannergren Selimovic 2018, 43), I will "inevitably take part in breaking as well as making and maintaining silences and voids" (ibid., 46). By multiplying the sources of information, and by conducting my research over a rather long period of time, I hope to have limited these shortcomings.

I primarily discussed with current and former male combatants, and spoke with them about their experiences of everyday violence in the bush, or in detention. I also collected testimonies of male and female refugees and displaced persons about the reasons that had led them to flee their region of origin, and about the types of violence they had experienced in their region of origin, during their flight and in their current place of residence. In many cases, especially during interviews conducted in the Great Lakes region of Africa, the issue of war rapes (against women) came up, and that gave me the opportunity to ask questions about potential male victims, as well as about other potential forms of sexual violence against men. This was a way for me to try to minimize as much as possible the risk of re-traumatizing my research participants by asking questions that might have sounded intrusive or even offensive, especially in a region where speaking about sex is particularly taboo (Hearn, Andersson and Cowburn 2007). A few of the people I spoke with mentioned episodes of wartime male sexual victimization they had witnessed, took part in or been victims of. Many did not, and in that case I did not push the matter. It is thus very difficult for me to have a precise idea of the proportion of my initial "sample" who has indeed been victim—or perpetrator—of such a type of violence; however, I do not consider this a problem, since my research belongs unambiguously to the qualitative realm, and its objective is to unveil and explain processes and patterns rather than to come up with figures, which a few others have begun to gather (see in particular Johnson et al. 2010).

In the Great Lakes region, the interviews were conducted in French or in English, as well as in local languages as determined by the participants' requests, with the assistance of a Burundian or a Congolese interpreter[6]. While the presence of an interpreter might have, at times, disrupted the interview process, I also believe that it has facilitated exchanges, especially when discussing local usages or contexts. In Northern Ireland and in the rest of Europe, the interviews were conducted in English. The interviews were always held in places chosen by my research participants, and where they felt comfortable to speak. Quite obviously, I have anonymized my data, and some dates/places mentioned in this book have been changed in order to protect the people I spoke to. At my research participants' request, I have almost never recorded the interviews, and instead used a notebook.

Much could be said about my position as a white, Western and female researcher gathering data on such an issue in one of the most unstable regions of Africa. Some local researchers have already told me that, because I am a M'zungu (a Swahili word meaning "someone with white skin"), local people were a lot more likely to speak to me, in the hope either of getting some money in return, or of having their situation somehow improved as a consequence of my research. Other Western researchers working in Africa have made similar observations, and this seems particularly true of male survivors (IRIN 2011). While I made sure to explain to the people I spoke to that my research was unlikely to have an immediate impact on their lives, and though I did not offer them any financial compensation, this might partly explain why some male survivors, and a few perpetrators too, were willing to talk to me. It was never an easy and swift process though, since most survivors of (wartime) sexual violence, male and female, experience difficulties with talking about what happened to them, and since perpetrators are usually more than reluctant to acknowledge their own responsibility in these acts. It is not uncommon for such stories to emerge years or sometimes decades after the event took place. My local anchorage in the region, as a co-director since 2009 of a Master Program in Gender Studies at the Université Lumière of Bujumbura in Burundi, undoubtedly played a role too, since it helped me to get to meet the relevant local, national and regional actors, and to gain their trust. I am, however, well aware of the very real possibility that some of my research participants were too traumatized, too intimidated, too mistrustful or too scared, to disclose their stories, and that those who did, did it perhaps partially, and chose not to reveal some important factors or details.

Taboos surrounding the issue of wartime sexual violence against men are not the only obstacle to the collection of empirical data, though. Many people, including professionals in the field of gender, or in the medical field, seem to be surprisingly unaware or oblivious of the problem. I have found, for instance, while trying to gather testimonies of local doctors or of local medical personnel in the Great Lakes region of Africa, that many confused male-on-male rape and even other types of male sexual victimization with homosexuality. That was not the case of course in some highly specialized places such as the Panzi Hospital in South Kivu, well known for its expertise in dealing with the consequences of sexual violence, especially obstetric fistula. Public awareness on these issues seems to be a bit higher in the DRC than in the rest of the sub-region (though still limited to hospitals and some specialized NGOs), but this is not a real surprise since over the past few years the issue has been brought up in the DRC by some international NGOs such as Médecins Sans Frontières. In Rwanda, because of the numerous trials and cases involving sexual violence that have been examined by the traditional tribunals, or *gacaca*, there is a growing awareness not only of the role played by women in violence (a fact that used to be taboo too) but also of the sexual violence perpetrated during the genocide on men, by both men and women. In Burundi, even those with a good awareness on issues pertaining to gender-based violence seemed to be mostly unaware of the issue, and most people I spoke to expressed surprise and dismay when I mentioned the matter and the cases or figures I had come across. This lack of awareness seems to be linked to the taboo existing in Burundi around homosexuality, as well as to its penalization[7]. Collecting information in Europe has been far easier, as all my informants, be they (former) members of paramilitary groups in Northern Ireland, or humanitarian and medical staff in Northern Europe, were well aware of the existence of wartime sexual violence against men. If the subject remains somehow taboo among non-medical staff, most agreed on the fact that it has, so far, received insufficient medical, policy and academic attention, and were willing to share their experiences with me.

Needless to say, researching wartime sexual violence against men hasn't been a smooth process for me either. Dealing with negative reactions, from open disgust—who, in his or her right mind, could possibly want to study such a gruesome topic?—to accusations of undermining feminist work, has been the least complicated. But collecting survivors', perpetrators' and bystanders' stories has brought its fair share of nightmares, anxiety and distress—especially when coming back from the field—which were also fed by my own doubts about using these very personal and intimate stories in order to write a book. I have sometimes had the feeling of being a voyeur and of profiting from the trust that my interviewees and local contacts, some of whom have become friends, have put in me. How to "reciprocate their generosity"? (Wood 2006, 382) I am deeply conscious of the power relations entailed in my work, from how I have selected my research participants, to interactions during interviews, to the fact that I am the one who has determined what is important in the stories that I have collected, and how to interpret them (Dauphinée 2007, 53). How can I speak "for" the victims, and, for that matter, "for" the perpetrators? How can I accurately convey their stories, safely back in the comfort of my everyday Western academic life? I am still unsure about what answer(s) to give to these questions. In the chapters that follow I have tried to accurately transcribe the diversity in their testimonies, and to convey the irreducible complexity of their journeys, emotions and choices. I hope that by choosing to focus on their truly gruesome experiences, I have not entirely obliterated the courage and resilience that often seeped through their stories.

PRESENTATION OF THE BOOK OUTLINE

The approach to wartime sexual violence against men developed in this book proposes to understand wartime sexual violence as a gendered performance that uses patriarchal and heterosexual norms in order to enforce or enact a new power order. The book begins by an examination of the available empirical evidence on wartime sexual violence against men, which has been collected by conflict scholars, historians but also medical doctors or humanitarian staff. Various patterns and recurrences in types and circumstances in which sexual violence against men is perpetrated are highlighted. The book then describes the theoretical foundations of the study, which are applied to different contexts and configurations of wartime sexual violence against men, from ethnic conflicts to insurgencies and to international interventions. The core empirical evidence collected during fieldwork is subsequently presented and analysed in two chapters dealing respectively with perpetrators and with survivors of wartime sexual violence against men. The book proceeds to presenting the context in which this type of violence can be understood, narrated but also addressed, either through support programs for survivors or through legal means.

Chapter 1, "Conflict-Related Sexual Violence Against Men: An Overview", opens up the discussion by providing a brief overview of existing theoretical frameworks on conflict-related sexual violence, and by highlighting how they have so far failed to mainstream the existence of sexual violence against men. Against this backdrop, the chapter details the mounting empirical evidence regarding conflict-related sexual violence against men in various settings, and underscores a clear diversity in patterns. The chapter shows that it is far from being a recent phenomenon, and that it can be observed in most contemporary conflict settings. Some variations in types of male sexual victimization are highlighted, showing, for instance, that sexual violence in detention displays different characteristics from sexual violence exerted in other types of conflict settings, and that the victims' profiles are also likely to greatly vary from one conflict context to another.

Chapter 2, "Making Sense of Wartime Sexual Violence Against Men", sets the theoretical foundations of the book and proposes to explore sexual violence against men as not only connected to other types of wartime violence, but also to wider societal relations. In particular, it shows how wartime sexual violence against men can be understood as an expression of power struggles between militarized groups, and the masculinity models that they embody. Conflict-related sexual violence can thus be read as an attempt to either impose a new hierarchy and order, or to reinforce and strengthen the existing one. This conceptual framework is then discussed in relation to different contexts and configurations of wartime sexual violence against men, from ethnic conflicts to insurgencies and to international interventions, showing that the phenomenon is not only more common than assumed, but also embedded in the same patriarchal principles that underpin patterns of sexual violence against women.

Chapter 3, "Perpetrators and Bystanders", builds on stories collected in the Great Lakes region of Africa, and presents diverse profiles and stories of perpetrators of wartime sexual violence against men. It discusses the various contexts and motivations underpinning male sexual victimization, as well as the resistances it creates among the groups that perpetrate it. It also outlines the diverse ways in which perpetrators make sense of, justify, and sometimes seem to regret their own participation in these acts.

Chapter 4, "Surviving Wartime Sexual Violence", mostly builds on stories and interviews with male survivors of sexual violence collected in the Great Lakes region of Africa since 2009, and in Northern Ireland since 2005. It explores the various types of suffering induced by sexual violence, from physical to psychological and to social, and presents the ways in which male survivors try to deal with the consequences of sexual violence. The chapter also discusses the long-term impact of this type of violence on individuals as well as on the communities to which they belong. The chapter ends with a discussion on the broader consequences of this type of violence on post-conflict and reconciliation processes, and shows that the silencing of male survivors' experiences is likely to impede the reconstruction of social links, and the stabilization of post-conflict societies.

Chapter 5, "The Elusiveness of Narratives on Wartime Sexual Violence Against Men", explores understandings of, and narratives on, wartime sexual violence against men, as well as some of the questions they raise. The chapter argues that gender representations that are dominating at local, national but also international levels hinder the acknowledgement of the existence of male survivors of sexual violence, and thus obscure our understanding of the underlying mechanisms sustaining wartime sexual violence. The chapter explores what accounts for such a silencing at the local, national and international levels, from representations of sexual violence where men stand as perpetrators, to patriarchal cultures associating masculinity to strength, protection and invulnerability.

Chapter 6, "Conceptualizing and Implementing Care and Support Programs for Male Survivors", reviews existing local and international programs and initiatives for the relief of male survivors, and highlights the important role played by organizations and groups led by survivors themselves. By putting the stress on the challenges faced by relief programs, the chapter also underscores the necessity for a contextualized and long-term prevention approach, as well as the importance of a combined study and strategy for alleviating the suffering of both male and female survivors of wartime sexual violence.

Chapter 7, "Prosecuting Wartime Sexual Violence Against Men", explores the difficulties associated with the prosecution of wartime sexual violence against men. It looks at how major institutions like the International Criminal Tribunal for the former Yugoslavia, the International Criminal Tribunal for Rwanda as well as the International Criminal Court have attempted to tackle the issue. The chapter discusses the recent and promising changes in international law, but also highlights challenges related notably to impunity, underreporting, gender biases, as well as to the existence of a fragmented legal and institutional framework for the prosecution of wartime sexual violence against men.

Chapter 1

Conflict-Related Sexual Violence Against Men

An Overview

Sexual violence against women within armies, or used as a "weapon of war" in conflict zones such as in Syria, the DRC and numerous other conflict areas, has recently attracted a lot of media and academic attention[1]. Overwhelming reports have been published since the end of the Cold War, revealing staggering numbers of women being raped in countries like the DRC, nicknamed the "rape capital of the world", but also during the war in Bosnia-Herzegovina, in Liberia and in Sierra Leone, to quote just a few examples. Recent research has also highlighted the multiple forms that wartime sexual violence can take (so that it is not just about rape, but also about sexual slavery, sexual torture, sexual mutilations and so on), variations in who is targeted (e.g. women of a certain ethnic or religious group, all women, women *and* men of a certain ethnic or religious group, etc.), in who are the perpetrators and so on (for an overview, see Wood 2006). Several types of conflict-related sexual violence, like sexual torture, rape or mutilation, seem to be used in different ways and with more or less frequency in different settings, with, for instance, a predominance of sexual torture in detention during asymmetrical conflicts. In most cases, however, and in spite of accumulated empirical evidence and testimonies, it remains extremely complicated to understand why some conflict actors seem to be more prone to perpetrate sexual violence than others, or why patterns of sexual violence often seem to change over the course of a given conflict. In this perspective, the chapter provides a brief overview of theoretical frameworks developed over the past decades in order to explain the occurrence of conflict-related sexual violence. It shows how these various theoretical frameworks have so far failed to mainstream in the analysis the existence of sexual violence against men. It also presents the mounting empirical evidence regarding wartime sexual violence against men, and details some of its most remarkable patterns.

1.1. UNDERSTANDING WARTIME SEXUAL VIOLENCE

Multiple explanations have been put forward to try to make sense of the occurrence and patterns of wartime sexual violence, with the objective to come up with a theoretical framework that would provide an overall explanation for wartime sexual violence. Scholarly debates have mostly focused on the question of whether sexual violence can be understood as a strategy of combatants using it as a "weapon of war", or whether it should be seen as the result of the combatants' opportunistic choices. If understood as opportunistic, sexual violence does not result from a planned strategy, but rather accompanies other types of violence like pillaging and looting, and is facilitated by the weakening of social norms. Both explanatory strands have received partial empirical validation, but the "weapon of war" thesis has become particularly popular at the international policy level, especially since the UNSC Resolution 1820 (2008), adopted unanimously by the UN Security Council, described rape as a "tactic of war". This thesis is, however, periodically challenged by the declarations of most concerned military and political authorities, who argue that sexual violence occurs without their consent. This suggests a potential lack of discipline within the ranks of armies and armed groups, as well as potential discrepancies between motives and interests of military leaders, and those of rank-and-file combatants (Leiby 2009, 448). Several authors have explored these dynamics and tried to solve this conundrum, like Wood (2006, 331), who proposes to explain conflict-related sexual violence by looking at the interplay between three levels of analysis, that of the relevant armed group, the smaller unit in which the combatants operate on a day-to-day basis, and the individual level, alongside the degree of access that combatants have to civilians. The idea that sexual violence is used as a war tactic, and in particular as an ethnic cleansing strategy, however, still dominates international policy debates, which frequently overlook the nuances offered by academics.

Research has also used gender-related analysis grids to provide a more detailed understanding of who is targeted by wartime sexual violence, and why. Many authors have thus put the stress on how gender roles, norms and relations come into play to enable and sometimes even increase the occurrence of sexual violence. Conflict-related sexual violence has, for instance, been analysed as a consequence of patriarchal gendered social norms (Brownmiller 1975), or of militarization of societies (Enloe 2000). Other authors like Miranda Alison (2007) stress the importance of heterosexual militarized masculinities and of particular constructions of gender, which intersect with ethnicity and other identity factors for explaining specific patterns of wartime sexual violence. In an attempt to map epistemological explanations of wartime sexual violence, Inger Skjelsbaek (2001a) has shown how, over the past decades, three main gender-based conceptualizations of wartime sexual violence have emerged, each based on different assumptions about human nature, gender and power relations: first, essentialism, according to which sexual violence, and especially sexual violence against women, is an inevitable part of war and a direct consequence of militarized masculinity (see, among others, Brownmiller 1975; Seifert 1993); second, structuralism, which points to structural factors as predisposing certain women to wartime sexual violence like marginalization, ethnicity, race or political affiliation, and which also sheds light on structural factors determining combatants' behavior (e.g. Lentin 1997; Wood 2006); and third, social constructivism (e.g. Shepherd 2008; Sjoberg 2013), which explains that "war-time sexual violence can be regarded as a transaction of identities between the perpetrator and the victims" (Skjelsbaek 2001a, 226), a transaction that reinforces the masculinity of the perpetrator and simultaneously feminizes the victim.

While none of these analysis grids (essentialist, structuralist and social constructivist) really provides a definitive answer to the above-mentioned tactics/opportunism debate, it is important to underscore that they are not systematically in contradiction with one another. Actually, they sometimes even overlap, and can be considered more or less valid depending on the conflict situation and the historical context. As noted by Kirby (2012, 800), the context always plays a major role in sexual violence patterns: "The apparent dispute between an account of wartime sexual violence in which all women are targeted and one in which men *and* women are targeted may tell us more about *contingent historical factors* (different wars and differing contexts may display different patterns of rape) or *analytical distinctions* (between acts that are essential to a strategy and those that are peripheral to it) than they do about the philosophical foundations of research". The sheer complexity and fluidity of conflict patterns seem to preclude monocausal explanations of sexual violence, highlighting the need to mainstream, beyond tactics, opportunism and gender factors, other dimensions such as poverty, collapse of law and order, past uses of wartime sexual violence and so on.

Most of these analyses also share a specific focus on rape as a major form of conflict-related sexual violence. There is, however, to date, no unified theory that consistently explains patterns of wartime rape that are observed at the empirical level (Gottschall 2004). Megan MacKenzie (2010), for instance, looks at how rape has been used as a tool of war and why it has been part of militant strategies throughout history. She argues that because it violates existing patriarchal norms, rape is used to create *dis-order* and to eventually turn women's bodies into battlefields. Other authors like Claudia Card (1996) interpret wartime rape as a martial weapon that is related to other types of violence, such as torture and terrorism. A series of authors like Stiglmayer

(1993) have more specifically focused on the bonding entailed by wartime rape, and argued that one of its main functions is to produce solidarity and friendship between combatants. Gang rape in particular appears to play an important part in combatant socialization for groups that have recruited their members through forcible means like abduction or pressganging (Cohen 2013). Recent research has also critically examined and challenged the "rape as a weapon of war" thesis, by showing its weak theoretical consistency, as well as the practical difficulties it entails for policy-makers trying to devise adapted responses (Kirby 2012). Eriksson Baaz and Stern (2013, 5) in particular develop an extensive critique of this narrative, arguing that wartime sexual violence can be the result of a carefully planned strategy such as in Bosnia-Herzegovina, or its exact opposite resulting from the breakdown of chains of command and lack of discipline, such as in the DRC. The "weapon of war" thesis thus seems to have a very limited applicability, and is far from providing an overall explanatory grid for wartime rape. Some authors like Buss (2009) have even argued that the idea of rape as a weapon of war erases women's individual experiences, as well as other types of violence that occur during conflicts, by inserting them in a globalizing narrative.

In spite of their diversity, these various approaches of wartime rape have left pending a series of questions, for instance, how wartime rape relates to other forms of wartime sexual violence, how it is fed by wider socio-economic issues, or how to account for male rape victims. Recent research has indeed highlighted that wartime sexual violence cannot be analysed in isolation from other types of wartime violence such as looting and pillaging (Wood 2006, 322), to which it is undoubtedly connected. But, as explained by Dolan (2010, 60), wartime sexual violence is also related to wider socio-economic and political factors, not just to patterns of violence; in that sense, it functions as an indicator of larger societal issues: "Rather than reading sexual violence simply as a consequence of impunity, we need to understand sexual violence as one, if not the indicator of ongoing, unresolved social and political conflicts, especially where those are technologically simple yet psychologically complex".

Because it lies at a series of nexuses, conflict-related sexual violence challenges and spills over existing taxonomies of violence: it can be elicited by political, military, social, economic *and* cultural factors; it can be triggered simultaneously by national *and* very localized issues; it is both public *and* private, individual *and* collective, political *and* sexual, normalized *and* extreme, set off by emotions *and* rational calculations and so on. In many ways, current analysis grids fail to capture this complexity, but also the multiplicity of consequences and suffering it occasions for the collective and the individual. Like other forms of conflict-related violence exerted against civilians, brutalization entailed by sexual violence can only be understood by trying to reconcile these multiple dimensions and levels of analysis, and in particular by paying attention both to micro-contexts of local power, and to larger orders of social force (Kleinman 2000, 127). In the absence of such an in-depth examination, requiring both conceptual instruments and thorough empirical work, current analysis grids can only be found lacking.

One of the most blatant shortcomings of existing theoretical models is that they fail to account for the occurrence of wartime sexual violence against men, to mainstream it in their analysis, not to mention to try to make sense of it. Some of the authors quoted above acknowledge male sexual victimization in footnotes, in two or three hurried sentences, or at the most dedicate a chapter to the issue (Meger 2016). It is as if sexual violence is triggered by different factors when it is committed against women, than when it is perpetrated on men. But is it really the case? Are men sexually victimized in different ways, for instance, in different circumstances, than women? If yes, what can account for these differences? Is rape of men—or castration, or male sexual humiliation, etc.—a "weapon of war"? Or a result of combatants' opportunistic behavior? Or something else? And if they are triggered by different factors, what is the relationship, if any, between sexual violence against men and sexual violence against women? Or can we assume that male sexual victimization is a sort of sub-category of sexual violence, just because available data indicates that men are less likely to be targeted for sexual violence than women? Before moving on to offer a more general and conceptual discussion on conflict-related sexual violence against men, it is worth having a look at the empirical evidence that has already been gathered on the issue and that provides preliminary answers to some of these questions.

1.2. AN ANCIENT AND WIDESPREAD FEATURE OF CONFLICTS

Instances of sexual violence against men have been documented in a great number of conflicts and wars, both ancient and contemporary. A number of factors have contributed to keep them well hidden from view, though. First, empirical evidence on wartime sexual violence against men is usually not elaborated upon, and much more stress is put on "other" forms of violence of which civilian and combatant men are victims, such as killing, maiming, and, to a lesser extent, imprisonment and torture[2]. Conversely, most published work on wartime sexual violence takes female victims as their unquestionable main if not unique object of analysis, and research on violence perpetrated on women during conflicts focuses primarily on sexual violence. Numbers and statistics about the sexual victimization of men are also difficult to come by, because male survivors tend to hide that they have been victims of such violence. Of course, both male and female survivors of sexual violence tend to underreport it, but there is evidence that male victims report these cases even less than women and girls do (Sivakumaran 2007). In addition, it appears that sexual violence against men is often not coded as sexual violence, but as torture or beatings (see Manivannan 2014, 643; Cohen et al. 2013). For instance, the Peruvian Truth and Reconciliation Commission coded male sexual torture as "torture", but female sexual torture as "sexual violence". Leiby (2012, 343) recoded and analysed the original testimonies of Peruvian survivors of sexual violence and found out that 29% of sexual violence victims were men, whereas the truth commission had found that only 2% were men. Finally, it seems reasonable to assume that because patterns of wartime sexual violence against men seem to differ from what we know of conflict-related sexual violence against women, they are not perceived as such. Wartime sexual victimization of women has set the norms for sexual violence more generally, and sexual violence against men does not always fit neatly within these established categories: men are less likely to raped, but are more likely to be victims of sexual mutilation, and of other forms of sexual torture like beatings of the genitals, which are usually not coded or perceived as gender-based or sexual violence.

In spite of these coding difficulties, some numbers have begun to emerge, signaling that the phenomenon is much more common and widespread than usually assumed. The attention of the wider public in Western countries has notably been drawn to the issue with the publication of some reports about sexual violence in armies, such as the figures published in 2012 by the US Department of Defense about the percentage of US male soldiers as victims of sexual assault: of an estimated twenty-six thousand soldiers who have been victims of sexual assault in 2012, 54% were men (Department of Defense 2012). Slowly, other figures collected in conflict zones are being published., for instance, a study conducted by Johnson et al. (2010) has reported that 23.6% of men and boys (39.7% of women and girls) living in Eastern DRC have experienced some form of conflict-related sexual violence. Such figures are in line with what has been observed in many other conflicts, and demonstrate in a striking manner that wartime sexual violence against men is, contrary to common assumptions, far from being an anecdotal phenomenon.

If researchers have only recently started to compile statistics, empirical evidence suggests that wartime sexual violence against men is probably as old as war itself. As explained by Sivakumaran (2010, 264), "the practice has been documented as dating back from almost time immemorial". In Ancient Greece, when enemy men and boys were captured, they were often used as sex slaves, or turned into "warriors' brides" in Mesoamerica (Del Zotto and Jones 2002). In the ancient world, Chinese, Persian, Egyptian or Norse armies, to quote but a few examples, castrated their male enemies, and publicly displayed their penises (Goldstein 2004, 357). Castration could be partial (cutting off testicles) or total (cutting both testicles and penises), and sometimes enemy men were circumcised, as a form of symbolic castration. In many pre-Colombian societies, like the Aztec in Central America as well as among Native American peoples, raping male prisoners was used as a way to assert domination, when male enemy combatants were not castrated before being eventually killed. In all these cases, sexual violence constituted a performative act underscoring the henceforth dominated and feminized status of male defeated enemies. Castration in particular was clearly meant to take away the enemy combatants' manhood, and, therefore, their symbolic and physical power. According to Zawati (2007, 33), in ancient wars and societies, wartime sexual violence against men, and specifically male rape was considered as a legitimate right of the victorious soldiers to declare the totality of the enemy's defeat, and to show that the emasculated and vanquished enemy could not be a warrior or a ruler anymore. If, as Del Zotto and Jones (2002) explain, these acts have been performed less and less publicly, it does not mean that they are not practiced anymore: "As western Judeo-Christian and Islamic taboos against homo-eroticism (including violent homoeroticism) became institutionalized, the above-mentioned acts became less public, and generally ceased to be part of triumphal spectacles of violence. They continued to be practiced nonetheless, but 'underground'". One should, however, be careful not to stretch interpretations of today's wartime sexual violence to existing evidence across ancient cultures and geographical areas. The fact that, in some ancient cultures like Ancient Greece, male-to-male sexual contact was not taboo suggests that it would be simplistic to read issues of gender relations and gender-based and sexual violence through the lenses of contemporary patriarchal and heteronormative societies. In that sense, the "undergrounding" of wartime sexual violence against men suggested by Del Zotto and Jones might have given these practices a whole new meaning, precisely by rendering them more taboo, inadmissible and, as we will see, feminizing. The plethora of historical examples nevertheless demonstrates that sexual violence against men has long been part of war and domination strategies.

Wars and genocides of the twentieth century also abound with examples of sexual violence against men. During the Armenian genocide, for instance, sexual torture of men was quite prevalent. Many Armenian men were castrated, forced to march naked or circumcised after they had forcibly been converted to Islam (Bjørnlund 2011). Another famous case is the "Rape of Nanking" in 1937, during which Chinese men were raped and forced to rape each other in front of Japanese soldiers. Horror did not stop there: "Cases were reported of castration, and even of selling penises for Japanese men to eat (supposedly to increase their potency)" (Goldstein 2004, 367). Cases of castration and rape of men have also been reported during the genocide in Cambodia (Studzinsky 2012, 92 and 106), among numerous other cases.

Recent conflicts offer ever more compelling evidence, and as attention is growing, cases of wartime sexual violence against men have now been documented almost all around the world. It has been used—though not always systematically—by soldiers, police officers, members of intelligence services, as well as by members of armed groups in civil wars, ethnic conflicts, interstate conflicts, genocides and so on. It is impossible to offer here a complete description of all known cases, but a few examples seem to stand out. In Bosnia-Herzegovina, for instance, a study of six thousand concentration-camp inmates in Sarajevo found that 80% of men reported having been raped (Stemple 2009, 613). Numerous cases of castration, mutilation of sexual organs, sexual humiliation, forced fellatio and prisoners forced to rape other (male and female) prisoners have been documented in official documents too (Bassiouni 1994). Survivors' stories have also been compiled and disseminated by non-governmental organizations, such as in the 2014 documentary *Silent Scream* (Nečujni Krik) on wartime rape during the war in Bosnia-Herzegovina, and which includes testimonies of male survivors. More generally, sexual violence against men seems to have been used extensively during conflicts related to the breakup of Yugoslavia, for instance, by Serb forces in Kosovo (Munn 2008, 153) or in Croatia (Oosterhoff et al. 2004).

The various conflicts raging in Eastern DRC since the beginning of the 1990s provide compelling evidence too. In addition to the statistics quoted earlier, a survey by John Hopkins University, in cooperation with the Refugee Law Project in Uganda, surveyed 447 male refugees (99% from Congo) and found that 38.5% had experienced sexual violence at some point of their life (Dolan 2014a). Some databases suggest that, in 2013, there were around one hundred thousand male survivors of wartime sexual violence in the DRC (Refugee Law Project 2013b, 13). In Liberia, Johnson et al. (2008) reported that approximately one-third of adult male ex-combatants in their sample had experienced sexual violence, a percentage confirmed by other studies[3]. Numerous cases have also been reported in Sierra Leone, especially among male child soldiers (Betancourt et al. 2011), in Colombia where 15% of victims of conflict-related sexual violence are male (Quijano and Kelly 2012, 490) and in Uganda where the rape of men has been referred to as "the pain of kneeling" (Oloya 2013, 49). Other known and documented cases relate, among many others, to the conflicts in Chile (Oosterhoff et al. 2004, 68), El Salvador (Leiby 2012), Guatemala (Perlin 2000, 409), Argentina (Skjelsbæk 2001b, 74), the former Soviet Union (Scarce 1997, 31), Ukraine (UNHCR 2017b), Greece (Lunde et al. 1980), Northern Ireland (McGuffin 1974; Murray and Faul 2016), Israel/Palestine (Punamaki 1988; Weishut

2015), Algeria (Peel 2004), Iran (Agger 1989, 305), Kuwait (Scarce 1997, 31), Afghanistan and Syria (Human Rights Watch 2012; UN 2015) where sexual violence has been identified as one of the main reasons for migration (UNHCR 2017a), Kashmir (Sengupta 2011), but also Sri Lanka (Peel et al. 2000; Sooka 2014; All Survivors Project 2017), Kenya (Sivakumaran 2010, 265), Sudan and South Sudan (UN 2015), Central African Republic (Sivakumaran 2010, 263; UN 2015), Burundi (Féron 2015) and Rwanda (de Brouwer et al. 2005; Mullins 2009).

Evidence from the fieldwork I have conducted in the Great Lakes region of Africa, but also to a lesser extent in Northern Ireland, is also quite compelling, and shows that in all these cases this type of violence has been frequent during conflict times, though silenced and overlooked by political authorities, survivors and relatives, as well as by non-governmental organizations. We will further explore these cases in the following chapters, but a few short examples will give a first overview of the phenomenon. At the Panzi hospital in Bukavu (South Kivu), for instance, the chief doctor I spoke with in 2012 reported two cases that had been treated the week before: the first was that of a driver who had been stopped on his way to Bukavu by an armed group, forced to rape all the people, male and female, who were in his van, and who then was himself raped by the members of the armed group (Panzi Hospital 2012, interview)[4]; the second was that of a young man who had been forced to help an armed group by carrying around goods that they had stolen from various houses (including the young man's) and had been subsequently gang raped by the members of the group. In both of these cases, there is a deliberate wish to instill terror, and to inflict pain and public humiliation (enforced rape and then gang rape in the first case, robbery and gang rape in the second). These cases are far from being isolated. Over the years, I have heard numerous similar stories, though the setting and identity of perpetrators obviously vary. According to a person working for the International Rescue Committee in the Great Lakes region of Africa (2012, interview), sexual violence against men, and more specifically male-on-male rape, has become just another strategy of war of armed groups active in the region, the ultimate aim being to force local populations into submission. Whether or not it is a predetermined strategy, sexual violence is successful in instilling terror among civilian populations, without putting the perpetrators at risk since victims are almost never reporting it. According to the survivors' and witnesses' stories I have collected, when this violence is perpetrated during raids on villages, men are often forced to rape their own family members (forced incest). This of course entails humiliation and trauma for both the rapist and his victim(s), and family relations can never be fully mended. But in many instances sexual violence seems to also happen during detention periods, or shortly after men and boys have been abducted by armed groups—a trend that also characterizes sexual violence against women and girls.

Survivors' experiences vary greatly, as do practices of sexual violence. Testimonies collected amongst refugees and internally displaced persons in Uganda by the Refugee Law Project (2013b, 18) offer a daunting overview:

- Oral rape, as well as rape using objects (e.g. screwdrivers, bottles);
- Having ropes tied to the genitalia and being pulled around by this rope;
- Having electric wires attached to the genitalia, through which electric shocks are administered;
- Linking two men using ropes tied to their genitalia and making them walk in opposite directions;
- Being made to dig holes in the ground, or in trees, and then to rub themselves in that hole to the point of ejaculation;
- Being forced to have vaginal sex with women of the same ethnic identity who are also being detained;
- Being forced to have anal or oral sex with fellow detainees, or with brothers or fathers;
- Being forced into sexual acts with your own spouse, while being watched by children, parents, etc.;
- Being used as a mattress while soldiers rape their family members on top of them;
- Being held for lengthy periods of time as sexual slaves;
- Forced circumcision, castration and other forms of genital mutilation.

In other settings, cases of forced bestiality, of acid poured on the genitals, of cigarette burns on the genitals, etc., have also been recorded. It is worth underscoring the fact that if sexual violence against men sometimes occurs during raids on villages or in a seemingly "random" manner, many of these cases take place in the specific setting of detention, where sexual torture is used in order to extract confessions, crush political dissidence or rebellion and/or for anti-terrorist purposes. In several cases, sexual torture seems to have been used by state security forces in an almost routine fashion. For instance, 21% of Sri Lankan men who were seen at a London torture treatment center reported sexual abuse while in detention (Stemple 2009), and in El Salvador, a survey of political prisoners at La Esperanza men's prison revealed that 76% had suffered sexual abuse perpetrated by prison guards or interrogators during their incarceration (Leiby 2012, 341), with a predominance of cases of forced nudity, genital beatings, electric torture and rape or threats of rape.

A comparison of statistics available on sexual violence against men in detention settings suggests that the most frequent types of sexual violence perpetrated are beatings of the genitals, electrical torture in the genital area, introduction of foreign bodies in the rectal area, as well as sexual humiliation such as forced nudity. In Abu Ghraib, for instance, male prisoners were forced to remain naked for days in a row and were photographed while being naked. Further, sexual torture at Abu Ghraib and Guantánamo seems to have been specifically tailored to include what was assumed to be the most humiliating for Muslim detainees: "A Briton released from Guantánamo alleged that, as in Abu Ghraib, sexual humiliation was identified by US officials as a way of breaking Muslim detainees. In Iraq it was the simulation of oral sex, forced masturbation and human pyramids, with people kept naked for long spells. In Guantánamo, according to one British detainee, naked prostitutes paraded before inmates to taunt them" (Dodd 2004; see also, for an analysis of these narratives, Puar 2004). In Syria, Amnesty International (2012, 11) has collected testimonies of former prisoners detained by Syrian official security forces who had been "hit in the genital region with truncheons, (…) forced to watch as a male detainee [was being] raped (…), forced to have a glass bottle with a broken top inserted into his anus, (…) raped with a metal skewer", among other abuses. Similar techniques of torture had been observed in the case of Sri Lanka (Peel et al. 2000, 2069).

1.3. PATTERNS OF WARTIME SEXUAL VIOLENCE AGAINST MEN

Is it possible to make sense of all these instances of violence? Quite obviously, patterns of wartime sexual violence against both men and women are tightly connected to the larger context. In particular, the conflict type (guerrilla war, civil war, genocide, interstate war, "war against terrorism", etc.), but also the status of combatants (state or non-state), the terrain, the type and number of weapons available, among other factors, all seem to impact on patterns of sexual violence. This means that similar trends in occurrence and type of wartime sexual violence can be observed in very different settings, but also that similar types of conflicts can generate quite divergent patterns of sexual violence. Military strategy and control (or lack thereof) might, for instance, have a strong influence on the spread of sexual violence, as explained by Myrttinen (2014): "Sexual violence (…) is not something that happens in a vacuum and the driving factors are not the same in all conflicts. Whereas, for example, in the concentration camps of the Bosnian war sexual violence was used systematically against women and men, in other contexts, such as in the Democratic Republic of Congo, it may be more due to a loss of military control and individual frustration rather than a planned strategy".

As we will further explore in the next chapter, wartime sexual violence against men can notably be interpreted as an expression of power struggles between militarized groups, and the masculinity models that they embody. As such, conflict-related sexual violence attempts to either impose a new social hierarchy and order, or to strengthen the existing one. It follows that the shapes that it takes are tightly related to how these power struggles are framed. In conflicts framed as "ethnic", for instance, men who belong to the "other" ethnic group become primary targets for types of violence like castration or mutilation, which aim to destroy their reproduction capacities, such as in Bosnia-Herzegovina, or they are bluntly killed. If the conflict is primarily political or ideological, sexual violence is more likely to be used as a repression tool aimed at opponents, often described as terrorists; in those cases, sexual torture aims at breaking their resistance by terrorizing them and by inscribing structures of power in their bodies and gendered identities, as the cases of Syria or Sri Lanka illustrate. And if the conflict takes on criminal features, and is more about social domination, control of economic resources and/or of territory, then men of any religious or ethnic group can be targeted, meaning that those who are less able to protect themselves, such as disadvantaged men, are particularly vulnerable to sexual violence, as empirical data collected in Eastern Congo demonstrates.

The ever-changing nature of conflicts, the emergence of new issues while some others lose relevance, the rise in power of new actors and so on significantly complicate the picture, though. Issues and framing of the conflict might differ from one region to another—the multiple Congolese conflicts being a good case in point. Actors within the same conflict might also have very different views on what is at stake, and thus employ dramatically different strategies and war tactics. Repertoires of action matter too, especially when it comes to torture techniques that have been tested and found efficient in the past. Patterns of sexual violence thus seem to be determined partly by structural factors and general conflict characteristics, and partly by individual combatants' agency and experience. For instance, Bjørnlund (2011, 29), looking at cases of sexual violence perpetrated during the Armenian genocide, argues that if the political and military hierarchy did not openly encourage or condone sexual violence, much was left to the appreciation of perpetrators: "Sexual violence during the Armenian genocide can at least partly be seen as a result of a thoroughly brutalized environment that left room for local initiatives when it came to the methods of killing and humiliation, initiatives that satisfied individual needs, not only for self-gratification but also for variation". This leeway left to perpetrators then comes to explain variations in the occurrence of certain types of violence, including during the same conflict episode.

Some researchers have already attempted to develop typologies describing abuses by types (see, for instance, Sivakumaran 2007, 261–67) or by objectives. Peel (2004, 65–66), for example, lists three patterns of conflict-related sexual violence against men: the first in Nigeria where rape and other forms of sexual torture are a part of the detention and interrogation process, the second in Algeria where sexual violence is part of a policy of intimidation and humiliation of opponents and the third in Sri Lanka where the rape of prisoners was common but not officially condoned. One of the main issues here is of course the scarcity of available data, which impedes generalization and makes typologies too case-dependent. How would other cases fit into this typology, especially if they display significantly different characteristics?

On the basis of the empirical evidence listed in the previous section, we can first observe that sexual violence perpetrated in detention seems to display specific characteristics, with a predominance of cases of sexual humiliation, forced nudity, genital beatings and electric torture and fewer cases of rape. These forms of sexual brutalization are clearly related, at least in a number of documented cases such as Abu Ghraib, to a wish to break the prisoners' resolve. In other settings and especially genocidal ones, rape and castration are more frequently practiced, and seem to be often related to a wish to turn male victims into "lesser men", into "womanized men", and to annihilate their reproductive capacities. It is, however, worth mentioning that some cases display both features, like Bosnia-Herzegovina. Sexual violence perpetrated on Bosnian prisoners indeed included sexual humiliation, forced nudity, genital beatings, electric torture and so on, alongside numerous cases of rape and castration. This case thus shows similarities both with other cases of sexual violence perpetrated in detention, and with patterns of sexual violence committed in episodes such as the Rwandan genocide. This hybridity probably pertains to the fact that no confession or conversion was expected from Bosnian prisoners, and that sexual violence was not used as a counter-rebellion or "counter-terrorist" strategy but rather took its meaning within a broader ethnic cleansing context. In any case, these cases strongly highlight the fact that, as is the case of conflict-related sexual violence against women, patterns of male sexual victimization are tightly related to broader conflict features, factors and issues.

Other patterns of wartime sexual violence against men can be highlighted, for instance, with regards to victims' profiles. The empirical evidence collected on known cases suggests that male members of marginalized groups, such as minority ethnic, religious or sexual groups, seem to be particularly vulnerable to wartime sexual violence. This is, of course, especially the case in conflicts that display a strong ethnic dimension, and/or of a genocidal nature, but also applies to cases of sexual torture in detention. As illustrated by the examples of Palestine, Kashmir, Northern Ireland, Sri Lanka, Guantánamo and Abu Ghraib, sexual torture in particular primarily targets political or military opponents, or people belonging to categories specifically targeted for repression, because of their ethnic or religious belonging. In that sense, sexual torture does not seem to differ from more general patterns of politically motivated torture. In addition, the vulnerability of these communities seems enhanced when membership to specific ethnic, religious or cultural groups intersects with other exposure factors, such as being a refugee, a homosexual or an internally displaced person.

In some cases like in Eastern DRC, the absence of a clear political division, the ethnic fragmentation, the multiplicity of active armed groups, as well as the blurred nature of cleavages and oppositions mean that almost every man living in an isolated, rural and deprived area is a potential target. If there are indications of certain ethnic groups being sometimes more targeted than others, most (male and female) survivors do not seem to have a particular political or religious profile, but rather a socio-economic one. Many live or used to live in small villages or camp settlements, more vulnerable to raids from armed groups, and mostly belong to disadvantaged socio-economic groups. According to the fieldwork data that I have collected in Eastern DRC and Burundi, many male survivors of sexual violence were young men or even adolescent boys at the time of the assault, and some of them were abducted or forcefully recruited into armed groups after being victimized.

Quite clearly, who is targeted by sexual violence, and how, also depends on how gender relations are structured in the relevant area, including, especially with regards to sexual violence against men, which masculinity models are valued by perpetrators. Most male survivors I have met did not embody what could be described as militarized or dominant masculinities, and lived simple lives before being attacked. Admittedly, a few cases of sexual violence exerted against community leaders have been documented, in Rwanda, for instance, (Mullins 2009), a trend that often signals a wish to challenge traditional power structures and weaken local communities. However, these cases remain comparatively rare.

As we will further explore in chapter 3, whatever the setting, most perpetrators of sexual violence against men are members of armed groups or of state security forces. If a few cases of sexual violence against men seem to be committed by partners and relatives, only a very limited number is indeed perpetrated by "non-combatant strangers" (see, for instance, in the case of Eastern DRC, Johnson et al. 2010, 557). Testimonies collected in various settings also suggest that new recruits or combatants are more likely to commit these acts than seasoned ones (Cohen 2013, 465). Most of the perpetrators I have met were in their twenties or even younger when they committed these acts. This also relates to the fact that sexual violence seems to be used by some armed groups as a bonding and initiation ritual for new combatants, who thereby prove their "toughness" and loyalty to the group. Worth underscoring also is the fact that most perpetrators of sexual violence against men are male, with a minority (for instance, around 10% in Eastern

DRC, see Johnson et al. 2010) of female perpetrators[5]. As we will see, this gender imbalance seems connected to the lower percentage of female recruits in armies and armed groups, and to their positioning within these groups. It is also related to a series of gender norms and expectations that most female recruits accept—by agreeing to have a lower status and a more passive role than their male counterparts—and a few decide to challenge—by enacting the same violent and militarized masculinity model.

Another regular pattern is that wartime sexual violence against men is often perpetrated publicly. The testimonies I have collected in the Great Lakes Region both with perpetrators and victims, as well as with professionals from the NGO and medical fields, indeed seem to indicate that sexual violence against men is often staged, choreographed and perpetrated in the presence of bystanders, who can be other combatants, civilians or even the victim's relatives. It is especially the case of sexual humiliation, forced nudity, forced incest or forced rape (Sivakumaran 2007, 264), but it also applies to other forms of sexual violence such as castration, mutilation and beatings of the genitals. Similar trends have been noted in many other conflict situations, such as during the war in Croatia (Oosterhoff et al. 2004, 74). As suggested in a UN report (2013, 12), this is likely a deliberate strategy to further shame the victim by making it impossible for him to hide what happened: "In many accounts, conflict-related sexual violence against men and boys is deliberately done with an audience, with the result that the violation is an open secret, known about by a number of individuals beyond the immediate perpetrator(s) and victim".

In some settings, sexual violence also seems to be frequently perpetrated collectively, in particular in the case of rape, with numerous instances of gang rapes. In the DRC, for instance, Duroch et al. (2011, 4) have found that 89.3% of male survivors of sexual violence in their sample had been gang raped[6], a finding confirmed by Mervyn et al. (2011, 234): "All the male survivors reported being raped by a group of male rebels or soldiers and the armed groups ranged in size from five to as many as thirty men. Male survivors reported being raped in front of their family and friends and others were raped at the same time as their wives and daughters". Other empirical data, mostly pertaining to cases of sexual torture perpetrated in detention, however, suggests opposite trends. Based on the testimonies of sexual torture survivors treated at Freedom from Torture (formerly the Medical Foundation for the Care of Victims of Torture), Peel (2004, 61) states, for instance, that "men (…) were almost always raped individually, alone. Unlike women, men are not usually raped in groups, adding to the feelings of isolation. There may have been several perpetrators involved, but generally they do not all rape the victim". Similarly, testimonies of LTTE militants tortured by members of

Sri Lankan security forces (Sooka 2014) seem to indicate that they had often been raped in their individual cells, and that gang rapes were relatively rare.

Although this would need to be further explored and confirmed by empirical data, this suggests that gang rapes of men are less frequent in detention settings than they are when sexual violence is perpetrated in a "lootpillageandrape" context, to borrow from Enloe (2000, 108). Testimonies collected by Mervyn et al. (2011, 234–35) aptly describe these dynamics: "Male survivors reported being captured by the armed groups with other men and women from their family and village. Some women and men were raped at the point of capture and then killed, while others were abducted and raped multiple times over weeks, months and even years by multiple male perpetrators before they were able to escape to safety. Survivors reported being held in captivity for periods of time ranging from one month to three years". One potential explanation for these diverging patterns is that the gang rape dimension presumably reinforces the political domination aspect of sexual violence, strengthening territorial control and ensuring the submission of local populations. In detention settings, these objectives are present but arguably less salient, because the detention system itself already enacts domination and control.

Another noticeable trend is that the use of extreme forms of violence like castration and mutilation seem to be particularly pregnant in cases of genocide, as the examples of Bosnia-Herzegovina (Bassiouni 1994), Darfur (Kristoff 2006) and the Armenian genocide (Bjørnlund 2011) show. Transgressing the taboos surrounding male sexual victimization is part of a strategy of escalation of horror, whereby male prisoners are, for instance, forced to bite off the testicles of other prisoners, or to perform acts of bestiality, like in Bosnia-Herzegovina. As explained by Mullins in the case of genital mutilations perpetrated on corpses during the genocide in Rwanda, these excesses are also a means to express total domination over bodies that are taken to represent a larger despised ethnicized body, thus signaling their vanquished and inferior status:

> Sexual mutilations, be they of men or women, are the most extreme form of this gendered destruction. The literal bodily destruction and ownership of sexual anatomies taken from dead bodies symbolically constitutes the strongest denial of agency (or, the strongest imposition of pure victimhood) both specifically on the victim in question and the community as a whole. Desecration of corpses in this highly gendered manner is the ultimate expression of control and power. (Mullins 2009, 24)

This is not to say, of course, that excesses are not committed in non-genocidal cases of conflicts. For instance, treating male prisoners as if they were women—sexually, but also with regards to social tasks, such as cooking and cleaning, which they are expected to perform—is or has been a relatively widespread practice in conflict areas like Burundi, which arguably has not recently displayed genocidal patterns. When men are raped by dozens of soldiers or combatants, such as in Eastern Congo, or when they are used as sex slaves, obvious dynamics of domination and of symbolic emasculation are at play. Such forms of punitive gendering have a long history, as the pre-Colombian *Berdache* practice, documented by Trexler (1995) testifies. Indigenous Americans forced their defeated male enemies to transvest and behave as if they were women—though the status of *Berdache* could also be adopted by personal choice by members of the community (Williams 1986). This practice, together with the above-mentioned case of Ancient Greece where captured enemy men and boys were frequently used as sex slaves, suggests that in the past punitive gendering was often part of a socially accepted as well as politically and militarily condoned policy. Nowadays, however, such practices are neither socially nor politically supported, but they remain nevertheless practiced by some armed groups, at an admittedly much smaller scale.

Variations in frequency and types of wartime sexual violence against men pose an obvious challenge to analysis, as does the fact that sexual violence—against both men and women—does not occur in every conflict, at least to the best of our current knowledge (Wood 2009). Our understanding of that type of violence is seriously hampered by the fact that available data is still limited and almost never systematic, meaning that many cases of sexual violence are never recorded, and that some types of sexual brutalization might be more affected by underreporting than others[7]. Awareness in both policy and academic communities is also still very low. On the basis of the empirical data that has been collected so far, we can, however, infer that there are indeed important variations in how and to what extent wartime sexual violence against men is perpetrated. A question that remains pending is whether this is just a question of salience, of dominant types in different conflict settings, or of opposite models. For instance, do differences in perpetrators' types signal a difference in nature? In Eastern Congo, for instance, perpetrators are both soldiers of conventional armies and members of non-state armed groups, whereas in Sri Lanka sexual violence has been mostly perpetrated by members of state security services, and in detention settings. And should we consider that variations in types of violence perpetrated are an indication that there is not one, but several models—and related purposes—of wartime sexual violence against men? In countries like the Congo, Burundi and Sierra Leone, for instance, there have been a few documented instances of sexual torture perpetrated by rebel groups involving the pouring of acid on the genitals, or the use of electric shocks, but these cases seem anecdotal as compared to the staggering number of rapes, sexual slavery, castrations and so on that they have been committing. During the Sri Lankan or Syrian conflicts, on the contrary, relatively few cases of sexual slavery, mutilation or castration have (so far) been recorded, whereas sexual torture for political motives, involving acid, electric shocks or beatings of the genitals, seems to have been much more common.

Another important and yet unanswered question relates to the potential differences between sexual violence against men committed during conflicts and during peacetime: are we dealing here with a difference in nature, or in degree? Empirical evidence collected so far suggests that it is both. Levels of male victimization in conflict zones are far higher than what is registered in "peaceful" countries, suggesting that sexual violence against men is indeed far more widespread during conflicts. But it seems also that it takes on new features. Episodes of castration, mutilation and male sexual slavery are, for instance, relatively rare in peacetime, suggesting a difference in nature that is maybe more salient than in the case of sexual violence against women. Further, the public and sometimes collective nature of wartime sexual violence against men, with an important number of gang rapes, public forced nudity, public sexual humiliation and so on also changes the meaning and impact of sexual violence. Even if sexual violence is always partly the result of wider societal and cultural norms regarding gender roles and expectations, societies usually treat it as a series of individual events; if, as in conflict settings, sexual violence becomes public, it takes on an unmissable collective meaning, and its consequences expand to affect the whole community, men and women alike.

Finally, it is worth underscoring the fact that all these patterns suggest the existence of multiple links and common characteristics between conflict-related sexual violence against women and against men, the extent of which still remains to be explored. Similarities also pertain to the way these two types of violence have been gradually integrated into political and academic agendas. The study of, and fight against, wartime sexual violence against men is currently facing the same hurdles that wartime sexual violence against women faced several decades ago—though, of course, the battle is not yet won on that front either. Lifting the taboo, raising awareness, conducting in-depth research and devising adequate responses will undoubtedly take time. But if sexual violence against women and against men are indeed two interrelated phenomena, they will need to be tackled at least partly jointly at the level of policy programming, and they will benefit from a renewed dialogue and cross fertilization between research on conflict-related sexual violence, and on conflict masculinities.

Chapter 2

Making Sense of Wartime Sexual Violence Against Men

Making sense of wartime sexual violence against men demands to solve a series of puzzles. Leaving aside cases in which sexual violence against men can be assimilated to homosexual acts—according to the data that has been collected up to now, these seem to be extremely rare—why do men in arms (and more rarely, women) rape, castrate, mutilate and sexually humiliate other men, when some of these practices could easily be interpreted as homosexual, thus potentially putting the perpetrator in an awkward position (Sivakumaran 2005)? And why do representatives of the State, such as soldiers or police officers, perpetrate such transgressive acts when so many other methods of torture have proven efficient to ensure the submission of prisoners and/or of political opponents? It also seems paramount to understand how this type of violence connects to other types of conflict-related brutalization, to the wider conflict, but also to societal relations of power, as determined by gender, class, caste, religion and so on. In this perspective, the fact that this type of violence is almost systematically silenced but seemingly frequently practiced is extremely intriguing, and calls for further investigation. What role does wartime violence against men play in the overall conflict, and in the relations of power that conflicts aim at challenging, or enforcing?

Scholarship has now well described and explained how gender constitutes a major dimension of social life and, most importantly for our purposes here, of conflicts (see, among many others, Goldstein 2004; Shepherd 2008; Sjoberg 2013; Yuval-Davis 1997). One of the most striking ways in which gender relations are played out in conflict situations relates to how conflict actors aim at affirming their own strength, defined as a masculine trait, by subordinating and disempowering feminized (male and female) "others". Depending on what the conflict is about, the targeted "others" may be singled out by their ethnicity, class, caste, religion, ideology, sexual orientation and so on, and sometimes by several of these factors at the same time. Exercising structural, physical as well as symbolic violence on them enacts their desired subordination, while it underscores and magnifies the assumed superiority of the perpetrator(s). One of the functions of violence, whatever its type, is to use pain in order to create distance between the perpetrator and the victim, at the ontological and psychological level, signaling the subjugation of the victim (Scarry 1985). In this perspective, wartime sexual violence plays a key role in power relations lying at the core of conflicts, because while it targets individuals defined by their ethnic, class, caste, religion and/or ideological positioning, it weaves together gender roles and values with these other social dimensions. However, what is important to underscore is that who is targeted for sexual violence, and how, is not just related to the characteristics of the conflict (say, who are the main conflict actors), but also to the multiple power relations that exist between and within groups in conflict. As research has now well established (see, for instance, Watts and Zimmerman 2002; WHO 2013), victims of wartime sexual violence do not just belong to the "other" group, and most conflicts also display high rates of "endogenous" sexual brutalization (Swaine 2018), for instance, perpetrated by relatives or community leaders. In that sense, sexual violence is not just embedded in the gendered ideology of the conflict; it is an inherent mechanism of reproduction of the wider social order.

Wartime sexual violence reinforces the feminization/masculinization processes entailed through the use of violence by underscoring their gendered meaning: targeted individuals are branded as inferior not just because they are being brutalized, but also because using their bodies as recipients of sexual violence further feminizes them—and thus further signifies their subordinate status. In parallel, perpetrators are (re-)comforted in their dominant masculinity. Other mechanisms can be at play, such as the wish to "demoralize" civilian populations one wishes to subdue, or to undermine their capacity to react, by breaking the capacity of their (masculine) members to play their role of protectors vis-à-vis their mothers, wives or daughters, but also vis-à-vis themselves. Wartime sexual violence is, therefore, never just related to gender issues; it is informed by other variables, and it lies at the nexus of relations of power—including patriarchal ones—within a given social order. This is why not paying proper attention to wartime sexual violence against men, as is the case in most existing accounts of sexual violence, deprives us from a full understanding of how wartime sexual violence participates in, and results from, larger political and social struggles.

In the following sections, I propose to explore the meaning of wartime sexual violence against men within the wider conflictual situation, but also in the context of the power struggles that cut across and between groups in conflict. Building on Butler's concept of gender performativity (1990) that highlights how bodies become gendered through the repetition of acts and practices that relate to known social norms, I show how gender, and by extension gender-based and sexual violence, and more specifically male sexual brutalization, take their meaning in relation to certain social norms. This approach allows me to understand male sexual brutalization as not only connected to sexual violence against women, but also to wider societal issues, as suggested by Vojdik (2014, 940): "Acts of sexual violence toward men and women are related and mutually reinforcing, operating within particular institutions and social systems of gender that privilege and empower masculinity as male and heterosexual". In other words, my aim here is to explore how wartime sexual violence against men can only be understood in relation to how power is distributed within and between the concerned groups, but also to dominant masculinity models and gendered social hierarchies.

2.1. THE GENDERED PERFORMATIVITY OF WARTIME SEXUAL VIOLENCE AGAINST MEN

Neither masculinity nor femininity are in principle attached to, respectively, male or female bodies. Both are played out in the process of configuring the social positioning of individuals and groups. It is thus important to recall the (potential) disconnection between models of hegemonic and of dominant masculinities, and the sex of those who perform them, as underscored by Cornwall and Lindisfarne (1994, 21): "(Masculinized) power is consistently associated with those who have control over resources and who have an interest in naturalizing and perpetuating that control. This means that in gender, class and race hierarchies, men and women who are pre-eminent may be included in particular gendered constructions of power which simultaneously disempower subordinate men and women". Nothing, in principle, prevents a man from claiming a feminine identity, or from being assigned one—just as, for instance, a female soldier can claim a masculine social role, or be assigned one. This inherent fluidity of gender, especially during conflict times as traditional gender identities and roles are put under considerable pressure (Enloe 1983), means that what makes individuals masculine, or feminine, changes over time and space, and that there are many ways to enact masculinity, or femininity.

In conflict settings, this plasticity of gender can be turned into a very powerful instrument of domination and subjugation. In particular, feminization is often used in social and political relations to produce and justify domination, not just between men and women, but also among men, and sometimes also, though this hasn't been much studied yet, among women. Feminization as a domination strategy can thus be enforced on female or male bodies, or on individuals who identify as neither (Hooper 2001, 71). It is important here to understand that feminization does not necessarily impose a straightforward feminine identity on men (or women). Rather, feminization can produce an array of effects on individuals that were previously identified as masculine: it can entail their downgrading to a lower (subordinate) masculine status (just like masculinization strategies can "upgrade" them), it can instill doubts on their masculinity and it can also assert a feminine identity on them, for instance, in the case of the previously mentioned *Berdache*. Thus, feminization operates as a major ordering principle between hegemonic, dominant, and subjugated masculinities, but also between masculinities and femininities, and between femininities.

Among the tools that conflict parties can use in order to enforce the feminization/subjugation of individuals belonging to the "other" side and, by extension, to suggest the feminization of the whole "other" group, sexual violence, against both men and women, occupies a choice position. While it enacts the feminization/subjugation of the victim, sexual violence also entails a parallel masculinization/empowerment of the perpetrator. Such process has been described by Jones in the case of male-on-male rape: "One of the most intriguing elements of male-on-male rape and sexual violence is the gendered positioning of rapist and victim: the way in which victims are feminized while rapists are confirmed in their heterosexual, hegemonic masculinity" (2006, 459). Though I don't think the concept of hegemonic masculinity applies in cases of perpetrators of wartime sexual violence against men[1], it is clear that the figure of combatant that is glorified through these practices is that of an extremely violent man, who intends to dominate physically, sexually, but also psychologically all the people, whatever their gender identity, he is in contact with. It is, however, important to underscore that if the gendered performativity of sexual violence contributes to (re-)imposing a certain gender order thanks to the subjugation of its victims, the twin processes of victims' feminization and of perpetrators' masculinization are not its necessary outcome. Rather, feminization and masculinization occur because of the existing gendered norms with which sexual violence resonates, and the way they structure gender relations. In other words, sexual violence seems to feminize the victim and to empower the perpetrator only because many of us—including most of the victims *and* of the perpetrators—adhere to the equation that is often made between, on the one hand, femininity/weakness/passivity/women and, on the other hand, masculinity/power/agency/men.

The gendered performativity of sexual violence highlights the limits of the division usually made between male and female survivors of sexual violence. The enforced feminization of male victims of sexual violence, alongside the fact that some perpetrators are female, demonstrates, as other studies have shown (see, for example, the case of travestis explored by Andrea Cornwall

1994), the absence of a direct link between the fact of being a man—in the sense of living in a male body—and the fact of having a masculine identity. It calls for a renewed understanding of (wartime) sexual violence, which would be more focused on masculinities and femininities than on the sex of its victims and perpetrators. Wartime sexual violence against men is embedded in the same patriarchal principles that underpin sexual violence against women, and both are part of a repertoire of violence that simultaneously produces, and is produced by, a certain social order. As such, wartime sexual violence is an interpersonal type of violence that connects the individual, group, societal, institutional and even international levels.

Further, it appears that wartime sexual violence is not just the product of the war situation but has to be understood as a continuation and an exacerbation of violence occurring in peacetime in various social institutions, and that tightly connects various norms, practices and values that support and legitimize the social order. Vojdik (2014, 927) has notably highlighted how sexual violence is part of a continuum of violence against both male and female bodies that occurs well beyond the specific settings of conflicts and wars. So while conflict-related sexual violence is as much about feminizing/subjugating the victim than about masculinizing/empowering the perpetrator, it is also meant to recast a social order in a context of tensions around who owns the State, the economic resources, etc. As such, it resonates with the structural violence of intersecting gendered, ethnic, racial and socio-economic hierarchies.

Looking at the wider context is thus key for understanding the relations of power from which sexual violence emanates, but also to which it gives birth. Wartime sexual violence usually occurs alongside numerous other types of physical violence, fed by an increased availability and circulation of weapons, and by an extreme militarization of societies. In addition, as shown by Enloe (1983), one of the reasons for the intensification of sexual violence during conflicts relates to the amplified polarization of gender roles, and to the disruption of traditional gender norms. In a context where displays of militarized masculinity become not just widespread, but also normalized, traditional masculinity models, often based on the performance of familial breadwinning functions, are weakened. Further, the destruction of local economies, the unweaving of social, communal and cultural ties entailed by displacement, killings and forced enrolment, considerably hamper the attainment of such masculinity models. And in contexts where traditional means to achieve masculinity are unavailable or extremely difficult to secure, physical violence turns out to be a key resource for enacting masculinity (Messerschmidt 1993). Sexual violence thus becomes one of the means—it is, of course, not the only one, which explains why sexual violence is not perpetrated in all conflict settings, and by all conflict actors—to (re-)assert one's masculinity and one's place in the gendered social hierarchy.

How does this all play out in the case of sexual violence against men? Simply put, male sexual victimization effectively undermines the masculinity of the victim, through an attack on what is supposed to epitomize it in most cultures, that is, male sexual organs. Simultaneously, it (re-)asserts the masculinity, power and control of the perpetrator, including when the perpetrator is a woman. As an apparently transgressive act that bears all the characteristics of a "runaway norm that overtakes cultural, religious, or legal thresholds" (Leatherman 2011, 29), wartime sexual violence against men seems to push the limits of horror ever further, with regards to the type of violence inflicted (gang rape, bestiality, castration, mutilation and so forth), to the targets of violence (civilians, helpless prisoners, boys, old men and others), and to the agency of violence (publicity, prisoners forced to rape other prisoners, fathers or sons forced to rape their male and female close relatives, and so on). This is of course not to suggest that wartime sexual violence against women is any less horrible, but that, because of the existing gender norms and representations, the sexual victimization of men is widely seen as more taboo, as more transgressive, and, therefore, as less tolerable. Overtaking thresholds accompanies feminization to (re-)establish hierarchies between masculinities, in a context where violence and sexual violence against women are likely to be widespread, and thus not "enough" as a stand-alone action to signal one's power and to distinguish oneself. Thereby, perpetrators of wartime sexual violence against men (re-)affirm their masculine domination, and emulate a "new" and more "powerful" model of masculinity. The performativity of wartime sexual violence against men is enhanced by the fact that the conflict context produces, and is produced by, empowered but also highly vulnerable masculinities: in particular, a powerful male soldier can lose his place in the conflict setting if he becomes victim of rape or of other forms of sexual violence, because his status is tightly connected to his ability to enact a strong masculinity model, and to abide by heterosexual norms. So male sexual victimization can be understood both as a masculinization/feminization performance, and as a reiteration of heteronormativity, just like in the case of sexual violence against women (Alison 2007, 77).

But the threat of sexual violence can also be enough to subdue populations, as shown by the numerous cases where sexual torture in prison includes threats of rape or of castration as part of a well-established repertoire (see, for instance, in the case of El Salvador, Leiby 2012). As Hooper (2001, 70) explains, "The threat of feminization is a tool with which male conformity to hegemonic ideals is policed. This threat works when subordinate masculinities are successfully feminized and then demonized". In the case of conflict-related sexual violence against men, however, it is not so much hegemonic ideals that are enforced, but rather violent and ultra militarized masculinities that seek to establish their control over economic, social and political resources. And this is effected by making it impossible for survivors to henceforth abide by the traditional key elements that are often used as a standard for measuring masculinity, for instance, being the breadwinner, being able to protect oneself and one's family, and so on. So if the twin processes of feminization and of masculinization are successfully performed, it is mostly because, as I will further analyze in chapter 4, the great majority of survivors feel deprived of their capacity to fulfill social expectations vis-à-vis men, not to mention hegemonic models of masculinity.

Male sexual victimization is often staged and choreographed in order to convey absolute domination: gang rapes, castrations, public humiliation, men turned into "bush wives", etc., are all meant as unquestionable statements of domination. They are part of a larger repertoire, including, for instance, enslavement, which aims at humiliating and feminizing the victims, and at designating more or less masculine and powerful men. Buss (2009, 159) notes, for instance, that "there is evidence that sexual violence including rape and forms of sexual slavery against men was a feature of the genocide" in Rwanda. Since most of the literature on the Rwandan genocide has so far focused on those men and women who were killed as well as on those who were raped, assumed to be mostly if not only women, this statement calls for renewed attempts to better articulate an understanding of sexual violence with other types of conflict-related violence. Male sexual brutalization in particular is a powerful instrument that, used together with military coercion, sanctions the domination of a certain type of individuals—mostly male—who embody an all-powerful masculinity. They enact a specific model of hyper violent militarized masculinity that uses violence and coercion to establish its dominance. In other words, they participate in the hierarchical (re-)organization of masculinities in a given society and as such play a key role in the gender order (Hooper 2001, 69). Patterns of wartime sexual violence against men thus underscore the malleability and fluidity of models of masculinity, especially in conflict contexts, and demonstrate how they can become part and parcel of war patterns.

It is important to stress the fact that this does not entail that sexual violence against men is necessarily a strategy or a "weapon of war". Empirical evidence suggests that, with a few exceptions mostly related to sexual torture in detention, it is not spelled out as such. Rather, the performativity of male sexual victimization is a consequence of how gender norms and roles support and underpin societal relations of power. And because patterns of masculinities have their own historicity and are inscribed in local cultures, conflict-related sexual violence against men always displays contextual specificities. What is important is thus not so much the specific shapes that male sexual brutalization can take, than the contextualized performativity of such acts. Although it would require more systematic and precise empirical records than what is currently available, existing data suggests that the perpetration of sexual violence against men varies according to what is considered, or not, as "proper" or "degrading" for a man to do in a specific setting. In the Great Lakes region of Africa, for instance, many male survivors I spoke with seemed more distressed of having been forced to perform the cooking, washing and cleaning duties "of a woman", than of having had their genitals beaten.

Similarly, and as we will further explore in the following sections, what the conflict is about, who it involves, and what shapes it takes, all impact on the characteristics of male sexual brutalization. In nationalist and ethnic conflicts, for instance, the nexus between ethnicity or nationhood and manhood underpins logics of domination and subjugation, in terms of masculinization and feminization. So while the appropriation and desecration of the other group's women are meant to humiliate them, the subjugation of male bodies via military victory and practices of male rape, sexual humiliation and castration underscore the dominated status of the vanquished. These processes are even more obvious during genocides, where the extermination of the other group entails the total annihilation of both its masculinities and femininities—hence cases where "enemy" men are first castrated before (or after) being killed. In detention settings, male sexual torture constructs a patriarchal, masculine authority, and reflects attempts to dominate and control those who are seen as challenging the existing power structure. And the performativity of sexual violence seems effective at the international level too, as it emphasizes an international security order, and buttresses an international political and military hierarchy.

Looking at the gender performativity of wartime sexual violence against men thus provides a general framework for understanding its occurrence. It demonstrates how patriarchal principles of social organization constantly adapt to tensions over power, and structure the position of individuals, both male and female, in relation to the violence that is perpetrated. However, in order to understand variations in prevalence, in types of violence, and of perpetrators, one has to dig deeper into specific models of masculinity, and into local configurations of power. In other words, feminization/masculinization and super/subordination processes entailed in sexual violence against men derive from, and in turn take on, different meanings in different settings and configurations.

2.2. SUBJUGATION, ETHNIC CLEANSING AND SOCIETAL (RE-)ORDERING

As the cases listed in the previous chapter suggest, wartime sexual violence against men is a regular—though by no means universal—occurrence in conflicts where ethnicity constitutes a major line of division between combatants. A closer look at this type of conflicts reveals that they share two interesting and interrelated common features that play an important role for explaining male sexual brutalization: patriarchy and patrilineality. Patriarchy, a system whereby men hold power at all societal levels, including within the familial cell, is usually described as a system that enhances male power and female subordination. In conflict contexts, this central role granted to men, however, turns them into primary targets for the "other" side, which explains that men are often singled out for killing in genocidal contexts, as the example of Srebrenica, among many others, shows. When men are targeted or weakened, it is the very backbone of the community that is sapped. This is why sexual violence against men is a very effective strategy for destroying family and community linkages. In the Great Lakes region of Africa, for instance, just like in most patriarchal societies (Sivakumaran 2007, 268), one of the key roles of men—and indeed, one of the key markers of masculinity—is to protect their wives, their children and their ageing parents but also the wider community. They are responsible for the security of the whole group. If they cannot protect themselves, if they are turned into victims, then their ability to protect the rest of the group will be questioned. The very same reasoning obviously lies at the core of sexual violence against women, as suggested by MacKenzie (2010, 206): "The act of rape becomes an effective strategy because it creates dis-order by desecrating the authority and property assured to males, as well as violating established norms relating to the family". One of the effects of sexual violence is thus to deeply undermine the concerned group's cohesion by attacking its patriarchal foundations. Men belonging to the subjugated group can no longer uphold the system, either because they have not been able to perform their protective function—when "their" women have been sexually assaulted—or because they have directly lost their masculine status—by being themselves sexually brutalized.

Male survivors of sexual violence cannot support the group's social organization any longer, and the attack on their masculinity equates with a destruction of the group's power structures. In this perspective, sexual violence is particularly efficient on civilian men, who don't have a status of combatant to help them uphold their masculine status. Turning them into victims, incapable of protecting themselves or their relatives, deprives them of their claim to masculinity (Myrttinen 2003, 42). As we will discuss in the chapter on male survivors, stories of men being ostracized by their own families and wives after their "unfortunate experience" became known are, for instance, very common in sub-Saharan Africa, and many of them are henceforth excluded from communal activities. In that sense, patriarchy multiplies the effects of sexual violence against men so that affects not only the survivor and his close relatives but also the whole community, which is left humiliated, unprotected and disempowered. These men cannot be men any longer, they cannot embody the dominant model of masculinity anymore. As a result, the communities to which they belong lose their ethnicity, they symbolically become communities of "women", of "homosexuals", symbolically and psychologically deprived of any ability to regenerate and perpetuate themselves.

In very patriarchal societies, where sexuality remains extremely taboo, and where male power and invulnerability constitute a core organizing principle, sexual violence against men seems to embody the ultimate transgression, the one that will underline the omnipotence of the transgressor, while depriving the victim of the means and the will to revolt. If sexual violence against women admittedly gives to armed groups and armies a sense of power and control, then sexual violence against men cannot but be seen as the ultimate form of control over populations, as well as over territory and resources, which local men usually "own". By sexually "owning" men, perpetrators of male sexual brutalization symbolically appropriate what these men used to own, power, territories, wealth, women, and so on. Sexual violence against men can thus be interpreted as an expression of territoriality for the group of perpetrators, whereby the symbolic possession of (mostly civilian) populations is achieved through the possession and breaking of their males. It is a form of territorial domination that is inscribed in bodies, and that builds on the destruction of core social links. Communities and individuals alike are broken, and thus more malleable and less likely to revolt against those armed groups or armies, who try to assert their rule over them. Interestingly, even the *potentiality* of sexual violence against men can be used as an element of propaganda against the other side in an ethnic conflict context. In Serbia and Kosovo, for instance, Kosovo Albanians were accused by Serbs and Kosovo Serbs of using rape, including male rape, to terrorize Kosovo Serbs and force them to emigrate (Bracewell 2000).

The other important feature from which wartime sexual violence against men can draw and increase its effectiveness is patrilineality. In patrilineal societies, descent and ethnic (and sometimes also national) belonging are traced through the male line. This grants men the power to allow groups to reproduce and perpetuate themselves. But what is crucial to understand is that patrogenesis, the fact that only men are considered generative persons for a given ethnic or national group, is a source of both strength and vulnerability for concerned men, as "males alone possess the ability to bequeath to their offspring certain identity categories, or what might be called 'social ontology', such as membership in a family, tribe, or religious, ethnic, or other group" (King and Stone 2010, 330). In such settings, attacking men by raping, castrating or sexually humiliating them stems from a similar strategy to that of raping women: an ethnic cleansing one (see, for instance, Carlson 2006, 20; Carpenter 2006, 89). In societies where ethnicity is seen as being transmitted by males only, it is indeed a very efficient way to target specifically the bearer of ethnicity and hence to destroy his own capacity to perpetuate his ethnic group. Attacks on sexual organs, especially castration and mutilation, directly target the ethnic group's capacity to reproduce itself in the future. As detailed by Sivakumaran (2007), in ethnic conflict settings perpetrators of wartime sexual violence against men seem to pursue three effects: emasculation/feminization, homosexualization and prevention of procreation, thus simultaneously resorting to the masculine/feminine dichotomy, the heterosexual norm and patriarchal principles. In the former Yugoslavia, for instance, men's genitals were beaten or even destroyed in what can be understood as an attempt to annihilate their reproductive functioning and to guarantee that they would not be able to produce ethnic minority children in the future. But sexually assaulting men of the "other" ethnic group also ensures the shattering of the social and cultural order, by using heteronormativity in order to instill confusion about the masculinity of those who are supposed to sustain patrilineality. This strategy often proves effective since, as we will see in chapter 4, most male survivors I have met feel confused about their gender identity, or have the feeling of having been "homosexualized", of having been deprived of their masculinity and of their capacity to support their relatives and community.

By contrast, the figure of combatant that is enforced through these practices is that of a strong, fearless and extremely violent individual, often male, who exerts absolute physical and psychological domination on others, both men and women. There is ethnographic evidence that patrilineality favors a "strong masculine identity" (Paige and Paige 1981, 10), which might feed hegemonic and dominant masculinity models by increasing competition between fraternity groups, and by rendering women "as, at most, nurturers and containers but not cogenerators-genitors of life" (King and Stone 2010, 331). It is, therefore, interesting to see that patrilineal systems also come to reinforce the feminization/subjugation and masculinization/domination effects of sexual violence, by underscoring the empowered status of victorious males. In these circumstances, assaulting or castrating men from the "enemy" group entails the symbolic appropriation of this group's masculinity. It demonstrates its weakness, and underscores its subordinate status (Zarkov 2001, 78).

It is also important to observe that the effectiveness of sexual violence against men is enhanced by the synergy existing in the way ethnic belonging and gender function. As Cynthia Cockburn has observed (2004a, 30), both are exclusionary and serve to produce "others": "There are both similarities and differences between gender and ethnicity in the processes they involve and in the effects they produce. They are alike in tending towards an 'othering' process in which a non-self is defined and excluded in the very process of defining the self". Both produce a certain societal structuring (creating hierarchies, differences, etc.) and function as legitimization resources for particular cultural, social, economic, political or military actors. Both also operate as cognitive shortcuts for making sense of the world, by creating simple dichotomies around which societies operate: masculinity is opposed to femininity, and in-group to out-group. In that perspective, wartime sexual violence against men performs a double othering on survivors, who are subjugated through both feminization, and ethnic domination (or annihilation). In other words, their masculinity is doubly negated: as males, and as patrilineal agents. This is what Chodorow (2002, 256), referring to genocidal situations, describes: "Challenges to ethnicity and nation threaten individual and collective selfhood, and the close developmental and experiential interlinking of selfhood and gender mean that masculinity is also threatened. Humiliation from men (the man-boy dichotomy) becomes linked with fears of feminization (the male-female dichotomy)".

Looking at how the synergy between gender roles and ethnicity affects the positioning of perpetrators of sexual violence against men proves very instructive too. In patriarchal societies that are also characterized by ethnic divisions, social domination follows complex patterns, determined by gender, by ethnic belonging and also by position on the social ladder. Combatants who have established themselves as unyielding defenders of the group and, maybe more importantly, as successful conquerors of the enemy, can hope to secure their status at the very top of the societal hierarchy[2]. Their masculinity display is doubly strengthened, as they have proven their worth by protecting the in-group, and dominating (including sexually) the out-group (see, for instance, the case of sexual violence perpetrated by Hindu nationalists, Anand 2007). In that sense, sexual violence (against both men and women) cannot only participate in (re-)producing a societal hierarchy between dominating/masculinized and dominated/feminized groups but it can also contribute to the creation, or maintenance, of a certain gender order within the perpetrators' group. To put it differently, perpetrating sexual violence seems to perform external as well as internal functions. It can ensure the domination of certain masculinity models over subjugated ones, as well as over femininities, be they attached to female bodies (women of both one's and the other community), to male ones (men of the subjugated group) or to LGBTQI individuals.

Thereby, sexual violence has a direct impact on hierarchies of femininities and masculinities, in relation to their ethnic and socio-economic foundations.

It is, therefore, clear that, at least in ethnic conflict settings, wartime sexual violence against men, and wartime sexual violence against women, stem from the same gender ideology, underpinned by ethnic and social differentiation processes. However, because they target the specific positioning of men and women in the social order, they seem to display different underlying logics: in the case of sexual violence against women, a logic of appropriation of female bodies, seen as "belonging" to the "other" males, is at play, whereas in the case of sexual violence against men, it is primarily the functioning of the "other" group that is targeted, with the ultimate result of preventing it from reproducing itself, and from surviving. This explains why patriarchal and patrilineal systems enhance the effectiveness of both male and female sexual victimization, and are likely to encourage its perpetration.

2.3. ENFORCING STATE'S DOMINATION THROUGH TERROR

As we have seen, sexual violence against men also regularly occurs when States are faced with internal political and ideological dissent. In these cases, sexual violence is part of a larger repertoire of torture mostly practiced in detention, which is legitimized by "anti-insurgency" or "anti-terrorist" policies[3]. In these configurations, male sexual brutalization is used in order to strengthen or reassert the State's socio-political dominance. It is initiated, controlled, regulated and perpetrated by agents who are motivated by ideologies and/or who are acting on behalf of a State. Whereas reports of sexual torture are often dismissed by military and political authorities as being isolated incidents committed by a few "bad apples"[4], the regularity of such occurrences suggests that they are intimately connected to the way States enforce their domination.

So why do States, including parties to the Geneva Conventions and democratic ones, use sexual torture on men? The empirical evidence described in the previous chapter suggests that sexual torture perpetrated in detention displays different characteristics from sexual violence perpetrated in nationalist or ethnic conflicts, with fewer cases of rape and castration, and a more widespread use of sexual humiliation, forced nudity, genital beatings and other forms of brutality such as electric shocks applied to the genitals. This suggests that the primary aim is not so much the destruction of the male prisoners' reproductive capacities (hence, patrilineality does not seem to play an important role here) as intimidating and subjugating them. In former prisoners' narratives (see also chapter 4), sexual torture is often described as an integral, almost normalized part of interrogation procedures, which seems to frequently crown the torture process, as a way either to extract confessions that other methods of torture have failed to produce, or to signify the prisoners' abject status.

For individual prisoners, sexual torture comes to reinforce the isolationist effect of detention by specifically targeting one of the most important social dimensions of their identity: gender. In that sense, it complements other types of psychological and physical violence used on prisoners, such as the practice of "white torture", entailing extreme sensory deprivation and prolonged periods of solitary confinement. The isolationist effects of sexual torture can even expand long after prisoners are released, because of the difficulties they experience in talking about what happened to them. In that sense, the taboo nature of these acts further ostracizes them from the rest of their community or social group. Seeking redress, exposing perpetrators means acknowledging what one has been through, and potentially facing mockery or incredulity, thereby further reinforcing the feelings of isolation and alienation of survivors, and of their close relatives. Sexual torture is thus very effective in separating mobilized individuals from their communities of origin, and while it strips them of their dominant masculine status, it significantly weakens their capacity to act as mobilizing—and, therefore, as opposition—agents. In other words, and contrary to other repressive methods implemented by States, sexual torture is not likely to produce martyrs of the cause, a consequence which would actually enhance their social and political status, and further their community's cohesion and determination. Instead, by highlighting the (gendered) vulnerability of prisoners, sexual torture undermines their position and contributes to unraveling the social links that rebellion might have created or strengthened. By feminizing prisoners through sexual torture, State agents also enforce their subordinate place in the gender order, and confirm the State, and its representatives, in their hyper masculine and heterosexual status. Further, within the frame of anti-terrorist or anti-insurgency policies, the feminization of male prisoners effected through sexual torture suggests a wish to depoliticize them, and to deprive them of their political agency.

The fact that the effects of sexual torture expand far beyond prisoners, and affect the communities to which these individuals belong, is, therefore, not surprising. This is especially the case of rebellion movements led by specific religious or cultural groups. As Ross (2002, 309) explains, (threat of) sexual torture, and in particular (threat of) rape and castration are very effective tools to reassert the superiority of the State and the subordinate status of these communities, sometimes with a racialized undertone: "The administration of a racial system requires the constant threat of torture as a means of managing surveillance and maintaining the ideology of mastery". By sexually brutalizing individuals who embody, for instance, minorities' struggle for equal rights, for self-determination or for any other political change, the State uses their feminized bodies to discipline whole sections of the population. In this perspective some of the mechanisms described in the previous section seem to apply here as well, in the sense that sexual violence perpetrated in detention is often directed at political, cultural, religious or community leaders, whose masculinity and, therefore, implied leadership capacities, are thereby undermined. Sexual violence thus equates to a strategy of political demobilization of opponents, or even more radically aims at destroying the capacity of opposition movements to act as groups, as suggested by Card (1996, 8): "There is more than one way to commit genocide. One way is mass murder, killing individual members of a national, political or cultural group. Another is to destroy a group's identity by decimating cultural and social bonds. Martial rape does both".

These acts aim at terrorizing whole communities by showing (and demonstrating) that they are defenseless. If their leaders can be subjected to such gruesome acts of violence, then these groups should certainly reconsider their participation in rebellion. And if those who were tortured were not community leaders, this is even worse: it means that anyone can be arrested and become a victim of sexual violence. It reinforces a feeling of impunity, and of arbitrary rule. Sexual torture demonstrates that the State is determined to enforce its authority, no matter the cost. They are "unforgivable" acts of violence that are perpetuated in such a way that they cannot be forgotten or expurgated. The excess, the transgression, breaking taboos are all part of a methodology of extremes, the purpose of which is to leave traces, to turn bodies into means of expressing an indelible message. This type of violence is part of a repertoire where the perpetration of unforgivable and imprescriptible acts signals a rationale of a "definitive breach", of barbaric extravagance (Féron and Hastings 2003). Male sexual victimization stands well beyond the accepted modalities of war, and, therefore, can never be fully accounted for. In official discourses, it is repeatedly described as the acts of an uncontrollable and disgraceful minority, and as such it does not "belong" to the war narrative, and, therefore, cannot be recounted as any other wartime injury. The excess epitomized by sexual violence pushes it in the realm of the anecdotal, of the footnotes. Because these acts are seen as degrading, as unacceptable and because many observers simply refuse to believe that they are perpetrated, they are relegated to a narrative limbo, whose existence undermines the group's solidarity networks—unless, of course, it is possible for male sexual torture survivors to revert the stigma, to somehow convert it into a badge of honor, by exposing it for what it is: a political act which is feminizing and subjugating only insofar as we still believe in its performativity. Testimonies of male survivors, as we will further explore in chapter 4, suggest that such reversion of the stigma is extremely difficult to accomplish. It is, however, interesting to note than in a series of cases, women's involvement in rebellion movements was actually triggered by sexual violence, such as in the LTTE case (Eager 2008, 140).

2.4. THE ROLE OF MILITARIZED MASCULINITIES

All the societies in which episodes of conflict-related sexual violence against men have been recorded are or were characterized by a very high level of militarization, in terms both of the number of combatants and of weapons in circulation, and of the societal penetration of military values. It is of course important to keep in mind that, as we will further illustrate in chapter 3, not all combatants are willing to perpetrate sexual violence against men, and that such practices can generate tensions within armed groups. However, the way militarization operates, and the way armies and armed groups function, favor the empowerment of highly violent individuals who are likely not only to vie for domination over civilian populations, but also to compete with one another. And the enactment of masculinity is a powerful asset with regards to both of these objectives. It should, therefore, not come as a surprise that wartime sexual violence against men is mostly perpetrated by men in arms, members of armed groups or soldiers and police officers. This feature, which characterizes wartime sexual violence against women too, seems to be slightly more pronounced when victims are male[5]. This suggests that militarized masculinities play a strong role in the perpetration of sexual violence against men, whether it is the outcome of a broader and carefully planned strategy like in Bosnia-Herzegovina, or whether it derives from a loss of control of military leaders over their troops, as the case of DRC illustrates. When conflicts stretch over long periods of time like in Eastern DRC or in the Central African Republic, wartime sexual violence against men can become a way to enforce a militarized heterosexual normativity, both within the perpetrators' groups and in the whole society that is subjected to military rule.

How can we make sense of these features? Here again, it seems that the way sexual violence against men is perpetrated performs both external and internal functions for the group to which the perpetrators belong. Committing these extremely violent and transgressive acts in public obviously reinforces their impact on survivors and on bystanders, and it also enhances the power of the perpetrators over civilian populations. Sexual violence against men is thereby staged as a performance of militarized masculinities where the power and the virility of the fraternity group are exalted (Price 2001, 216). As such it is a way for armed groups or armies to impose their power and domination, and to contest or abase the masculinity of civilians, which is seen as "soft" or "weak" as compared to the militarized models. This is not without echo to the practice of shaming war objectors for weakness and cowardice, and to submit them to homophobic stigmatization (see, for instance, Conway 2008). Glorified militarized masculinities are opposed to the civilians' feminized ones, and their assumed lack of virility is substantiated by their emasculation through rape or other forms of sexual brutalization. Sexual violence thus establishes the combatants' superior status and legitimizes their predatory behavior on civilian populations, especially when, like in Eastern DRC, the conflict increasingly takes on criminal traits. As observed by Daley (2008, 234) in the case of Burundi, militarization is often accompanied by violence exerted upon subordinate and marginalized masculinities: "Military men's intolerance of alternative forms of masculinity often leads to the most brutal atrocities being inflicted on men who don't fight or belong to the other social and political categories". This means that those who are targeted are not necessarily singled out because of their ethnic or religious belonging, or because of their political opinions. Instead, sexual violence, as part of a larger repertoire of violence, is used as a form of social control that cuts across gender, socio-economic, ethnic or religious categories.

In societies torn apart by decades of warfare and/or of instability, and even in the absence of a strong State, militarization entails the penetration of military values in the social fabric. Ideologies of domination are underpinned by a violent heterosexual normativity, which is enforced upon all sections of society. In this context, sexual violence against both men and women is normalized; it becomes part of the militarized culture, as a way to impose a certain social order, where men displaying violent, militarized and heterosexual masculinities subjugate the rest of the population. As Leatherman (2011, 155) explains, sexual violence helps to reinforce their hyper violent and militarized masculine identity: "This identity is predicated on the opposition of Self and Other, so that 'I am because you are not'. These maneuvers circle around social processes of de-humanizing, treating the other as evil, subhuman or object of revulsion". In other words, perpetrators promote their hyper masculinized self by feminizing others. Rebellion groups can even use the transgressive nature of sexual violence against men to contest existing rules—for instance, traditional structures of power—and to impose their own militarized power. Precisely because it often appears random, transgressive and extreme, sexual violence against men is a very effective tool for challenging existing power structures, for turning populations into submission, and for asserting a new social order. By breaking taboos, cultural norms and values, and by seemingly ignoring traditional (hegemonic) models of masculinity, perpetrators of sexual violence against men emancipate themselves from existing power structures, and use fear and terror in order to underpin their own desired alternative. Social control is thereby implemented through the gender order.

There is also mounting empirical evidence suggesting a desensitization of combatants and a parallel dehumanizing of victims, which lead to the use, in many contemporary cases of conflict, of ever more extreme forms of violence (Wood 2009, 139). This is especially the case of prolonged conflicts, where the disruption of normal life seems to lead to a gradual loss of values. This is what Oloya (2013, 53) describes in the case of Uganda: "The absence of an overarching moral umbrella in times of war provides the opportunity for 'anything goes' because of the uncertainty over what is normal or abnormal, real and unreal, acceptable and unacceptable". The frequent uprooting of combatants who are usually recruited extremely young, and who move from one combat site to another, entails the dissolution of preexisting social, and in particular familial links. By fully embracing militarized and aggressive masculinity models, combatants acknowledge their belonging to a new group, and their adhesion to its norms.

In parallel, it appears that the perpetration of sexual violence against men also performs internal functions for armed groups. Just like sexual violence against women has been shown to promote bonding between perpetrators (see, among many others, Alison 2007, 77; Goldstein 2004, 365; Leatherman 2011, 155; Price 2001, 16), male sexual brutalization, especially when it is perpetrated by a group, promotes cohesion and complicity. Perpetrators are bonded by horror, by the transgression of taboos, but they are also empowered by the very nature of their deeds, and by the process of bonding itself. Because they are often perpetrated collectively, these practices serve to foster group solidarity, which is always likely to falter in the tough conflict conditions. In addition, when several individuals participate in these acts, it entails a dilution of responsibility, meaning that the responsibility for this transgression is shared by the whole group of perpetrators, and not by its individual members. Nobody is innocent, but no specific individual bears the responsibility either. As I further detail in chapter 3, there is also some evidence that these episodes of sexual violence are sometimes orchestrated as bonding practices, initiation rituals and rites of passage for young and/or new combatants (Amir 1971). They can constitute a means of combatant socialization (Cohen 2013, 461), whereby new recruits are expected to enact the hyper violent and militarized models of masculinity that are valorized by the group.

It is also interesting to look at cases where sexual violence is perpetrated internally, on male members of the armed group itself. The empirical evidence I have collected in the Great Lakes region of Africa indicates, for instance, that those, men or women, who have just joined an armed group are much more likely to be targeted for sexual violence by their own colleagues. It can seem paradoxical to submit new recruits to forms of violence that are likely to break them and to undermine their capacities to fight, but Belkin and Terrell (2012, 560) suggest that sexual violence is something that a soldier has to learn to endure, a kind of test that proves that s/he is strong enough to be a soldier: "When male troops are raped, penetration can conjure up multiple meanings in military culture, including the notion that the victim is too weak to fend off attack, and hence not worthy of being a warrior (and so abjected), but also that he is strong enough to take it like a man". In that sense, sexual violence perpetrated within armed groups can be interpreted as a masculinity performance for both the perpetrator and the victim if he is strong enough to defend himself and foil the attack or, failing that, if he manages to demonstrate his (masculine) resilience. Further, sexual violence can also be used to construct and maintain hierarchies of masculinity between combatants. More specifically, there are indications that sexual violence exerted on new (male) recruits is used as a strategy in the competition between combatants to reach leadership positions. That is, those who are unable to defend themselves when sexually attacked, and who are thereby feminized, are deemed unable to incarnate and to lead the group in the future: "The capacity to resist is also diminished by reducing the pool from which leaders are drawn; known victims, for example, are less likely to access leadership or military positions" (UN 2013, 12). Though this has to be nuanced as the perpetration of sexual violence against men often raises internal oppositions[6], this suggests that perpetrators are also driven by their own ambition, and that the performance of an aggressive masculinity can in some cases constitute an effective tool to enhance one's status within the group.

2.5. STRUCTURING AN INTERNATIONAL AND RACIAL GENDER ORDER

While many reported cases of conflict-related sexual violence against men seem to occur during internal and asymmetrical conflicts, such as in Eastern DRC or in Sri Lanka, there is also considerable empirical evidence that male sexual torture in detention has regularly been used in international conflicts or interventions, for instance, to enact prisoners' submission, or to extract information. It has been documented in both recent and more ancient conflicts, such as by the Japanese in Manchouria, where they used various forms of sexual violence against men, including rapes, forced intercourse with family members and/or the dead (Chang 1997). Other types of conflict-related sexual violence against men, such as the sexual exploitation of local men and boys by international troops, have also attracted attention over the past few years, for instance, in the case of the Central African Republic (Deschamps et al. 2015). Admittedly, these types of violence are constantly and strongly condemned by international political and military authorities. But the fact that the sexual brutalization of men continues to occur at the level of day-to-day interactions between combatants, in spite of these condemnations, calls for attention.

As part of a broader repertoire of coercion, there are clear indications that sexual violence against men can be used as a way to secure the position of certain models of masculinity at the top of the international security order (Razack 2002). Though there certainly are relations between performances of masculinities and the distribution of power at the international level (Hooper 2001), I am not suggesting here that any international actor deliberately and systematically uses sexual violence against men as a strategy to establish its dominance at the international level, but rather that the gendered performativity of this type of violence, as described in the previous sections, holds when perpetrators and victims belong to different national and cultural universes. In other words, sexual violence against men, whether perpetrated by a few "bad apples" or endorsed by a large number of combatants, echoes and replicates wider strategies of domination. In that sense, it conveniently captures, as Razack (2005, 342) describes about the sexual torture perpetrated in Abu Ghraib, the articulation between racial, sexual and political power that is played out in so many international conflicts: "A pyramid of naked male prisoners forced to simulate sodomy conveyed graphically that the project of empire, the West's domination of the non-West, required strong infusions of a violent heterosexuality and patriarchy". When international combatants representing opposing sides are faced with one another, and in particular in detention settings where the body of the other is at the mercy of his (or her) enemies, sexual violence can enact domination and discipline, help with extracting confessions and bolster one's masculinity. In other words, bodies of opponents, of political prisoners, of rebel combatants, are one of the loci where international power relations and power struggles are spelled out and waged.

Gender-related and sexual violence against both men and women has long been part of a wide array of techniques to subdue "inferior races" and to enact the supremacy and dominance of "superior", often white, ones. As explained by Connell (2000, 25), colonial empires were highly gendered institutions, which not only destroyed local gender orders, but also applied violence to impose a new hierarchy dominated by the colonizers' violent masculinities: "This process was the beginning of a global gender order, and the colonizers' masculinities were the first globalizing masculinities". Colonial order was maintained through the use of various kinds of gender-related violence, including feminization (Krishnaswamy 1998). This gender order was subsequently contested and disrupted during decolonization and national liberation wars, which sometimes entailed the adoption, by indigenous communities, of Western-inspired militarized and violent masculinities. By the same token, in societies characterized by a racial-based order like the pre-1994

South Africa or the United States before the abolition of slavery, social control was frequently implemented through male sexual brutalization. Nancy Dowd (2010, 47) shows, for instance, how in the United States black masculinities were debased through the practice of lynching: "Manhood was at the core of lynching, a violent response to the perceived threat of black men being equal to whitemen. Lynching commonly included castration, and it was a public event". The political performativity of sexual violence against men, enhanced by its public nature, enacted the subordination of the whole group to which the victim belonged. Similarly, Ross has demonstrated how, in the context of African Americans' slavery, sexual violence against men including castrating and raping had been used in order not only to violently enforce a racist domination project, but also to establish the superiority of white masculinities upon the willingness of white males to commit such acts: "In symbolizing racial domination through rape, it is the act of genital dismembering rather than penetration, that signifies masculine supremacy. Proper manhood is defined not only by the normativity of the impulse towards masculine violence but more subtly by an injunction not to fear enacting such violence on others. The male who fears beating up a faggot cannot be truly masculine, must be a faggot himself" (Ross 2002, 315).

The use of sexual violence against men, and especially of sexual torture, during more recent international wars and interventions has been amply documented, like in the Congo by Belgium, in Kenya by Britain, in Vietnam by the Unites States and in Algeria by France. In Israel too, as explained by Weishut (2015, 79), recent examples of sexual torture of Palestinian prisoners can be interpreted as both a political and a cultural project: "Put in a broader context, sexual violence toward Arab men by non-Arabs can be viewed as a way to superimpose one culture over another and break down social codes". But the example that has probably been the most commented on and discussed is that of the torture perpetrated in the Abu Ghraib prison in Iraq. US soldiers and personnel of the Central Intelligence Agency have used sexual abuse, sexual humiliation but also rape and sodomy as part of interrogation techniques. "Militarized and masculine presumptions about the oriental other were at the heart of the acts of sexual domination at Abu Ghraib", remarks Nusair, stressing how the simultaneity of sexualization and racialization of the Arab/Muslim prisoner epitomized the domination over a feminized (inferior) Other (Nusair 2008, 183). Pictures and videos in which male prisoners were "sexually dominated, degraded and forced to simulate homosexual acts" marked off the perpetrators' "position as well as the nature of their domination over Iraqi others" (p. 184) through their hypermasculization and patriarchal authority. Guantánamo male detainees have reported similar practices. In all of these cases, feminization, racialization and subjugation of the "enemy" have been implemented through violence exerted on sexual organs, and/or through sexual means. As explained by Patricia Owens, what is primarily asserted through these practices is a hierarchy of masculinities, and the superiority of the masculinity of American combatants: "The hegemonic masculinity of American combatants, for example, is made possible through a continual effort to define its sexuality relative to the sexuality of inferior others, setting it apart and protecting it" (Owens 2010, 1042). Though the use of the concept of hegemonic masculinity should, here again, be qualified[7], a clear mechanism of subjugation of non-militarized masculinities is at play. As such, the use of sexual torture on political prisoners is an instrument of power that glorifies the masculinity of the winner, and that prolongs other tactics of subjugation. Such practices are underpinned by colonial stereotypes and build, among other assumptions, on the supposedly specifically homophobic male culture among Muslims. Their main aim is to (re-)assert the international security order by reaffirming the superiority of some combatants (mostly Western) on others, thanks to a demonstration of their alleged stronger masculinity. But, as observed by Butler, the torture of prisoners in Abu Ghraib and Guantánamo did not just aim to debase their masculinity, it also ambitioned to compel them to adopt their assumed "Arab" identity (2008, 16). In that perspective, sexual torture was doubly performative, by feminizing prisoners/empowering perpetrators and by coercively creating a Muslim figure along the lines of its assumed abjection and backwardness. Looking at the full repertoire of horrors that were committed in these prisons indeed demonstrates a wish to deprive Iraqi prisoners of their dignity, to treat them as trash—which echoes dehumanization practices described in the previous section. Prisoners have been urinated upon, forced to stand with human excreta smeared on their face, neck, chest and stomach, threatened by dogs and snakes and so on. Here, humiliation clearly conveyed a message of super/subordination. In all these examples, sexual violence against men belonging to other nations, as part of a wider repertoire of coercion, builds upon and perpetuates what Quijano has called the coloniality of power, which is "based upon racial social classification of the world population" (Quijano 2007, 171).

Episodes involving international peacekeepers as perpetrators of sexual violence against men confirm the idea that sexual violence is both an emanation and an enactment of the international security order. Peacekeeping and international interventions can even be described as colonial encounters that are often underpinned by rampant racist practices (Brodeur 1997). The recent example of sexual violence against men perpetrated by UN peacekeepers in the Central African Republic, involving French, but also Chadian and Equatorial Guinean soldiers (Deschamps et al. 2015) is very interesting in this respect. It suggests that the nationality of origin is less important than the actual positioning of perpetrators. By embodying a certain type of internationally dominant and even, arguably, hegemonic masculinity, peacekeepers enjoy privileges that are beyond local populations' reach. In that sense, sexual violence exerted by peacekeepers, what Paul Higate has called "exploitative social masculinities" (2007), can also result from a mixture of impunity, and of cultural and socio-economic privilege. Further, it is worth remembering that UN blue helmets have been socialized and trained in national armies, and, therefore, often exposed to, and pushed to adopt violent and militarized models of masculinity.

All these violent and localized practices participate in the imposition of a "global gender order" as described by R. W. Connell (2005, 83), which is also underpinned by global ideologies undermining local models of masculinity, and which generates resistance, in particular through the reaffirmation of local gender hierarchies. Local men, faced with an external (overwhelmingly masculine) force which pretends to impose itself upon all others, and which tries to force an order upon them, strive to retrieve/reenact their masculinities. Their cultural references and values, already questioned by the situation of conflict itself, are put under further stress by non-physically violent practices, such as internationally celebrated gender mainstreaming programs which often try to enforce Western-inspired models of gender equality and gender roles. In that context, extreme forms of violence, and especially sexual violence against co-nationals, or, as Fanon (1963) would have it, against other colonized persons, can be understood as a way to "retrieve" one's masculinity. It has been shown that gender-based and sexual violence against women can result from a backlash to perceived local women's empowerment through westernized gender mainstreaming programs (see, for instance, Wendoh and Wallace 2005). Some of the testimonies I have collected suggest that such processes can also be at play in sexual violence against men and other extreme forms of brutalization, whose transgressive nature seems to convey a statement against imposed international norms, and to reaffirm local combatants' autonomy and of masculinity. Richard, the leader of a Congolese armed group active in North Kivu, stated, for instance, (2009, interview):

> "[In response to my mentioning the international community's disapproval of the use of sexual violence]: We don't care about what they think in America! It is not America here, it is our country and it is not up to them to decide what we can do or not" [8].

This suggests that extreme acts of violence, and among them sexual violence against both men and women, serve in some cases to reassert the agency of local men, and participate in a wider struggle over international power structures.

In parallel, the way episodes of sexual violence against men are told also perpetuate a symbolic and discursive violence towards men in the developing world, reaffirming their lower status. The understanding and framing of how and why gender-based and sexual violence is perpetrated in conflict areas are tightly related to how masculinities of femininities of the "Global South" are viewed. More specifically and as we will further explore in chapter 5, narratives on sexual and gender-based violence that can be found in humanitarian discourses notably endorsed by the UN often perpetuate colonial representations whereby men in the developing world cannot control their sexuality, have to be "educated" in sexual matters and are inherently violent[9]. Often implicitly considered as irrepressible and impervious to gender equality values, they are seen as responsible for the very high levels of (sexual) violence against women, as well as against other men. As such, these narratives entail a pathologization of (post)colonial sexualities and a dehumanization of men of the developing world, which then further strengthen the idea that their masculinities are lesser masculinities. Such representations have also been present in discourses on "enemies of the West", particularly during US interventions in Afghanistan and Iraq, with recurring depictions of "enemy combatants as sexually deviant" (Owens 2010, 1042). These discourses thus use representations of sexuality and of gender roles as indicators of progress and civilization (or lack thereof), and place Third World masculinities at the bottom of the international ladder, far below the masculinity models epitomized by peacekeepers or GIs.

The scattered accounts of episodes of sexual violence against men participate in reinforcing this gendered hierarchy, because humanitarian organizations, as well as policy makers both nationally and internationally, struggle to make sense of the phenomenon, which is presented as extraneous, random and uncontrollable. These depoliticized accounts of sexual violence against men symbolically deprive men living in conflict areas of strategy and of political agency, thus further legitimizing their position at the bottom of the international security order. Consequently, men who are victims of sexual violence are implicitly seen as bearing some responsibility for their own fate, if only by never questioning the highly patriarchal models that are said to be valued in their societies. But because men are seen as dangerous to others (that is, to women and children) as well as to themselves, these narratives come to justify not only interventionist and paternalistic policies, but also military, economic and cultural dominance. Descriptions of the "plight of Third World Women" are, for instance, key for legitimizing interventions to "save" them from violent masculinities, as was apparent at the time of the US intervention in Afghanistan. These narratives construct and strengthen a binary division of the world (the "West" vs. the rest of the world), which is used to define what the "West" is, what its missions vis-à-vis the rest of the world are and to justify wars and interventions. As explained by Owens (2010, 1043), "The Orient at war is an historical construct, an image, a site of cultural production and power made possible by other discourses, those of sexuality, gender and race". The global gender order is thus naturalized, and sexual practices as well as gender values and roles act as key markers of differences in civilization and progress.

Sexual violence against both men and women in warfare undoubtedly stems from the same process of appropriation and destruction. In both cases, power is what is at stake, and domination is effected through the performance and display of certain types of masculinity. Because of the central position of men in cultural, social and political structures, sexual violence against men interrogates and weakens the cultural, social and political order that victims embody. It also asserts a new hierarchy at the local, national and even international levels, which builds on, among other elements, the feminization of survivors induced by the gendered performativity of sexual violence. Shedding light on the role that sexual violence against men plays in the constitution or reproduction of local, national and international gender orders helps to question commonly held assumptions about how war is waged and won, and further unveils the role played by militarized and violent masculinities in conflict. In addition, it helps to situate conflicts within the wider dynamics of power, bringing to the surface the implications of the gender bias that often informs theories and analyses of violence, but also peacekeeping and conflict resolution policies.

The analysis provided above does not imply that the phenomenon of sexual violence against men is present in all conflicts or practiced by all parties in a conflict. It however highlights the existence of variations in types of sexual violence against men perpetrated in various contexts, and proposes explanations for such differences. In fact, a growing body of empirical literature on the subject is shedding light on the conditions and contexts in which such practices become integral to the conflict dynamics. Yet, it seems urgent to develop a conceptual approach capable to account for variations in wartime sexual violence against men while situating them within a wider theory of masculinities, gender and power. This book also aims to encourage a more systematic integration of existing and future analyses into the theoretical discussions on the gendered dynamics of conflicts and their wider social and political implications. Such a conceptual move transcends gendered distinctions between victims, and between perpetrators, which hinder a more organic and integrated understanding of sexual violence against women and men in conflict situations.

Chapter 3

Perpetrators and Bystanders

While a few researchers have explored the motivations of perpetrators of sexual violence against women in conflict zones (see, for instance, Eriksson Baaz 2009; Eriksson Baaz and Stern 2013; Skjelsbæk 2015), very little is known about those who perpetrate sexual violence against men. Are they the same people? How do they justify these acts? What consequences does the experience of perpetrating sexual violence against men have on the social inclusion of perpetrators? Do they get access to some sort of additional "patriarchal dividend" (Connell 1987, 1995) as a result of their acts?

This chapter mostly builds on interviews I have conducted in Eastern DRC and in Burundi since 2009 with former combatants, both male and female. Collecting perpetrators' testimonies has been a long process, complicated by the fact that I could not rely on pre-existing methods or experiences to do so. For these reasons, and before detailing the information that I have collected over time, this chapter's first section elaborates on how I proceeded to gather primary data, and what difficulties and dilemmas I have faced.

3.1. RESEARCHING PERPETRATORS OF SEXUAL VIOLENCE

Undertaking research on perpetrators of sexual violence entails a series of ethical, methodological, security and legal dilemmas for the researcher. As I discussed with men who had perpetrated such atrocities, I could not shy away from what they had done. At the same time, I knew that most of them had also, at times, suffered atrocities, faced the loss of relatives, lived in more than precarious conditions, known hunger and fear, been injured and so on. Some of them, in the Congo, for instance, had been kidnapped, abused and forcefully enrolled in an armed group, before seemingly embracing militarized and hyper-violent masculinity models. Some of the perpetrators I have met have expressed deep regret for what they had done, while others seemed indifferent to the suffering they had caused. The concept of perpetrator attaches a single, and deeply stigmatizing, label on individuals whose lives have been everything but simple, everything but linear. Perhaps more than any other concept used in social sciences, the category of "perpetrators" raises more questions than it clarifies, and if anything, it only sheds light on the incredible complexity of conflict settings. It obscures the important nuances existing between those who perpetrate these acts without any second thought and who sometimes take pleasure in the suffering of others, those who perpetrate those acts under duress, those who are complicit, those who resist calls for violence, those who try to help survivors and so on. Like the oppressor/oppressed dichotomy, the perpetrator/victim opposition hampers a more nuanced understanding of the tension between individual agency and coercive models of masculinity (Robinson 2002, 152). So even if I do not want to find any excuse for what they have done, it is only reluctantly that I am using the concept of perpetrator, acknowledging its practical use, but still wary of how it might be instrumentalized, and of how it might oversimplify the lives, values and motives of those who have perpetrated sexual violence against men.

As I further detail in this chapter, there is some empirical evidence of the existence of female perpetrators of sexual violence against men (and women), but although I have also conducted interviews with female former or current combatants in various locations, none of them ever admitted that they had sexually tortured or abused a male combatant, or a male civilian. This might be a reflection of my sample and of the case studies I have chosen to collect data on, but it might also be a consequence of gendered taboos and positioning, preventing my female interviewees to recognize in front of a Western, female researcher that they had committed such acts. Worth repeating also is that most of the perpetrators I have come across were interviewed as former or current male and female combatants, not as perpetrators per se. A few of them turned out to be survivors of sexual violence, even fewer admitted to be perpetrators, and most of them said they were neither. The questions I asked them related to their experience as combatants, notably their experience of fighting, of taking prisoners, of using violence or torture and so on. More often than not, they reflected upon their experience of the war, and explained their choices, hopes and regrets. Clearly none of them was comfortable speaking about sexual violence against men, and most preferred to use circumlocutions and ellipses to describe cases they had participated in, witnessed or heard about. However, I was surprised that some were willing to admit their responsibility, even if rather defensively. This suggests, as we will see in the next sections, a certain degree of normalization of the use of sexual violence against men, at least in a war setting.

In spite of all the precautions I have taken, conducting research on perpetrators has at times been challenging, both practically and psychologically. I have tried to constantly abide by international recognized principles, such as the protection of my research subjects and the minimization of risks for the researched as well as the researcher, and informed consent, among other key criteria. There are very few guidelines on how to do research with perpetrators of sexual violence (as an exception, see, for instance, Hearn, Andersson and Cowburn 2007), much less in a conflict setting, and I was sometimes left to wonder whether I should have reported cases I was hearing about. But in most of the countries where I have been conducting research, like in the Congo or in Burundi, sexual violence against men is not a recognized offence. I also had no way to find those who had been victims of the violence, and who might be needing help—though most of the acts I have been informed of had seemingly been committed in a rather distant past. Needless to say, some of these interviews were psychologically challenging, just as listening to survivors' stories has been distressing.

Finally, as it is a question that has sometimes come up when I was presenting my preliminary fieldwork results, it is worth mentioning that I have almost never felt threatened in the presence of these "perpetrators". I have always paid great care organizing the interviews[1], which often took place in the premises of local NGOs or, in a few cases, in private homes. I have also tried to ensure, with the exception of the interviews for which I needed a translator, as much privacy as possible to my informants. My position as a M'zungu (a Swahili word meaning "someone with white skin") certainly played a role in the respect and attention the people I spoke with showed, but many of them seemed also rather happy or relieved to be invited to tell their stories. Undoubtedly, as we will see in the subsequent sections, some perpetrators also wished to seize this opportunity to explain, justify or downplay what they had done.

Before moving on to detailing perpetrators' and bystanders' narratives on sexual violence against men, the next two sections highlight and discuss the main patterns that have come out of my research, regarding the perpetrators' main profiles and motivations.

3.2. A GREAT DIVERSITY OF PROFILES

Since not much research has yet been done on wartime sexual violence against men, many preconceptions attached to sexual violence against women taint representations of this type of violence too (Skjelsbæk 2015). One of these is that wartime sexual violence against men is usually perpetrated by men in situations of power, and more specifically by high-ranking military officers. And indeed, if we rely on the scattered survivors' stories that are available in the media, it is tempting to assert that perpetrators are always very powerful men, like military officers or warlords. Such representation is in my view partly misleading. Sexual violence is, as we have seen, an act of power, but this does not necessarily imply that those who are perpetrating it are men holding societal or military positions of power. If the perpetrators' testimonies that I have collected are to be believed, many of them were just rank and file soldiers or combatants, sometimes freshly (and forcefully) enrolled, just like some of the survivors. But power is of course relational, and the men and adolescent boys who have been subjected to sexual violence and torture certainly felt powerless as compared to them.

Both State security organizations and rebel groups have been known to perpetrate sexual violence against men—though this is by no means a general rule, as shown by Wood (2009) and Butler et al. (2007)—and the data that I have collected on the ground seems to confirm this finding: in Burundi, for instance, the people I spoke with recounted ghastly stories about male sexual victimization perpetrated by the Burundian army, but also by rebellion groups such as the Forces Nationales de Libération (FNL), the Conseil National Pour la Défense de la Démocratie–Forces pour la Défense de la Démocratie (CNDD-FDD) and so on. In the Congo, stories point at the Congolese army, but also at the Mai-Mai, or at the Rwandan Forces Démocratiques de Libération du Rwanda (FDLR, a Rwandan Hutu rebel group), among many others. In conflict settings all around the world, there is no doubt that sexual violence against men is perpetrated by men and women in arms, sometimes belonging to national armies, sometimes to rebel armed groups. There is, for instance, a wide range of evidence, collected by NGOs, researchers and international organizations, that demonstrates the overwhelming responsibility of State security institutions in the perpetration of sexual torture against men. In Sri Lanka, for instance, there is ample and compelling evidence that most national security organizations have participated in sexual torture against both male and female Tamils, accused of being members of the LTTE (Sooka 2014, 31; Human Rights Watch 2013). Similar evidence has been collected in other secessionist and political conflicts all around the world, including in Israel and Palestine, where research conducted by Weishut (2015, 75) has shown the implication of Israeli soldiers and border police, secret service, police and jail officers in the sexual torture of Palestinian men, either during arrest or during interrogation. In Peru, the State was recognized responsible for most episodes of sexual violence against men that occurred during the conflict, but evidence of public castrations and of other forms of sexual violence perpetrated against male "traitors" by the Shining Path have also been documented (Leiby 2012, 331 and 344). Other contemporary examples include sexual torture perpetrated by US and UK soldiers on male prisoners at Abu Ghraib and Guantánamo (see, among others, Razack 2005) and by the British Army during the 2000 decade in Iraq and previously in the 1960s and 1970s in Northern Ireland (McGuffin 1974). Similarly, rebel groups in Liberia and Sierra Leone, to quote two well-known examples, have also perpetrated sexual violence against men at a seemingly very large scale. The number of Liberian male ex-combatants who have been sexually victimized during the latest conflict by combatants of their own, or of the other side, has, for instance, been estimated at one third overall (see Johnson et al. 2008, 38). My fieldwork data thus does not stand as an exception, but rather comes to confirm the scattered empirical evidence available in other conflict settings.

In parallel, some authors have argued that, genocidal contexts aside, the most extreme and transgressive displays of violence—to which, I argue, sexual violence against men belongs—often occur in ideological vacuums, and are perpetrated by organizations with weak institutional cultures. Barker and Ricardo assert, for instance, that "historically, African armed insurgency movements with clear ideologies, as in the case of Tanzania and South Africa, generally have promoted some degree of restraint in the use of violence, including collective decision-making about the use of violence, social control over members who seek to use excessive violence and often used violence after exhausting non-violent means" (2005, 26). This would suggest that armies are somewhat less likely to perpetrate sexual violence against men, with the exception of sexual torture in detention, which often fulfils clear strategic objectives. Such statements have, however, been contested by other authors. For instance, in their critical review and assessment of the stereotypes surrounding perpetrators of wartime sexual violence against both men and women, Cohen et al. (2013) underscore the fact that contrary to what most believe, sexual violence is not necessarily more common among rebel groups than State militaries.

Based on the empirical evidence that I have collected on the ground, and on existing research, it seems that these divergences in interpretation are mostly due to the fact that many cases of sexual violence against men, and in particular sexual torture in detention, are not coded as such, as I have explained in chapter 1. In other words, on average conventional armies are not less likely to perpetrate sexual violence against men (or women), but they tend to favor the use of different types of violence, which are more likely to be considered as belonging to a torture repertoire. On the one hand, and setting genocidal contexts aside, my fieldwork data shows that State militaries often use sexual torture as a means of putting pressure, extracting confessions and enforcing domination; they are more likely to use sexual humiliation, to apply electric shocks to the genitals and anus, to insert objects through the anus or assault the prisoner's genitals. On the other hand, many of my research participants mentioned examples of rebel groups using forced nudity, enforced incest and enforced rape of other female or male prisoners but also sexual slavery and especially gang rape on male prisoners or new recruits. Quite obviously, more empirical evidence needs to be collected to further document these potential differences, which, if confirmed, could pertain to the context in which these two types of groups operate, their members' training, their organizational cultures and so on. The fact that military cultures are extremely diverse, and shape different models of masculinity and associated practices (Enloe 1993) is likely to prevent any further generalization, though. And given the remaining strong taboos around these issues, as well as the low level of reporting of male survivors, it will also be complicated to gather systematic evidence.

One of the issues that has been raised by researchers working on wartime sexual violence perpetrated by military groups is that the perpetration of such acts often generates tensions within these groups (see, for instance, Wood 2009). Tensions can arise either because the military hierarchy explicitly forbids the use of sexual violence, or because it raises moral concerns among combatants themselves or because it is seen as benefiting the individual to the expense of the collective (Cohen 2013, 465). The empirical evidence I have collected, however, suggests the absence of a general rule regarding the condoning, or condemning, of the use of sexual violence against men by military hierarchies, and the existence of extremely diverse levels of tolerance. In fact, it seems that in many cases sexual torture has been used simply because it produces "results"—though the quote below also suggests a wish to distantiate oneself from the sexual dimension of the act:

> When you fight, when you have enemies, you do what needs doing, you don't ask questions. We didn't intend to … we didn't mean … what I want to say is that we did what we did because that was needed. For instance, if we needed information, then we would do whatever it took to get it, whatever. We didn't mean anything else by it. (Pascal 2013, interview)

As we will see, if there is a general tendency to condemn the use of rape against both male and female civilians, as well as against fellow combatants, attitudes are a lot more ambiguous with regard to sexual torture exerted against male and female prisoners. In Burundi, for instance, as explained by a former officer I met in 2013, the rebel group of the Forces Nationales de Libération (FNL) used to officially punish the rape of women by death penalty, but has also been known to use sexual torture on male and female prisoners (Alexis 2013, interview)[2]. The idea that the military hierarchy is in entire control of soldiers' behavior also overlooks the fact that very few of them correspond to military ideals, and eventually downplays "the agency of soldiers themselves, who are not simply passive recipients of training, but engage in various forms of coping strategies and resistance" (Eriksson Baaz and Stern 2013, 72). As shown by Cohen, perpetrating sexual violence and other atrocities might also be initiated by combatants themselves in order to reinforce group bonding, like in the case of the Revolutionary United Front (RUF) in Sierra Leone, where cohesion was low because of the forced and random recruitment of fighters (2013, 464).

In any case, whereas "lust rapes" of civilian women, to borrow from Eriksson Baaz and Stern (2010b), can sometimes be considered as a kind of personal war bounty for individual combatants, according to my empirical data no such representations appear to apply in the case of wartime sexual violence against men. Even if perpetrators can take sadistic pleasure in inflicting pain, in venting frustration or in transgressing taboos, sexual violence against men seems to generate much less tension between the individual and the collective levels than sexual violence against women. It is also worth underscoring the fact that if rape is often not tolerated by military hierarchies and by armed groups alike, it is not necessarily the case of other forms of sexual violence. In addition, in many developing countries, the concept of rape applies to women only, leaving men out of the interdiction's scope. With very few exceptions, sexual violence against men seems to be considered as a tool to enforce domination, subjugation and fear, and which might benefit the whole group, not the individual combatant perpetrating it:

> In a war-like situation you have to make sure that people respect you, that they understand that they have to cooperate. So, yes, such things have happened, but not because we liked it, but because some combatants thought it was the only way to get local men to obey them. (Jean-Baptiste 2011, interview).

It does not mean, of course, that the use of sexual violence against men does not give birth to oppositions between perpetrators and the wider group. As shown by this testimony from a Congolese officer of the National Congress for the Defence of the People (Congrès national pour la défense du peuple, CNDP), it unveils important tensions and disagreements over morality, means and ends:

> This is wrong, plain wrong. We all know that it is forbidden to do these things on women, but to a man? That is an abomination. I have always condemned these acts and refused to participate, but some of my fellow officers think differently. It is sometimes difficult to say it when you don't agree. But God will be the only judge. (Néhémie 2009, interview)

The question remains, however, of how much of wartime sexual violence against men is organized from the top down and implemented collectively, or results from individual acts that have neither been planned nor endorsed by the hierarchy. Speaking about wartime rapes in general, Goldstein (2004, 368) argues against the idea of wartime rape used as an overall military strategy: "Notwithstanding such cases as Bosnia and Nanking, most wartime rapes are organized not from above, but by small units and individuals. Commanders' attitudes range, in various wars, from relative tolerance or even encouragement, to relatively strict punishment, of rape". In cases of genocide, however, sexual violence against both men and women appears to have almost always been part of the military strategy, even if the specific details of how exactly it should be implemented were left to the appreciation of individual combatants, as the cases of Bosnia-Herzegovina and Rwanda exemplify. Studies on gender-based and sexual violence during the Armenian genocide like Bjørnlund's have produced similar analyses, arguing that if sexual violence was not planned from above, it was far from being discouraged (2011, 30).

There is even less doubt that various military hierarchies all around the world have not only condoned, but also largely organized the sexual torture of male prisoners. In the case of sexual torture perpetrated against Iraqi male prisoners during the second Gulf War, for instance, and though this is contested by the official investigation report that was published afterwards[3], the pattern of sexual abuse clearly followed established interrogation techniques described in CIA manuals (Dodd 2004). Similar observations had been made with regard to sexual torture perpetrated on male Republican prisoners by the British Army in Northern Ireland (McGuffin 1974). What might sometimes give the impression that sexual torture against male prisoners results from abuses perpetrated by individual soldiers, rather than from an officially condoned strategy, is the fact that in survivors' narratives, perpetrators' behavior is frequently pictured as irrational (Weishut 2015; Feldman 1991, 119), and, as confirmed by some of my research participants, they are often drunk (Aimable 2010, interview)[4]. But, as explained by Sooka in the case of sexual torture perpetrated against members of the LTTE in Sri Lanka, these occasional "blunders" should not hide the fact that sexual torture is almost always part and parcel of a larger, systematic and well-organized system of abuse and repression (Sooka 2014, 64).

Even if perpetrators of sexual violence against men are first and foremost recruited among armed groups and State security institutions, there is also some scattered evidence of civilian involvement. The proportion of wartime sexual violence against men that is perpetrated by civilians, and in a civilian context, is, however, extremely difficult to assess, let alone quantify with precision., for instance, if sexual violence perpetrated by intimate partners in conflict areas is obviously favored by the overall violent and militarized context (see Cohen et al. 2013, 7), it is difficult to establish exactly whether and when it is conflict-related. In many conflict settings, distinctions between armies, armed groups and civilians in arms are really fluid (Swaine 2018), and the number of cases of sexual violence against men perpetrated by "non-combatant strangers" (thus excluding violence perpetrated by partners and relatives) is usually so low that it is difficult to establish whether they might not sometimes pertain to cases of misidentification[5].

Sexual abuse against men and women in conflict areas has also been repetitively perpetrated by peacekeepers, an issue that has attracted a lot of media attention and debate over the past few years. Though I have never met any male or female survivor who said that he or she had been victimized by a peacekeeper, empirical evidence of multiple cases of abuse perpetrated against adolescent boys has been collected, especially committed by French soldiers of the Sangaris operation in the Central African Republic (Deschamps et al. 2015). The case of "Johnny Jean", a young man assaulted in 2011 by Uruguayan troops part of the MINUSTAH in Haiti, has also attracted a lot of media attention, as well as three investigations, one by the Haitian authorities, a second by MINUSTAH itself and a third by the Uruguayan Defense Ministry (Klarreich 2015).

The fact that, contrary to common representations, all perpetrators are not male also has to be underscored. There is solid evidence that female soldiers and combatants have been taking part in the sexual torture of male (and female) prisoners (Sjoberg 2016), though the implication of women in the perpetration of this type of violence seems more common in armies than in armed groups. The implication of three US female military police officers in abuses committed in Abu Ghraib is, for instance, well documented (Sjoberg and Gentry 2007, 54–87), two of whom have later argued that they had no choice and that the blame should have been put on their hierarchy instead. Many other cases of female military involvement in sexual torture against male prisoners have been uncovered, for instance, in Israel (Weishut 2015, 75) and in Sri Lanka (Sooka 2014, 31; see also Human Rights Watch 2013).

There is less empirical evidence regarding the involvement in sexual violence against men of female combatants belonging to armed groups. In many armed groups, women seem more likely to adopt the "bystander" role, witnessing sexual violence but not directly participating. A few of the survivors I have spoken with have mentioned that female combatants had "participated in their torture" (Félicien 2010, interview), but such involvement seems to be the exception rather the rule. This is likely to be related to the fact that women are less numerous than men in armies and armed groups, and to their status in these groups: women are indeed often used in an auxiliary capacity and not as frontline combatants. Though some armed groups, like the LTTE in Sri Lanka, are or used to be more egalitarian than others, in most cases women are less likely to occupy positions of command. In patriarchal societies like the Congo, Rwanda or Burundi, for example, women help rebel groups to function not just because some of them fight alongside male combatants, but first and foremost because they provide services that men do not have the time or the will to ensure, like finding and cooking food, providing medical help, washing and tending clothes, etc. But instead of being valorized as providers of much-needed services while still playing their armed role at the frontline, female combatants are often despised for it. During an interview, a former leader in a Burundian armed group once described women enrolled in the rebellion as "sandugu" (Déo 2011, interview)[6], a Kirundi word for wooden boxes—in other words, (useful) items that are not meant to take any initiative and to move and act on their own. Given that women are likely to occupy subaltern positions in rebel groups, and to be denied any agency, it is not surprising that cases of sexual violence against men perpetrated by female combatants are comparatively rare[7]. Conversely, cases where female fighters are clearly expected to "prove themselves" as worthy combatants, to be "tougher" than men, can explain their involvement in the perpetration of torture and other atrocities, as shown by Coulter (2008) in the case of Sierra Leone. Looking at sexual violence against men thus highlights the weight of gender roles and expectations that female combatants have to deal with, and suggests that those who want to achieve some sort of equal status with their male colleagues have to enact the same militarized masculinity model, which might entail, in some settings, the perpetration of extreme forms of violence.

3.3. INSECURE MASCULINITIES

Thinking about conflict masculinities and about perpetrators of sexual violence notably requires reflecting on the effects that prolonged and protracted conflicts have on models of masculinity, and on the possibilities men (and sometimes also women) have to enact them. It is well known that conflicts are accompanied (and in turn shaped by) a sharp militarization of masculinities and of societies more generally, which often partly contradicts traditional masculine ideals. Coming up with a detailed and systematic mapping of this impact is an almost impossible task, though, because we are speaking here of extremely diverse situations in terms of conflict duration, intensity and actors. For instance, the impact of war escalation on models of masculinity will not be the same for "local" combatants as for soldiers in "intervention" armies such as the US Army in Iraq or Afghanistan, or for peacekeepers. What is more, as many authors have already highlighted, gender relations and models are constantly evolving and vary across local configurations. As explained by Barker and Ricardo in the case of sub-Saharan Africa, generalizing the impact of war means misrepresenting multiple, fluid and ever changing models of masculinity upon which violence, itself varied and changing, leaves its mark (2005, 4). What is clear, however, is that in concerned countries and regions, the prolongation of conflict and war over time induces a blurring of the pre-existing distinctions between military and civilian cultures, and that the omnipresence of armies and armed groups entails a diffusion of militarized values and models, if just because so many men and boys (and, in many cases, women and girls) are participating in warfare (Lwambo 2013).

We can nevertheless trace some common trends in how men in patriarchal societies are affected by conflict escalation and maintenance. These similarities derive from the core functions men are expected to perform at the family and community levels, and from the fact that all models of masculinity need to be constantly performed and reasserted. With the irruption of war, the structural and discursive conditions in which masculinity models usually unfold change, and this logically impacts men's individual capacity to enact these models, and it affects power relations between groups of men embodying them too. Joining the army or an armed group frequently entails leaving one's family behind and, therefore, abandoning at least part of one's familial responsibilities as a breadwinner and as a protector, which constitute core aspects of hegemonic masculinity models in most countries around the world:

> I had to abandon my family to fight. I am proud of my family, of my children, but it was tough being away from them, because I didn't know what would happen to them, I couldn't give them any money to buy food anymore. It was hard for them. One of my daughters died while I was away. But I had to do my duty and fight. (Serge 2010, interview)

For some of those who enroll in rebel groups, there might even be a stigma attached to the fact of not having a "respectable" job—especially when the armed group does not have a clear ideological or political profile. For those who choose not to fight, displacement, loss of livelihoods and of dwelling places, extreme poverty, violence exerted by armies, armed groups and rebel movements, dehumanizing practices sometimes echoing the worst memories of colonization, as well as the presence of peacekeeping forces, all render the enactment of traditional models of masculinity more complicated. And there is also a well-known stigma attached to men who refuse to fight for their country or their communal, religious or ethnic group, whose (heterosexual) masculinity becomes suspect (Price 2001, 222).

What is important to emphasize here, and what might contribute to understanding the specific stories that we will explore below, is that in the context of war, whether a man chooses to fight or not almost always entails a tension and even a contradiction with traditional masculine models that are valued in peaceful times. In societies that haven't recently experienced war, values and behavior traditionally attached to hegemonic masculinity models are put under stress by the escalation of violence. War is accompanied by the emergence and/or the strengthening of alternative role models, which do not necessarily garner wide social and cultural support—that is, they do not become hegemonic in turn. For instance, combatants participating in displays of extreme violence are more likely to provoke repulsion than adherence among the civilian population. That is not to say that the figure of the soldier or of the combatant defending his or her home country is never a popular one, especially when wars start and end, but that it often stands in contrast with masculine models that had been valued up to then.

In many ways, young men and women living in conflict areas are in a no-win situation. Those who choose to invest in a militarized masculinity model, and who enroll, or are forcefully enrolled, in rebel groups or armies instead of trying to follow more traditional masculinity or femininity scripts, will not be guaranteed to gain social respect and power. For instance, in the Great Lakes region of Africa, men are expected to ensure their financial independence, to own a house, to have a family and to be the breadwinner. But reconciling these objectives with a life as an armed combatant is complicated:

> You see now I am 23. I should have married a long time ago. I should have children, a woman waiting for me at home. I think my parents would be disappointed in me. But I am proud of what I do, of fighting for my country, for my community. (Laurent 2014, interview)

Respectability and power, whether understood in a Gramscian or a Foucauldian sense, are not necessarily achieved by the use of physical violence, as many of my interviewees discovered. This is what Alexis, a former officer in the FNL in Burundi, explains:

> I was fighting for my country. But people don't respect you even if you risk your life for them. Today we are back in the same situation than before, sometimes I feel like it was all for nothing. (Alexis 2013, interview)

And indeed, in societies like the Congo, Burundi and Rwanda, traditions define a "real man" by his ability to refrain from using physical violence, by his self-control (Lwambo 2013, 52). Many of the combatants I have met also resent the difficulties of clandestine or military life, especially when they had been expecting riches and an easy life. Hunger, sleep deprivation, serious medical issues due to a lack of hygiene and of access to medical care and so on make up their everyday life. In these conditions, some have the feeling that all that remains available to them is their ability to threaten and terrorize others thanks to their gun. As one of the combatants I spoke with somewhat cynically noted:

> At least I have my gun, with it I can eat and get what I need. (Jean-Baptiste 2011, interview)

His words were echoed by several other research participants, including former combatants who confessed that they were considering taking up arms again:

> You only need a gun. With a gun I could feed my family. (Serge 2010, interview)

This resonates with Messerschmidt's assertion that crime, violence, aggression and in particular sexual aggression can be used to reassert masculinity for men who are under psychosocial stress and who are unable to perform as they think men should (1993, 85). If, as explained by Silberschmidt (2001, 668), this desire to restore self-esteem is primarily expressed through sexual aggressiveness towards women, it is clear from my fieldwork that it can target other men too.

In many conflict zones, this belligerence seems to primarily target civilians. The Congolese soldiers interviewed by Eriksson Baaz and Stern, for instance, connected their involvement in sexual violence to their frustration at having a bad reputation and a low status in the wider society, as well as at receiving low salaries (2013, 81). If civilians are particularly targeted, it is also because militarism equates soldiers with the figure of the strong man, embodying male power and dominance over society, in particular women and feminized Others, that is, those who do not fight (Daley 2008, 234). This is also consistent with the perpetration of sexual violence against civilian men, as a way to use feminization to reaffirm super/subordination relations. One of the pernicious effects of these violent practices is that they are in turn likely to be self-perpetuating, since breaking taboos by committing random violence—and particularly sexual violence—can generate hatred of oneself, fear of being wrong and distress among combatants, which in turn might cause more violence, as shown by Price in the case of war rape in former Yugoslavia (2001, 217).

Some authors, following Fanon (1963), also convey a (post)colonial analysis grid to explain that in (post)colonial settings the perpetration of the worse dehumanizing atrocities on fellow men "is not compensatory humiliation but rather doing exactly what white men do, following the hegemonic script" (Dowd 2010, 46). In light of recent scandals regarding UN peacekeepers involvement in sexual trafficking and sexual violence, or regarding sexual torture in Abu Ghraib or Guantánamo, these interpretations cannot but be appealing. In their study of masculinities in sub-Saharan Africa, Barker and Ricardo (2005, 25) hint at the role played by violent versions of manhood such as Rambo, which are propagated by Western movies, in the recruitment and socialization of young combatants. And indeed, such role models transpired in some of the interviews I conducted:

> You know when I got enrolled I had all sorts of images in my head, on how things would be. About how I would fight for my country, for democracy in my country. And that it would become a great and powerful nation like in Europe, that we would become a model. How I would be a courageous soldier, like in the movies. I was a bit naïve, I was very young you know. (Alexis 2013, interview)

In that sense, sexual violence and other acts of extreme violence might be triggered by versions of manhood and masculinity that are neither directly inspired by local traditional models nor inspired by the immediate experience of conflict. Mimicking movie characters, but also borrowing from other conflict scenes—which is facilitated, among other things, by the circulation of mercenaries across countries—constitute obvious sources of inspiration for combatants. The institutionalized circulation of violent practices say, of methods of torture, as discussed in the case of Northern Ireland by McGuffin (1974) or by Faligot (1992), is also a clear indication of the fact that our understanding of sexual violence should not be restrained to local influences and patterns.

It is important to underscore that my purpose here is not to find "excuses" for perpetrators of sexual violence. I recognize that it is easy to infer from the above discussion a rather simplistic explanatory model whereby the difficulty to enact socially respectable masculinity models in a war situation leads to frustration and resentment, as well as to violence and aggressiveness to restore male self-esteem. Perpetrators of sexual violence against both men and women would then just be the unsuspecting victims of gender models and of the war context. But as we will see in the next section, most of them have a choice not to commit these atrocities, and actually—and fortunately—most use their free will and decide not to participate. Convening gender analysis, together with an examination of the social, cultural and economic factors that might impact on the perpetration of sexual violence, does not entail a negation of individual agency, but invites an improved understanding of how it can be constrained, or on the contrary enhanced, in some specific configurations. In that sense, some testimonies I have collected confirm the thesis according to which the perpetration of sexual violence against both men and women can to some extent, and in some cases, be related to individual frustration and humiliation, emotions that are themselves tightly related to a wider institutional and cultural context. In these cases, the individual decision to initiate and/or to participate in sexual violence can be interpreted as a performative act to regain power and respect, values that are in many cultures strongly associated to masculinity. But as we will explore in the next section I have also collected testimonies qualifying existing explanations for the perpetration of sexual violence against men, as well as testimonies clearly questioning the masculinity model enacted through the perpetration of such acts.

3.4. PERPETRATORS' PERSPECTIVES AND STORIES

There is a wealth of literature, especially in genocide studies (see, for instance, Baum 2008; Waller 2007), trying to establish the psychological profiles of perpetrators of extreme violence. So far, however, apart from a few very interesting case-study-based publications (see, for instance, Eriksson Baaz 2009), there has been no major research undertaken on perpetrators of sexual violence in general, much less on perpetrators of sexual violence against men. Skjelsbæk (2013, 3) has listed a series of potential psychological profiles of wartime sexual violence perpetrators against both men and women, among which are those with "psychopathologies such as deviant sexuality; traumatized individuals, i.e. people with a history of trauma, which may include experiences of sexual abuse and/or extreme violence; dysfunctional individuals who are seeking misplaced emotional comfort; ideological dispositions that would render the person prone to dehumanizing others; paranoia, delusions, sadistic personality traits". Genocide studies have also shown how the heavily militarized and violent environment in which individuals are placed facilitates the acting out of individuals with such psychological traits. It is, however, unclear whether such characteristics can apply irrespectively of the gender of victims, and my own interviews do not entirely support such a typology: some of the perpetrators I have met were at the time very young recruits who did not seem to be particularly deviant, but who, if their stories are to be believed, lacked strength of will to resist peer pressure. And given the lack of detailed and systematic empirical data on perpetrators of wartime sexual violence, it is difficult to say whether perpetrators of violence against men display a different profile from others.

Of course, it seems that in some cases sexual violence against both men and women is perpetrated by the very same individuals, but there is also indication that at least in the case of Eastern DRC there are differences in terms of profiles (proportionally more civilian perpetrators in the case of sexual violence against women, for instance,) and of gender (40% of female perpetrators in the case of sexual violence against women, vs. 10% of female perpetrators in the case of sexual violence against men) (Johnson et al. 2010). Empirical data and evidence is unfortunately still too scarce to be able to say if this applies to other case studies—say, Bosnia-Herzegovina or Sri Lanka— and if differences in profiles highlighted in genocide studies—for instance, between organizers, executors, fanatics and so on—apply in the case of wartime sexual violence against men.

Several researchers (see, for instance, Skjelsbæk 2015; Eriksson Baaz 2009) have proposed a typology of narratives offered by perpetrators of sexual violence themselves, or of the ways they are depicted by others. These typologies, pertaining to perpetrators of sexual violence against both men and women, display some resemblances, but also some remarkable differences, with the stories I have collected. The Congolese soldiers interviewed by Eriksson Baaz (2009), for instance, rationalized rape in different ways, as pertaining to their identity as heterosexually potent fighters, as a result of their sexual needs and desire or as a consequence of their moral disengagement and of the normalization of violence. Interestingly, these categories overlap to a certain extent with those highlighted by Skjelsbæk (2015) in her study of the sentencing judgments of the International Criminal Tribunal for the former Yugoslavia (ICTY). According to her analysis, these legal texts built three main narratives on perpetrators: the "narratives of chivalry", portraying the perpetrators as protective or driven by their sexual desire, the "narratives of opportunism" describing perpetrators, some of them sadistic and abusive, as taking advantage of the situation, and finally the "narratives of remorse" whereby perpetrators were entering guilty pleas and expressed remorse. If opportunism, context-related variables or remorse clearly appear in the stories of sexual violence against men I have collected, it is not the case of chivalry or sexual desire, perhaps logically considering the heterosexual norms within which most combatants operate. An alternative, but minority, discourse on the "usefulness" and "necessity" of using sexual violence against men also emerged. In their own ways, each of the narratives I have collected provides "excuses" for the perpetration of sexual violence against men, and attempts to downplay the individual responsibility of the narrator. Most perpetrators or bystanders I spoke with, whether soldiers or members of armed groups, expressed discomfort if not remorse at what they did or let happen without reacting, and all strongly emphasized the role played by the context and/or by peer pressure. Such narratives of "reluctance" can be interpreted as a genuine expression of remorse, or can pertain to a more down-to-earth wish to improve my opinion on them.

It is worth underscoring the fact that my sample is context-specific. The narratives I am describing in the forthcoming paragraphs are a series of plots or of stories that I have collected in a specific region, the Eastern Congo,

Burundi and to a lesser extent Rwanda, during a specific period (2009–2014). There are good reasons to assume that narratives in, say, Sri Lanka, Bosnia-Herzegovina or Israel/Palestine would display at least partly diverging characteristics, if just because the conflict settings and institutional contexts are themselves vastly different. The lack of existing research focusing specifically on perpetrators of wartime sexual violence against men[8] unfortunately prevents me from relying on comparable work elsewhere, and it is in my opinion not possible to assume that their stories are entirely similar to those of perpetrators of wartime sexual violence against women. In addition, the people I spoke with are former or current soldiers or members of armed groups who had at the time of the interview never had to answer for their crimes in front of a court—or to provide testimony for what they saw. This prevents a systematic comparison, for instance, with the testimonies collected by the ICTY regarding the few men who were accused of sexual violence against both men and women in Bosnia-Herzegovina, and whose narratives had probably been impacted by detention, by the need to come up with a proper defense strategy and so on.

Lastly, and before further detailing these narratives, it is interesting to reflect on the discursive strategies that the perpetrators I spoke with deployed in order to talk about what happened. How do they locate themselves in these stories? Do they accept responsibility and use "I" instead of a more diluting "we", or of a discharging "them"? Not surprisingly, few accepted their own direct responsibility in the perpetration of sexual violence against men, and when they did, they downplayed it by denying being at its origin, or by depicting their own role as minor, or justified it by the abuse of alcohol and drugs, or by peer pressure. Oftentimes the shift from "I" to "we" or even "them" occurred as soon as the issue of sexual violence against men came up, many adopting the position of the bystander, and using "they". The few individuals who admitted that they had directly taken part in sexual violence against men, and who had thus started their stories using "I" almost always switched to "we" or "them" when it came to explaining why these acts were committed. As I was sometimes meeting survivors and perpetrators during the same research stay, over quite short periods of time, I was struck by how their refusal to endorse the role of agents echoed with the way many survivors describe sexual violence, as if it had been inflicted on others and not on themselves. In the stories I have collected, it seems that sexual violence against men is so shameful and stigmatizing that neither victims nor perpetrators want to be directly associated with it—it is an "othering" violence, perpetrated on others by others.

"War Is War"

As we have seen in chapter 2, one of the main consequences of sexual violence is to "feminize" the victim and "masculinize" the perpetrator. It is a powerfully performative act, which underscores the subjugation of the victim. In Burundi or in the Congo, it is even considered as a way to symbolically turn male victims into "women" and to reinforce the masculinity of the perpetrator. It is an instrument of power that structures or maintains relations between masculinities, and between masculinities and femininities, and that affirms the superiority of the perpetrator's masculinity (Jones 2006, 459). None of the perpetrators I spoke with seemed to think that their masculinity could be questioned because of their participation in sexual violence against men, quite on the contrary. Even those who had participated in the rape of men reacted strongly to the idea that what they did might be perceived as an homosexual act by the rest of the society—thus suggesting that they understood the perpetration of sexual violence against men as a heterosexual and militaristic performance:

> EF: But isn't that considered as shameful for a man to do that to another man?
> Serge: I cannot say that I am proud of what we did, but I am not ashamed, certainly not! I am not ashamed, they [the male victims] are the ones who should be ashamed. We did what we did because it was war. That was how it was done. We did our duty as combatants, that is all. (Serge 2010, interview)

While speaking with men who had either perpetrated or witnessed (without opposing it) sexual violence against men, my questions were often dismissed as a kind of naïveté, as if it was obvious that the conduct of war necessitated the perpetration of that kind of violence. Admittedly, my position as a Western researcher, living in a peaceful country, as well as my gender positioning—being female obviously largely discredited me with regard to military matters—partly explain this dismissal, but the "it is/was war, you know" argument regularly came back, in various forms. Of course, as we will see in a subsequent section, not all of the people I spoke with condoned the use of sexual violence, but many of them saw it as an unavoidable part of the necessary evil entailed by the conflict situation. More precisely, some interviews suggest that sexual torture was employed as part of a more general war strategy destined to extract confessions from prisoners, or to collect information from civilians:

> [Talking about events that occurred during the Burundian civil war]
> Joseph: Yes, some have beaten male prisoners and sometimes also civilians quite badly. Some have been badly tortured, and used, you know, like women.

EF: Like women?

Joseph: Yes, some of the men were drunk, they were excited and angry, and they had the prisoners pretend they were their wives. As if they were women.

EF: As if they were women ...

Joseph: Yes, have them cook for them, clean their clothes, even sleep with them, things like that.

EF: And they were also tortured?

Joseph: Maybe not tortured that much really, but beaten, yes. Some died, others I am not sure, sometimes we had to move on and we could not carry them.

EF: What kind of beatings?

Joseph: First we would threaten them, and then if they did not cooperate or confess we would start punching them, try to hurt them by maybe stabbing them or cutting parts of them ...

EF: Parts of them?

Joseph: Fingers sometimes, but more has already happened, like a hand, or private parts. You know this was war, there was no other way. Our security was at stake.

EF: So you have taken part in all this?

Joseph: I took part in some of the beatings, yes, may God forgive me. Sometimes we had no other choice you know, some prisoners did not want to cooperate. But I never participated in ... in the other things. (Joseph 2013, interview)

This exchange suggests that sexual violence against men belongs to a broader strategy of brutalization that is not only sexual in nature. It is part of a continuum of violence, and many of the perpetrators I have met did not really differentiate between the perpetration of sexual violence against men, and other methods of torture, especially when applied to prisoners. It might of course be a discursive strategy attempting to diminish the existence and weight of such violence, but some testimonies still suggest that sexual brutalization is often inscribed within a larger project of power assertion. In some interviews, sexual violence was presented as a "last resort" method for punishing prisoners, justified by the war context:

[After hearing about the case of a prisoner who had a bottle inserted in his anus, among other brutalities]

EF: But why do that?

> Richard: He had passed on important information about us to the army, so the men wanted to show him what happened to those spying on us. We can't tolerate that kind of behavior. We had to set up an example. (Richard 2009, interview)

There is a real possibility that some perpetrators did not fully understand these forms of sexual torture as *sexual* violence. In many accounts, sexual violence against men was described as the most efficient and quickest way to inflict pain, to extract confessions, and so on. Of course, there are good reasons to assume that the fact that the violence was exerted on sexual organs largely explains its "efficiency", but this never came up clearly during my interviews. Similarly, for some of the people who had witnessed—but said they had not participated in—such episodes of sexual violence against men, sexual torture in particular is part of torture more generally, which itself is part of war. These narratives were particularly present in my interviews with female combatants:

> During war everybody is at risk, so it was us or them. If they were a threat because of their activities or because they were passing on information, we had to do something. That was not nice, what was done, but it was necessary. (Béatrice 2011, interview)

> I didn't like it, but we were told to keep our mouths shut. So we obeyed. If they did it, there was surely a good reason for that. (Violette 2011, interview)

A Necessity for Ensuring Submission

A second explanation, given by a small number of interviewees, presents the perpetration of violence (against both men and women) as a kind of necessary evil, especially for "taming" young combatants or people forcefully recruited for auxiliary purposes. It is worth remembering here that forced enrolment is widely used in the Great Lakes region of Africa, and that the integration process of these new combatants or followers is rarely smooth. Déo (2011, interview), for instance, who used to be high in command in the Burundian rebellion, insisted that both men and women who had been kidnapped to be used as auxiliaries or as future combatants had "to be broken, to be tamed", because they often did not want to perform the tasks they were required to do. The efficiency of such "integration" techniques is, however, doubtful, and is likely to generate more trauma than adherence., for instance, Dionise (2011, interview), a former combatant in the Burundian rebellion, did not openly recognize that he had been sexually abused, but used metaphors to speak about it. He explained, for instance, that when he was abducted and forcefully integrated within the ranks of the combatants, he was first treated with great brutality, beaten, tortured, but that he, as many other men, had to choose between the acceptance of "being treated as a nobody", of "being used like a female slave", or being killed. After this traumatizing period, he was apparently allowed to join the ranks of combatants. Dionise recognized that he had subsequently witnessed the perpetration of sexual violence on other men, especially civilians, but adamantly denied his own involvement in these acts. He has stayed two years in the rebellion, and now feels broken, and incapable to "resume a normal life".

This is somehow consistent with Cohen's finding (2013) on how forced recruitment is related to high levels of gang rapes, though in Cohen's study rapes were assumed to be mostly perpetrated against civilians or outsiders to the group. But some interviews also confirm Cohen's hypotheses, and show that cases of sexual violence against civilian men follow the same logic:

Willy: You know sometimes we don't need more combatants but we need help for doing other things like carrying weapons and ammunitions. Usually women carry weapons or ammunition in their baskets because soldiers think they are carrying food, but sometimes when the weapons get heavy ... women tire easily, so sometimes we also ask civilian men to carry heavy things for us. And it has happened once or twice, but not more than that, that they were very stubborn and even when we beat them they still did not want to do the work ... So a few others decided to teach them respect and were really brutal with them ...

EF: They were really brutal ...?

Willy: You know, beating them and that sort of things.

EF: What did they do apart from beating them?

Willy: Things like forcing them to go naked, joke about them, trying to shame them ...

EF: Shame them? About their body?

Willy: Yes, joking that they were going to use them as wives, and asking them to bend and laughing ...

EF: And what else?

Willy: No, no, nothing else. If anything else happened I did not see it. (Willy 2009, interview)

Some combatants described episodes of sexual violence against civilian men as bonding and initiation rituals for young and/or new recruits. In one of the rare cases where an interviewee recognized his direct participation, he somehow presented sexual violence against men as an ongoing practice for the group:

> They had done it before, so I thought I had to do it as well ... I wasn't given any choice, really. I was new in the group, I just did what I was told to do, what the others were doing as well. (Serge 2010, interview)

This is in line with what some authors have shown about ritual violence in gangs. Moolman, in her study of masculinity models in gangs, explains, for instance, how new recruits are asked to perform a particularly challenging first deed as a way to test their endurance, as well as to reaffirm the centrality of violence in the masculine definition of the group (2004, 115). Once gang members have successfully gone through these initiation rites, they are allowed to exert their domination over land, but also over bodies. In that sense, if sexual violence against women and girls admittedly gives to armed groups a sense of power and control, then sexual violence against men and boys cannot but be seen as the ultimate form of control and ownership over civilian populations, as well as over territory and resources, which local men, in patriarchal societies, usually "own". In this perspective, many forms of conflict-related sexual violence can certainly be read as a way to subdue victims, regardless of their gender, and to reassure perpetrators about their dominant, though precarious, role. The perpetration of sexual violence thus tries to ensure that power is stabilized and that dissent is policed through a violent gendered hierarchy.

A Result of the Context of Extreme Violence

Another, more common, narrative was that perpetrating sexual violence against men is an "abnormal reaction to abnormal (or extreme) situations", to borrow from Skjelsbæk (2015, 58). Perpetrators insisted on their "normality", but described the context as conducive to all sorts of excesses. Both sexual violence against men and against women were presented as deriving from the "craziness" of war, and from a diluted sense of right and wrong. Déo (2011, interview), talking about new recruits, explained:

> Déo: Some of them were lazy, pretending to be too tired to do the work. And some women did not understand why they should accept. ... You see women can also get some protection if they behave in the proper way. ... If they can get a guy to look after them ...
>
> EF: You mean, if they have intercourse with them?
>
> Déo: Yes, yes, there were many unions. You know even during the rebellion some marriages were celebrated. Of course not real ones, but that gave women a protection from ... from other men who might have wanted to abuse them
>
> EF: So some combatants were not behaving properly?

Déo: War is war, it is difficult to control everything, men get nervous and all that. Everybody has to be cautious, because during war men tend to really get astray.

EF: You mean that men were also likely to be confronted to that type of improper behavior from other men?

Déo: That did happen as well, yes, yes, but people don't want to talk about that, and all sorts of other terrible things happened at that time.

Bystanders likewise used words like "hell" or "beasts" to speak about what happened during war. Discussing episodes of sexual violence against men he admits to have witnessed, but not participated in, René reflects:

Yes I have seen that happen, that and many other horrible things, done to men, women, children, babies, old men, old women, everyone. But we don't talk about it. I don't want to talk about it. War is horrible, men become beasts, hell is on earth. I am not the same man anymore, because of the things I have seen. (René 2014, interview)

This largely echoes what Eriksson Baaz says about Congolese soldiers' description of "evil rapes": "'Evil' rape, they explained, stems from a sense of moral disengagement that accompanies the climate of warring and violence in which they have been living; previously unthinkable behavior becomes conceivable and even dedramatized through the process of dehumanizing and 'normalization' of violence and killing" (2009, 510). Undoubtedly, the availability and proliferation of small arms as well as the deep militarization of civilian society facilitate the perpetration of sexual violence, not just because they allow those who own weapons to brutalize others, but also because they participate in the glorification of militarized and violent masculinities. Many combatants have the feeling they are invincible, that for them nothing is prescribed or forbidden, including the transgression of taboos:

You know with a gun you can get everything that you want. Everything you need. You just have to go to someone, and if you have a gun, they will do whatever you want, give you food, work for you, sleep with you. ... You can be the boss. (Jean Bosco 2009, interview)

Possessing a gun is clearly equated with power over others, particularly civilians, who have to satisfy every whim of combatants often crazed by fighting. And, as Price explains (2001, 217), exerting extreme forms of violence eventually gives birth to a vicious cycle, made up of low self-esteem, excitement, intoxication and feelings of impunity.

Some of the stories collected also justify sexual violence as a sort of preemptive violence, resulting from the fear of being caught by "the other side", and then from a fear of being subjected to castration and to torture if it were to happen. This fear of what might happen, some people I spoke with explained, triggered the perpetration of similar acts on some men who were abducted:

> During the war everybody gets crazy, so we did ... we did things we would not have done at home, we would not have done if it wasn't war. It was not us, it was because there is violence everywhere, and some of us were really scared of what could happen to them, of being wounded, of being caught by others. So sometimes I think they did bad things because of fear, and because violence was everywhere. (Jean Bosco 2009, interview)

Laurent (2014) expressed similar ideas:

> Laurent: You are always scared of being left behind, of being caught. If you are too badly wounded then you won't be able to carry on. You will be left behind. And what will happen then? What will happen if the army catches you, or others? They will kill you, torture you, or worse.
>
> EF: Worse?
>
> Laurent: I have heard stories ... about bad things they do to those they catch. I would rather die than being caught. But what they would do to us, we do to them. That is the only way. (Laurent 2014, interview)

This can be related to the "lootpillageandrape" dynamic described by Enloe (2000, 108), or to the concept of "forward panic" developed by Collins (2008) and also quoted by Eriksson Baaz and Stern (2013, 76), which describes moments of excessive physical violence when fear is at its peak. Not surprisingly then, several interviews suggest that episodes of sexual violence against men (and women) are more likely to occur either during or immediately after raids on villages, or after military confrontations:

> After a fight, you can get really excited. Maybe you are happy to be still alive, maybe you are happy you have won, or maybe you just want to celebrate with others. At these moments bad things can happen. For instance, the guys would drink a lot, they would have sex with the girls from the villages, they would be violent with them and also with the prisoners. It is forbidden of course, but after a fight you often have a lot of energy, you don't care, you just want to celebrate. (Serge 2010, interview)

Here, we can clearly see how sexual violence loses its taboo, and how the context of conflict—and of celebration—provides an excuse for transgressing rules, and for using sexual violence as entertainment. Sexual violence is also clearly a way to assert domination, to crown victory by claiming ownership of the prisoners' bodies. This is far from being specific to the Great Lakes region of Africa, and is present in other conflict settings, including those where the confrontation displays completely different characteristics, including in terms of involved actors. Peel et al. describe, for instance, cases of recreational sexual violence perpetrated by Sri Lankan soldiers, forcing male Tamil "friends to rape each other in front of soldiers for their 'entertainment'", among other abuses (2000, 2069–70). Interestingly, some of the narratives I have collected did not seem to really differentiate between circumstances in which rapes and other types of sexual violence were committed against men, and when they were committed against women. In some cases, and especially in pillaging contexts, men and women seem to be victims of the same types of torture and violence, even though, because of sexual and gender-related taboos, people were much more willing to speak about sexual violence when it was committed against women. This certainly calls for caution when trying to understand the reasons why sexual violence against men is committed, as the context in which sexual violence is perpetrated is likely to have a strong impact on the identity and gender of the victims, as well as on the motives of the perpetrators.

One recurrent theme in these stories is the consumption of drugs and of alcohol, which is used as an excuse for explaining excesses, and for relieving perpetrators of their responsibility. Alcohol and drug abuse has also been described by survivors, and it is present in almost all perpetrators' stories I have collected, as well as in those compiled in the Bassiouni Report (1994) on the former Yugoslavia, by Eriksson Baaz on the Congo (2009) and by Sooka (2014) on Sri Lanka:

> We did crazy things. Some were fun, we had good times. I did not take drugs, but some others did, but when we could afford it we shared beers, alcohol, cigarettes, that made life easier. ... And yes, some of us could get drunk and then do bad things, very bad things. But when you are drunk you don't really know what you are doing, and it makes bad things come out of you. (Jean Bosco 2009, interview)

There is also some evidence that perpetrators of sexual violence use alcohol and drugs as a way to numb their emotions and escape their own doubts and uncertainty vis-à-vis their actions (see also Price 2001, 217):

> Willy: War is hard, very hard. It is dangerous, you can die every day, and sometimes you have to do things you don't like, because it is necessary.
>
> EF: You mean, to commit violent acts?

Willy: Yes. We don't kill other people because we like it, but because it is necessary in the fight. It is difficult for many of us. So everyone tries to get courage somewhere and cheer up. Some think about their families, they will fight for their families, and some will fight for their country. But some also try to find courage in alcohol and that sort of things.

EF: So alcohol gives you courage?

Willy: Maybe not always, but you can forget about war for a time, you can forget about your nightmares, you can forget what you have seen and done. (Willy 2009, interview)

Group Solidarity and Peer Pressure

War and genocide studies have long established the importance of peer pressure for explaining why soldiers perpetrate atrocities. In the case of the Holocaust, for instance, Christopher Browning (1993) has shown that while most men of Unit 101 of the German Ordnungspolizei participated in the killings out of obedience to authority, other factors such as peer pressure, but also the fear of being called "weak" or "coward", or the fear of "losing face" in front of other members of the group, played a central role. Jean Hatzfeld (2005) has come up with similar findings in the case of the Rwandan genocide. My own fieldwork data suggests that the perpetration of sexual violence against men can be interpreted as the result of internal group dynamics and of peer pressure too; it performs internal functions for the groups responsible for its perpetration, and has an impact on their functioning. For new recruits as well as for more seasoned combatants, opting out is seemingly complicated, because it would indicate a reluctance to share the fate of others, and would, therefore, mark the objector as suspect, either in his loyalty to the group, or in his masculinity, or both. The collective perpetration of rape and of other acts of sexual violence also signals them as products of the group, not of individuals: they participate in combatants' bonding, while diluting their individual responsibility. This is not anecdotal, especially when one thinks about the combatants' conditions of living:

> When you are in the bush, life is hard, really hard. You might die any time. You don't know whether you will see your family again. So you have to be united, you have to stand together with the other guys. You cannot get in a fight with them because of bad things they do. You have to side with them. (Jean-Baptiste 2011, interview)

The need to enact solidarity and group cohesion might explain why sexual violence against both men and women is often perpetrated publicly in that region of the world, as I have already detailed in chapter 1. In that sense, what Cohen says about the participation of new recruits in gang rape (of women) seems to apply more generally to all combatants, and to episodes of sexual violence against men, not just against women: "By participating in group rape—and perhaps by bragging about the individual rapes they have committed—combatants signal to their new peers that they are part of the unit and are willing to take risks to remain in the group" (2013, 465).

Further, collectively perpetrating sexual violence against men, which is clearly seen as reprehensible both legally but also morally[9] by perpetrators themselves, is meant to demonstrate to the rest of the world that the group sees itself as being above the law, as being able to set its own rules. It is a clear affirmation of collective power, of an arbitrary rule that is imposed on other groups:

> [After discussing the use of sexual torture on male prisoners]
> We have a conflict here. You can't expect us to respect the rules. It is those who are the most powerful who impose their rule. The others have to obey, whether it pleases them or not. (Richard 2009, interview)

Transgressing such ingrained taboos gives to combatants a feeling of invincibility, of invulnerability, which in turn feeds their will to carry on their struggle, and/or their various operations of looting, kidnapping and racketing, in the numerous cases where greed seems to be the main motivation of the armed group.

Remorseful Perpetrators and Objectors

All the former or current combatants I interviewed about their experience of everyday violence had heard about cases of sexual violence against men, and if a majority denied that it had happened in their group or battalion, some recognized that they had personally witnessed episodes of such violence, and fewer still admitted that they had participated in some way in its perpetration. Their attitudes changed whether we were speaking about sexual violence against women, or against men. On the one hand, speaking about "bush wives"—that is, girls or women more or less forced to provide sexual services to combatants under the cover of so-called "marriages"—was absolutely not taboo and was even expected from a Western, female researcher. On the other hand, however, the issue of sexual violence against men, and in particular male on male rape, often elicited strong reactions, from a flat refusal to discuss the matter, to long and animated speeches about how evil this is. Several interviewees, such as Néhémie, vehemently condemned these acts as "plain wrong" and positioned themselves as strong objectors to these practices:

> Which man would do this to another man? It is against nature, it is not how God has made us, it is evil, real evil. There is no excuse for that. (Néhémie 2009, interview)

In this quote Néhémie directly questions the masculinity model that is enacted through such acts, and opposes it to a "natural" (that is, in his view, God-made) finality, reminding us about the potential contradictions between traditional (and hegemonic) understandings of masculinity, and violent militarized ones.

Interestingly, perpetrators who expressed remorse, as well as those who condemned the perpetration of such acts, often used the religious register to do so, probably because it conveys a sense of morality, of distinction between right and wrong. Many of the combatants I interviewed—regardless of their participation in acts of sexual violence against men or not—thus spoke at length about the "normalization" of violence that occurs during war, and about their own growing confusion about what was right or wrong. In particular, those who are strongly religious could not reconcile what they did or were asked to do with their religious beliefs:

> We did what we did because it was war, and in war you have to do what is needed. But now I feel bad about what I have done. I have bad dreams, sometimes I cannot sleep at all. I am asking myself "Did God want this? Did He want to test me?" I don't know, but I am not proud of myself. (Jean Bosco 2009, interview)

Some argued that the violent context had changed them, and that somehow it is not really *them* who committed those acts, though they still feel remorse for what they have done:

> When I think about what happened, I can tell you, it is not me who did that. I am not like that, I am a good man, I pray and I go to the Church and I take care of my family. But somehow, all this violence, all this killing, all of this drove me insane. I am ashamed of some things I have done. (Joseph 2013, interview)

The narratives collected for the purposes of this chapter are remarkably diverse, and also largely case-specific. It is, however, striking to see that, with very few exceptions, most stories weave episodes of sexual violence against men together with wider conflict dynamics. Even when it is narrated as resulting from the craziness of war, and even when it is condemned as evil, this violence is still somehow related to the war context, to security imperatives and to power relations with civilians or other militarized actors. Sexual violence against men is also often understood in relation to other forms of violence exerted against civilians or prisoners, both male and female. What these narratives thus come to confirm is that wartime sexual violence against men is neither exceptional nor disconnected from broader conflict issues and strategies. It is part of a continuum of violence that is affected both by local group dynamics and by broader societal and political relations of power.

Chapter 4

Surviving Wartime Sexual Violence

The capacity of male survivors to cope with what happened to them and, more generally, the ability of the wider society to deal with, and to overcome the sequels left by, sexual violence are inevitably dependent upon their own cultural background and positioning; the violence's scope, duration and motivations; and also upon the other types of violence the survivor has been subjected to. However, somewhat paradoxically, the scope and severity of sexual violence sometimes seem to entail divergent consequences for individuals and for the wider society to which they belong. For instance, and as we will see, the more widespread sexual violence against men is, the more difficult and lengthy it is for the relevant community or society to mend its wounds, whereas if there are a lot of other survivors with whom to exchange and on whom to rely upon, recovery might become a bit less complicated for individual survivors[1] (Edström et al. 2016). This apparent paradox derives from the social and symbolic functions that men are required to play in social groups, and from the masculinity models they are expected to enact, especially in times of war (Dudink, Hagemann and Tosh 2004).

This chapter, exploring male survivors' stories, mostly builds on interviews that I have conducted in various conflict zones during the past decade, and more specifically in the Great Lakes region of Africa (primarily in Eastern DRC and in Burundi, and with survivors of the Rwandan genocide) since 2009, and in Northern Ireland since 2005. I am not suggesting that the findings and trends exposed in this chapter are universal. Notions such as masculinity, femininity, violence or power, and the values and roles that are attached to them, vary according to the context, and it would be very surprising if all male survivors of sexual violence reacted in the same ways to their experience. And indeed, as we will see, contrasting narratives that I have collected in Burundi or in the Congo, with those from paramilitary group members who have been imprisoned in Northern Ireland, highlight quite significant differences. Also, it is likely that the experiences of, and reactions to, sexual violence vary according to the victim's gender identity and sexual orientation. However, none of the survivors I spoke with suggested in any way that they had considered themselves, at the time of the assault, as gay, bisexual or transsexual. In spite of these limitations, most of the key trends exposed in this chapter are confirmed by data compiled by other researchers in different settings like Bosnia-Herzegovina or Sri Lanka, or by survivors' groups themselves[2].

Before moving on to detail how male survivors try to deal with their experience of sexual violence, and what consequences this type of violence has on post-conflict and reconciliation processes, this chapter's first section briefly outlines why and how I began collecting survivors' stories, and what kind of obstacles and problems I have faced.

4.1. EXPLORING SURVIVORS' STORIES

My field experience in conflict areas spans over two and a half decades, and I had met numerous male and female survivors of conflict-related sexual violence before getting specifically interested in this topic. I have long failed to grasp the significance of what they were recounting, and of the immense trust they were demonstrating by sharing their stories with me. It is surprisingly easy to overlook veiled references to episodes of sexual torture, especially when narrated by male survivors, when this is not what you are expecting to hear. During a research on former political prisoners in Northern Ireland that I undertook more than a decade ago (Féron 2007), for instance, several former male paramilitaries told me about the "abuse" they had experienced during interrogation and then in prison. At the time, and much to my embarrassment today, I had not fully understood what they meant, nor how frequent those experiences had been. I had been fooled by the fact that they had mentioned it almost in passing, without elaborating much—a typical feature of survivors' stories, as we shall see—and that they were putting a lot more stress on other dimensions of their experience of detention, like their bonding with other prisoners. As we will see, in highly politicized settings such as Northern Ireland, experiencing sexual torture in detention takes on a strong political meaning for survivors. This political understanding and framing of sexual torture seems to make it a bit less difficult for them to put it in the perspective of other types of violence they have been victims of. Putting this experience into perspective seems somehow more complicated for survivors who are unable to ascribe a strong political or cultural meaning to it, thus failing to integrate it into a consistent narrative. In any case, the Northern

Irish male paramilitaries I met at the time had done a great job of weaving this experience into their own consistent narratives of resistance, and of tying it back to the wider social and political context. Some of them also told these stories of abuse as if it had happened to other prisoners, but certainly not to them—another typical characteristic[3]. Re-reading the field notes I had compiled at the time, I am now puzzled at my own distraction.

But facts are stubborn, and often find their own way back to attention. The issue of conflict-related sexual violence against men came up again in 2009 while I was conducting several rounds of interviews with former combatants (both male and female) on the issue of daily life within armed groups in the Great Lakes region of Africa, and more specifically in Eastern Congo and Burundi. Both male and female combatants regularly spoke about sexual violence against women, and described it as an almost ordinary feature of their everyday life. But when one female combatant told me at the end of an interview, and in an almost confidential tone, "You know it happens to men too" (Fabiola 2009, interview), I decided that I could not ignore the matter any longer.

Collecting male survivors' testimonies has been anything but smooth, though not necessarily because of disclosure issues. Some obviously did not want to talk about it—and of course in these cases I never insisted—but some others seemed almost relieved to be able to tell their stories, though I am not sure talking to me has in any way alleviated their distress. Oftentimes, I had the feeling that people in the Great Lakes region of Africa treated me as if I belonged to a "third gender" (Partis-Jennings 2017), so remote from their own cultural and practical experience[4] that it eventually made it easier for them to confide their stories. I was neither a masculine competitor, nor a local woman who would judge them for their "lack" of masculinity or manhood. Of course, it is almost impossible for me to tell whether, and if yes how, they altered their narratives because of who I am, or because of what they assumed I wanted to hear. In several instances, survivors also expressed their satisfaction that, at long last, someone was paying attention to them.

Being familiar with some of the literature on the business or "commercialization of rape" in the Congo and other conflict areas (Eriksson Baaz and Stern 2013), I have at times wondered what my research was "doing to the field", not just in terms of possibly turning attention away from female survivors—which I obviously do not want—but also by inadvertently giving male survivors an entry card in that business. Without a doubt, male survivors need to be supported, and I sincerely do not think that those I have met were in any way trying to make money with their stories, and neither do I think that this is why they told me their stories. Undoubtedly, the support attracted by female survivors of sexual violence, paralleled with the almost total obliviousness regarding their own suffering, irritates some of them. But most do not look ready to pay the price of exposure that being part of such business would entail.

Dealing with the survivors' psychological and physical suffering, but also with the hopes that my attention to their stories was generating, and with my own helplessness in the face of their situation, has obviously not always been easy. Like many researchers interacting with deprived and disadvantaged people, I did not want to give them too high hopes about how my research would have an impact on their lives, but at the same time I still want to believe that my work, together with the recently published work of other researchers, will somehow participate in raising awareness of the plight of male survivors, and will generate more adequate prevention and support policies.

4.2. A MULTIFACETED SUFFERING

Surviving sexual violence means first and foremost dealing with and overcoming the suffering induced by such violence, but that is complicated by the fact that the consequences of sexual violence span across the physical, psychological and social realms at the same time. As underscored by Ronald E. Anderson (2014, 8–27), suffering is almost never just physical, it often co-occurs alongside mental and social suffering, and the suffering induced by wartime sexual violence seems to be no exception to this rule. While many authors have highlighted physical (e.g. fistula, HIV infection), mental (e.g. anxiety, humiliation) and social (e.g. social rejection, distrust) consequences for women who have been victims of sexual violence, including in conflict settings (see, for instance, Okot, Amony and Otim 2005; Ahuka et al. 2008), in-depth research on what it entails for male victims is still lacking. Reports by male survivors themselves have, however, demonstrated that their suffering spans across these three dimensions too, with dire consequences. Before moving on to detail these, it is worth remembering that sexual violence almost always occurs alongside other types of brutalization, which dramatically hamper the survivors' recovery capacities. It is also important to keep in mind that sexual violence is not necessarily what all survivors would describe as "the worst" that happened to them:

> [After alluding to having been "used as if he was a woman"]
>
> I don't know if one can live a normal life after suffering abominations like that. But what I can never forget is what they did to my family, how they killed my father in front of me. ... I never saw my mother again, I don't know what happened to her, I think she is dead now. And I lost all my brothers save one. I had 5 of them. It is the hardest, losing your family, seeing them suffering, and not knowing if they are alive or dead. (Didace 2014, interview)

Physical Suffering

As it is the case for female victims of sexual violence, male victims suffer from various types of physical pain, which can be related to total or partial castration, genital infections, ruptures of the rectum, etc. However, because they are too ashamed to ask for help, many victims prefer to bear the suffering on their own, with sometimes fatal consequences. According to the medical staff I have met in various places in Eastern DRC and Burundi, male survivors do not seek medical support unless they really have no other choice and have severe health problems like festering wounds or serious hemorrhage (see also Gettleman 2009). In addition, many of them face physical sequels that further add to their shame and further undermine their masculinity in the eyes of their relatives, such as physical impotence or urinary incontinence (Refugee Law Project 2014, 8). Because they are likely to demonstrate that survivors are neither powerful nor in control anymore, even the most serious of these physical sequels often remain unreported and, therefore, uncured. Male survivors I spoke with were very reluctant to detail their physical pain, enduring it on their own:

> I am still in pain, yes, some parts of me still hurt. But I don't want to ... I can't really speak about it. So I have to live with it, and pray that it goes away. (Jean-Paul 2009, interview)

Many were adamant that they could not mention their physical pain to anyone, least of all to their relatives:

> I hurt, a lot. I cannot eat what I want, and even sitting is painful. But it won't change anything to speak about it. I don't want my family to know that I am suffering. This isn't proper. (Jacques 2013, interview)

The expectation that men will bear physical pain without complaining plays an important role in the low level of reporting. As a consequence, the survivors' unspeakable physical and often chronic pain locks them in solitude and deprives them of much needed support (Misra 2015, 170).

But even when they report the assault, the lack of training and of preparation of medical staff and health care professionals regarding sexual violence against men can put survivors in further danger. Physical symptoms are frequently overlooked, and they are thus often not addressed in time. Even in regions where sexual violence against men is widespread, such as in the Great Lakes region of Africa, there seems to be very little understanding that men can be victims of that type of violence, and more particularly that they can be raped. In a rural hospital of South Kivu, for instance, one of the doctors I spoke to did not really understand what I meant when I was asking him about sexual violence against men, and thought that I was speaking only about forced incest, or of cases where men have to watch other female family members being raped. Surprisingly in a region where the prevalence of male sexual victimization is so high, he said he had not heard about men being raped or castrated (FOMULAC Hospital 2012, interview). This oversight, combined with the shame felt by survivors, leads them to underestimate the consequences of the violence they have been victims of, and to requalify sexual violence into types of violence that medical staff is likely to understand and be knowledgeable on. As a consequence, both survivors and sometimes also health care professionals tend to use more abstract categories for describing sexual abuse, such as beatings, which veil its sexual nature and overlook its deep impact on survivors' gender identities and social status. By symbolically stripping episodes of sexual violence from their sexual characteristics, the medical staff thus overlooks the fact that the gendered nature of these acts is likely to profoundly affect the survivors' capacities for recovery.

What is more, and as we will further explore in chapter 6, most programs fighting sexual violence and offering support to survivors set up by international or national organizations in conflict areas specifically target female victims of sexual violence. Men are sometimes not even accepted in these facilities, thus impeding their access to adequate and indispensable medical care (Dumas 2011). Aside from these humanitarian support programs, medical treatment and support is sometimes available, mainly in large cities like, for instance, in Bukavu in South Kivu, where the Panzi hospital has specialized in treating victims of sexual violence. But because many survivors come from deprived communities, even when they live close to a large city they cannot afford to spend money on medical expenses. The costs of a reconstructive surgery, regardless of its necessity, are prohibitive for them. In addition, spending time in a hospital would often mean losing their job, which they cannot afford because nobody would then be able to cover their daily expenses. As a consequence, some male survivors who can afford it try to cope with the physical pain by taking painkillers, which of course are far from being sufficient.

Psychological Suffering

Male survivors of sexual violence also face an intense mental and psychological suffering, which is in many ways similar to what female survivors of sexual violence experience. Commonly reported symptoms include loss of appetite and of sleep, exhaustion, anxiety and nightmares, all consistent with a post-traumatic stress disorder syndrome (Christian et al. 2011, 236; Loncar, Henigsberg and Hrabac 2010). A lot of male survivors also experience extreme mental fatigue, haziness, disinterest and withdrawal: "Just thinking about what happened to me makes me tired" (Vandecasteele 2011). Suicidal thoughts and self-disgust are also common. Jean-Claude, a Burundian who was abandoned by his wife and children when they heard about what had happened to him, is in extreme distress:

> I'd rather be dead. They should have killed me. I don't have a life anymore. (Jean-Claude 2011, interview)

Léonard, a Congolese man who has now been living alone for several years, expresses feelings of loss and confusion:

> They did things that I cannot speak about. I cannot … I still cannot understand what happened, how that could happen. What I know is that I am not the person I was before it happened. I am here, but at the same time it is like I am not here, I don't want to be here. (Léonard 2014, interview)

Similar testimonies have been collected elsewhere, notably among Bosnian survivors of wartime sexual violence: "Later when I play it all in my mind, if it were to happen again I'd rather be killed than to go through that again. (…) I was the happiest when I was taken out to be shot" (male survivor interviewed in *Silent Scream/Nečujni Krik* documentary).

Some studies claim that male survivors of rape display higher levels of anxiety and hostility symptoms than female survivors, especially among former child soldiers (see, for instance, Betancourt et al. 2011). Similar findings, pointing at higher post-traumatic stress disorder rates, and higher suicidal tendencies among male survivors, have also been described in the case of former combatants and rape survivors in Liberia (Johnson et al. 2008). However, such results have to be interpreted with a lot of caution since male survivors are known to be even less likely than female survivors to report episodes of sexual violence, either to relatives or to medical staff. Thus, the male survivors under scrutiny in these studies are more likely to be those who have been through the most horrendous and destructive episodes of violence, and perhaps displaying higher levels of depression, trauma, mental illness and anxiety. Considering also the additional public shame that those who report these acts have to face, it is also probable that reporting, if not accompanied by serious psychological support, constitutes a further source of anxiety for male survivors.

Empirical evidence indeed clearly shows that men only report sexual violence when they really have no other option, most often because physical pain has become unbearable. Because what they have gone through is taboo not just for themselves, but also for the wider society, they won't talk about it and seek help. While there are places where raped women can go and get some psychological help—though it is well documented that many of them don't or can't take advantage of these facilities—nothing of that sort exists for men. But even if there was, it is likely that many of them would still be too ashamed to ask for help. Most of the male survivors with whom I spoke had the feeling of having been deprived of their masculinity, or that their masculine status had somehow been damaged. And many of them found it impossible to report the assault they have been victims of, as complaining would symbolically reinforce their feminization by adopting the status of victim that is usually reserved to women:

> I don't need help. I don't want to speak about it. (…) [In response to my mentioning clinics and some local and international NGOs helping survivors of sexual violence:] They are treating only women over there. They do a good job, but this is not a place for me. (Aimable 2010, interview)

Such findings are consistent with existing research on post-traumatic stress disorder in armies and armed groups, showing a strong reluctance of combatants to recognize that they have been traumatized. Recognizing that one is in need of psychological support is considered as feminizing and goes against the ideal of militarized masculinity (Whitworth 2008). Anxiety and other types of psychological suffering are, therefore, repressed by male survivors, possibly precipitating the occurrence of mental illness. The feminization intended through sexual violence induces "gender trouble" and confusion, to borrow from Butler (1990), leading many survivors to question their gender and/or sexual orientation. Most of the survivors I have met in Burundi and in the Congo were wondering whether they could still be fully considered as men (especially following episodes of partial or total castration), or as women in men's bodies, as lesser men, or something else, neither entirely male nor female:

> I don't think I can have a family now. Of course I would prefer not to be alone, but I am not sure I can marry. I don't know what to do. I am not sure of what I want, of who I want to be. … I mean what is there for someone like me? I don't know what God's plans are for me. (Dionise 2011, interview)

Some survivors also think that they have somehow been turned into homosexuals, especially when they have had an erection or when they have ejaculated while being raped—which are mechanical reactions and not an expression of desire (Sivakumaran 2005). As a consequence, some experience confusion with regard to their sexual orientation, which proves particularly complicated to handle in societies where homosexuality is strongly penalized, at the social if not also at the judicial level. It also leads them to question the very core of their identity, to feel abjected and rejected from society, as they have the feeling that they do not belong anymore to either of the two genders and sexual identities that are deemed socially acceptable. As argued by Clark (2014), sexual violence attacks the victim's sense of self, and can, therefore, be considered as a "crime of identity". Sexual violence against men not only attacks the victim's bodily integrity, but also his gender and sexual identity. Male survivors consider that they have failed to abide by heterosexual norms, and that they, therefore, stand outside of the national, religious, ethnic, political or cultural community. It prevents them from relating to others, and explains why wartime sexual violence against men is unspeakable. It has a strong isolationist effect on survivors:

> Sometimes I don't know who I am anymore. What am I supposed to do? How can I go on and live after that? I can't sleep at night, I always think about who I was before, the family I had, and now what? No one is here with me, and I can't trust anybody. I barely have enough money to survive, I can't be the man I was before. (Jean-Claude 2011, interview)

It is also worth underscoring the fact notably highlighted by Goldstein (2004, 358) that the fear of sexual violence, and especially the fear of castration, has long been a major source of anxiety among male combatants. It was, for instance, a common theme of the post–World War I literature, and of the literature on the Vietnam War. Often seen as the soldier's greatest fear, it is, therefore, no surprise that when it turns into a reality, sexual violence generates considerable levels of trauma among survivors, be they combatants or civilians, especially in contexts where models of militarized masculinity are valorized and influential. Such contexts render the feminization that is enacted through sexual violence especially difficult to cope with (Seidler 2006). Armies take this risk very seriously. For instance, after the first Gulf War during which several US military personnel were captured and sexually assaulted by Iraqis, the US army decided in 1993 to implement a "sexual exploitation training program", "designed to prepare recruits for what could happen to them if they should ever be captured as prisoners of war and subjected to sexual violence" (Scarce 1997, 48).

Survivors of sexual violence thus struggle against feelings of emasculation, of shame, of guilt, and they also fear retaliation by perpetrators, if not a repetition of their ordeal. This seems to leave many survivors angry with themselves:

> Happiness has left me. I always feel angry, so I don't see my family and friends as I used to. They don't know what happened to me. They don't understand why I am angry all the time. I used to go out and have drinks with my friends, but not anymore. I have too much anger in me. (Vincent 2014, interview)

They often blame themselves for what happened, and fear that they no longer will be able to function as men, that is, as men are expected to behave in their societies of origin. In many patriarchal cultures of the developing world, a man is indeed defined by his ability to cope with what befalls him. Male victims of sexual violence often think that they have to bear the mental and psychological suffering just as they have coped with the physical pain. Seeking help and speaking out would be another acknowledgement of the fact that they cannot act anymore as requested by dominant models of masculinity.

Social Suffering

Suffering is obvious at the social level too, although it is likely to be influenced by the type of environment in which the survivor finds himself. In particular, survivors are likely to face different kinds of difficulties whether they live in a refugee camp, in their country of origin or abroad, in a city or in the countryside. Male survivors who flee and find shelter in refugee camps, located either in their own or a foreign country, can hope to escape the stigma attached to their sexual victimization. But if their "experience" is known or even just suspected, they can face negative reactions such as ostracism and discrimination on top of racism and hostility for being an outsider. Bernard, a Congolese refugee who fled the Congo after being detained by an armed group and sexually assaulted, explains:

> Bernard: When I left the Congo I stayed for a while in Musasa [a refugee camp located in the north of Burundi]. Things were hard for me there. I tried to earn a bit of money here and there, but it was difficult because I was so tired, I was still bleeding from my wounds from time to time. My smell was bad. I was alone, and nobody wanted to give me work. I think they could tell that something was wrong with me, they could smell it. People did not trust me.
>
> EF: Who do you think did not trust you?
>
> Bernard: Nobody trusted me, not in the camp, not outside. I was a foreigner, and I was alone. They thought I was sick. They thought I would bring trouble. (Bernard 2013, interview)

In rural settings too, where communities are usually more tightly knit, it is complicated for survivors to hide what they have been through. They are thus also likely to face discrimination and ostracism, unless they flee. This is what happened to Aimable, who used to live in a small village in the Cibitoke province, in north-western Burundi:

Everybody discovered what happened, and I couldn't stay anymore. It is not right, what they did to me. Because of that, I had to leave. I could not face the shame, and I have lost my whole family. (Aimable 2010, interview)

Whatever the setting, however, several common patterns are identifiable. Male survivors of wartime sexual violence are, for instance, likely to experience marital problems, alcohol and drug abuse, lack of trust, but also, if what they have been through becomes publicly known, ostracism, segregation or even discrimination on the part of their communities of origin. Ostracism can be provoked by security concerns, for instance, based on the idea that the survivor might attract the attention of perpetrators and thus put the whole community or neighborhood at risk. But it also seems that most other men try to distance themselves as much as possible from so strong a source of shame that it might eventually contaminate them, and undermine their own masculinity. As Adhiambo Onyango and Hampanda explain: "Social expectations of what it means to be a traditional man in most societies (i.e. strong, tough, self-sufficient, and impenetrable) are contradictory to male victimization in general and especially with regard to sexual victimization" (2011, 241). Just like it is sometimes complicated to accept that women do not respect traditional gender roles and refuse to play the role of victims in need of protection (Gibbings 2011), men are not supposed to deviate from traditional conceptions of masculinity and manhood that exclude the possibility of sexual victimization.

So when survivors speak out, many others, men, women and children, ridicule them; they cannot embody traditional masculinity models anymore. In sub-Saharan Africa, male survivors of sexual violence are sometimes called "bush wives"—a reference to women who have been forcefully abducted by armed groups and forced to marry combatants—to further shame them, and underscore their feminization. "Bush wives" are usually expected to both serve as sexual slaves and to take care of chores that are commonly considered as being women's work, like cooking, fetching food and water, carrying goods for combatants and washing clothes. Calling male survivors "bush wives" thus doubly endorses the strong performativity of sexual violence, which impacts both on the assumed sexuality of the survivor and on his "social" gender. Not surprisingly, therefore, many of the survivors I have met choose to avoid social contact, especially in public places[5], and to mostly stay at home, thus symbolically renouncing to some of the most valued masculine privileges. Here, the social impact of sexual violence against men is clearly visible, by weakening the traditional structures of the groups to which victims belong. Elias, a Congolese man I met in Bukavu in South Kivu, has greatly suffered at the hands of a rebel group. He has trouble walking, misses several fingers, and seems to be blind in one eye. The scars he bears are obvious for all to see, but he says I am the first person he tells about being sexually victimized. He explains that his ordeal has aged and weakened him, and that it has also weakened his ties to the wider community:

> You know when they held me prisoner they made me suffer in many ways, they beat me, they tortured me, they treated me like a slave, like a woman. Many horrible things were done to me, I have lost limbs, I have lost my dignity, I have lost everything. I am only 28, but I am old now. I am old inside, and my body is old. And nobody understands me, they don't understand that I have not the strength. I feel like I don't belong, like I am not welcome anywhere. (Elias 2014, interview)

I have also heard several stories of men being ostracized by their own families and wives after their "unfortunate experience" became known, either because "there cannot be two wives in the same house", as a common local saying goes, or because male survivors are henceforth assumed to have adopted an homosexual identity:

> My wife and children thought it had happened because I was homosexual. I could not be their father anymore. (Jean-Claude 2011, interview)

It is thus not surprising that most male survivors of sexual violence prefer not to tell their spouse what befell them. In some cases, such confessions might actually help mend relations between husband and wife, especially when both have been victims of sexual violence or when sexual violence has provoked the husband's impotence, thus raising his wife's concern (Halla 2016, interview). But for many male survivors, the risks of speaking out are just too high, and silence is seen as preferable.

What is striking is also that the male survivors' relatives themselves can bear part of the consequences of sexual violence, so that the shame and stigmatization often extend to include the survivor's wife, but also his children: "Not only do other adults mock survivors and their wives, children in the village will say to the children of male survivors, 'your father is a woman', stigmatizing the children of survivors" (Christian et al. 2011, 239). Considering the patriarchal nature of many societies where wartime sexual violence is happening, such trends are not surprising. The man, as husband and father, is expected to uphold and represent the honor and dignity of his whole family, so his shame reverberates upon them: "When a man is raped, his family is also raped (...). The whole family is not respected—his wife is considered lower than other wives in the community" (IRIN 2011; see also Christian et al. 2011, 238). This means that even if the act of sexual violence itself might be directly targeting individuals, its consequences actually impact on a much larger group of individuals.

4.3. COPING STRATEGIES

The survivors' capacity to cope with what befell them is often impeded by the other conflict-related plights they have had to face or are still facing, like losing family members, being forcefully displaced, having their belongings destroyed or taken away from them, etc. Their ability to face and recover from the consequences of sexual violence is, therefore, influenced by a number of other factors that increase their vulnerability. In other words, the suffering induced by wartime sexual violence intersects with other types of suffering, and it cannot be understood without taking into account the context in which the violence has been committed, and in which survivors find themselves.

Trying to Make Sense of What Happened

Understanding why they have been victims of sexual violence is particularly complex for survivors finding themselves in conflict settings where lines of divisions between warring parties are blurred and shifting, and where ideological or political oppositions are not at the center of the conflict, such as in Eastern Congo. Many explanations put forward by the survivors I have met revolved around the apparent "madness" of perpetrators, the loss of values in the context of war and the breakdown of traditions and social links:

> These men believe in nothing. They have no family, no proper job, no home. Some say they are true men of God, but it is not right, what they are doing. They do not show any respect of what their fathers have told them, they only know how to destroy, how to bring pain. (Félicien 2010, interview)

These explanations implicitly build on the assumption that sexual violence is perpetrated in a random way, that it is the product of madness, therefore, both unpredictable and uncontrollable. Almost all express puzzlement and even bewilderment, like Bernard, a Congolese refugee in Burundi:

> Every day I ask myself why, why me.... What if I had chosen to do something else, to be somewhere else the day when it happened? (Bernard 2013, interview).

Some of my interviewees even challenged me to come up with an explanation, to explain to them why they had been targeted:

> You who are studying this, can you tell me why they are doing this? What is their goal? Why doing this to me? I am not someone important you know. (Aimable 2010, interview)

Most of the male survivors I have met in Burundi and in the DRC didn't seem to have been specifically targeted for sexual violence, at least in terms of their political, ethnic, religious or geographic belonging. But all came from rather poor families, and very few inhabited, at the time of the assault(s), in a large city. In other words, all were vulnerable to violence committed by roaming armed groups. Many of them had been abducted by armed groups during raids on villages, or while they were in the countryside running some errand. And many had the feeling of having been at the wrong place at the wrong time. The apparent random nature of these acts makes it extremely difficult for survivors to come to terms with what has befallen them. While some thought that sexual violence against women could be explained by the sexual "urges" of combatants, they did not understand why this would happen to them, and what relation it might bear with the other types of violence they are victims of:

> They rape our women, they beat us, they kill our cattle and they take our food, but why doing this to me? They can have our food without doing this. When they beat you, when they take everything you have, when they burn down your house, they have what they want! So why did they do that? (Jean-Paul 2009, interview)

In these cases, incomprehension dominates, and most survivors seem to fight a nagging feeling that perhaps there is something that they cannot yet grasp, that would help them understand what happened, and thus hopefully overcome it. But because this explanation rarely comes, most survivors opt either for silencing the matter, or for re-labeling what has happened. Castration and rape are, for instance, re-qualified as torture or beatings, and many survivors use metaphors to speak about what happened to them, or describe it as if it had happened to someone else (Halla 2016, interview).

Things are somehow different in cases where survivors have the (right or wrong) feeling of having been singled out, especially in cases of sexual torture for political or ideological motives. In the testimonies collected by Feldman (1991), former political prisoners in Northern Ireland spoke almost casually about sexual torture: "They don't say a word, they just beat you rabbit punches, squeezing the testicles, anything at all. Just general brutality. (…) It was very clear then strip searching wasn't a method for finding anything: it was an opportunity for them to do whatever they were going to do on you" (128, 158). The Northern Irish paramilitaries I have met also inscribed their experiences of sexual violence in detention within a larger narrative on their political struggle:

They [interrogators] would beat me down there [gesturing at his groin], because they had tried everything else, and they couldn't break me, see? So they tried that too, trying to break me, but of course that didn't work. (Jim 2006, interview)

For some of them, it was an almost natural part of prison experience, an additional vindication of their wish to bring down this abusive system. And instead of depriving survivors of their agency, living through this kind of violence was seen as a proof of their (masculine) strength and resilience:

And yes of course like many others I was abused, you know, that is part of what you go through in there. But in a way that made our resolve stronger, because this is wrong, just like the whole system is wrong. It made us more determined to do whatever we can to bring it to an end. (Kieran 2005, interview)

Everything was done to make you feel like shit, like you are a piece of meat, you know? So whatever humiliation they put you through, whatever indecency they could do to you, like put their fingers in you or things like that, it was nothing. What was done to us is nothing as compared as to what they do to our families and to our communities. This is what counts. (Pat 2006, interview)

In Sri Lanka too, male survivors acknowledge that political motives triggered their arrest and torture, and put forward explanations pertaining to gender roles and local cultural values: "To be subjected to rape in front of other people is a shameful thing. If other Tamil people come to know they will look down on me. They did this to make us ashamed" (quoted in Sooka 2014, 41). Unlike many survivors I have met in the Great Lakes region, those who have been victims of sexual torture because of their political beliefs, or their ethnic or religious belonging, do not seem to struggle with the "why me" question, or with the "why sexual violence" one. But it is not necessarily the case for their (surviving) relatives. Claire, a Tutsi *rescapée* from the Rwandan genocide, speaks about her brother who was castrated in front of her, before being eventually being "cut"[6] by the Interahamwe (radical Hutu militias). She was eight years old at the time:

I don't understand, I really don't understand. Why did they have to do that before cutting him? (Claire 2012, interview)

Other *rescapées* of the Rwandan genocide shared similar stories, suggesting that this practice was, if not common, at least not exceptional during the genocide:

Nina: With my mother we decided to flee, cross the border and ask a cousin living in Burundi to help us. (…) We saw so many bodies on the way, at night. They left them there, rotting in the streets, in the houses, everywhere. They didn't care. Some of the bodies were half naked and mutilated, especially the men's.

EF: Mutilated?

Nina: Yes, mutilated. Cut. Some men's and boys' bodies were cut, down there.

EF: Why do you think they did that?

Nina: I don't know, I don't understand. Wasn't it enough to kill them? (Nina 2013, interview)

Fleeing

In Burundi and the Congo, male survivors' difficulty to comprehend sexual violence is frequently mirrored by the incapacity of their communities of origin to show understanding towards them, often precipitating their decision to leave—and also, in some cases, to commit suicide. This explains why the percentage of victims of sexual violence is so high among refugees[7]. Isolation, self-imposed exile and flight thus often characterize the experience of survivors. But flight can of course also be triggered by the situation of conflict itself, inducing mass killings, forced displacement, destruction of crop and cattle, bombings and attacks, epidemics and so on. But even in cases where violence is sporadic, some survivors prefer to leave their communities of origin for fear of another encounter with perpetrators (Refugee Law Project 2014, 8). And this insecurity often seems to follow them in exile, as if their incapacity to make sense of what happened had led them to assume that they would never be safe anywhere.

Evidence shows that migration can most of the time be explained by several reasons, and even for male survivors the experience of sexual violence is not necessarily the triggering factor. For people having experienced sexual torture in the hands of a national security agency, for instance, other experiences of control, repression, harassment and threat by security forces can precipitate the decision to start a new life abroad (see, for instance, the case of Sri Lanka, Sooka 2014). For them, leaving is a way to try to start anew, and to retrieve some agency and control over their lives:

> I came to Burundi because I wanted to try to live a normal life, to find a job, maybe start a small business. I had also thought about Rwanda, but it is less complicated here. It is not easy and it takes time but with God's help I will manage. (Bernard 2013, interview)

Fleeing allows male survivors to escape shaming by their communities of origin, or persecution for political, religious or other motives, and decreases the probability that they will have to face again the perpetrators. At the same time, it creates new burdens for survivors, who still have to cope with the physical and mental consequences of their ordeal, as well as with the difficulties related to settling, integrating and finding a job in another country, not to mention facing the hostility of populations in countries of settlement. If, as we will see in chapter 6, a few support programs are available for male survivors of sexual violence and torture in Western countries and especially in Northern Europe, they often face indifference and hostility in developing countries, especially in regions where all acts that can somehow be assimilated to homosexuality are penalized. It should also be noted that being a refugee increases the vulnerability of both male and female survivors, because without the protection of their relatives and communities of origin, they are likely to be targeted for sexual violence and all sorts of trafficking and exploitation, especially in refugee camps (UN 2013, 12). By fleeing, survivors thus often expose themselves to significant difficulties, and possibly also to further episodes of violence.

Coping with Feminization and the "Compensation" Hypothesis

Where is the male survivor's gender identity located, in the interplay between masculinities and femininities? As we have seen, sexual violence is a feminizing and subjugating act that seems to leave most male survivors in a limbo, as many of them think that their gender identity, and their social status, have been affected. However, especially during post-conflict and reconstruction processes, and unless they flee their regions of origin, they have to act according to dominant models of masculinity again, to take up their responsibilities as family heads, as breadwinners, and so on. But the memory that they have symbolically—and sometimes physically—been "unmanned", and maybe also forced to perform as women (for instance, in cases of imprisoned boys and men used as "bush wives" by armed groups in sub-Saharan Africa), stays on. The "material incorporation" (Connell 1987) of the feminized gender identity assigned by sexual violence is sometimes even visible at the corporeal level, as has been made apparent during several of my interviews. By keeping their eyes down, their voice hardly audible even when secrecy was ensured, and by staying as still and discrete as possible, many male survivors[8] abide by the social and cultural norms that a woman living in this region of the world is expected to respect. Of course, their behavior can also be explained by their wish to remain anonymous and not to attract attention, but experiencing sexual violence often seems to provokes a corporeal feminization, as well as a silencing of survivors—two effects that are obviously interrelated:

> I don't like going out, there are too many people outside, and there is too much noise. I prefer to stay at my place, where it is quiet, and I don't need to talk. And I don't like it, when people are looking at me. (Léonard 2014, interview)

If the survivors' plight becomes public, their communities of origin or of adoption when they try to settle elsewhere often consider them as neither women nor men: they are women in men's bodies:

> Nobody supported me. I was a wife who had a wife (Aimable 2010, interview).

Again, this is not without echo to how the military treats soldiers with post-traumatic stress disorder, mocked as "hysterical men" (Cornwall and Lindisfarne 1994, 18; Whitworth 2008), though there have been indications that a number of armed forces now take the issue of post-traumatic stress disorder more seriously, notably by investing a sizeable amount of resources in treatment and prevention. In any case, the feminization that is enacted through sexual violence seems to render survivors ineligible to any "respectable" masculinity model, and their assigned gender identity contradicts the one displayed by their bodies. Even when what happened to them stays hidden, many male survivors still have to struggle with a feeling of emasculation that hampers their capacity to enact traditional masculinity models, not to mention post-traumatic stress disorder symptoms interfering with their sexuality and capacity to still act as fathers to their children.

A minority of male survivors seem to react to enforced feminization by strongly restating their masculinity, by displaying heightened levels of violence towards others, by falling into criminal activities, or even by becoming perpetrators of sexual violence themselves. In the course of my African fieldwork, for instance, I have met survivors who had been abducted by armed groups, been sexually assaulted, and consequently stayed in the group and become perpetrators of sexual violence themselves. In the rare cases when such information was shared, male survivors have recognized having subsequently participated in the rape of women during raids on villages (for instance, Félicien 2010, interview). It is, however, worth noting that none of the male survivors I interviewed ever mentioned subsequently perpetrating sexual violence against men. Such mechanisms of compensation, through the perpetration of violence, have also been observed by medical staff working with male refugees from the Middle East who have been sexually tortured (Halla 2016, interview).

These findings are also in line with the work of Messerschmidt showing that crime can constitute a resource for enacting masculinity (Messerschmidt 1993, 85). The idea that perpetrating violence, and specifically sexual violence, for redeeming one's masculinity, has sometimes been called the "compensation hypothesis", whereby "feminized" men reassert their masculinity by performing feminizing acts on others (Mechanic 2004, 22; Leatherman 2011, 140). This would suggest that sexual violence against men is likely to generate a vicious cycle of further violence, by potentially increasing the incidence of gender-based, domestic, sexual and other types of violence against women, men and children. This also strongly implies that patterns of sexual violence against women, and against men, are even more tightly interrelated than usually assumed. At the policy level, such findings further underscore the need to come up with prevention programs addressing in an encompassing way wartime sexual violence against both men and women.

One should beware of simplifications, though. The proportion of male survivors turning into perpetrators of sexual violence is unknown, and seems unlikely to be very high. Many survivors are physically and mentally broken by what they have been through, and are more likely to display a self-destructive attitude than aggressiveness towards others. Moreover, it has been shown that in some cases, and especially if the survivor's partner has also been victim of sexual violence, male survivors can display more egalitarian behavior in their own couple, and more understanding towards gender equality issues (see, for instance, Edström et al. 2016, 32).

Retrieving Agency

One of the main characteristics of sexual violence, related to its feminizing nature, is that it is a physically and psychologically disempowering act that underscores the victim's weakness and subordinate status. Retrieving agency is not an easy process for survivors, be they men or women, especially when they have to face hostility on the part of the rest of the society; but it is also an indispensable one for male survivors in patriarchal societies that see men's mental strength and will to act as a key masculine requirement. As we have seen, for many male survivors, going back to performing their duties as chief of household, father and husband can be a real challenge, not least because they sometimes face the hostility of their own relatives. Many, however, strive to achieve it:

> I try to act normal, as if nothing has happened. But it is hard, I am tired all the time, I don't have any energy. I want to act normal for my children, for my family. (Jacques 2013, interview)

For many male survivors, fleeing, alone or with their families, is a way to reassert control over their lives, to "leave the past behind", and to try to find a better and more secure environment for themselves and for their families

(Halla 2016, interview). Some male survivors, notably those living in refugee camps in Uganda, have organized collectively and formed groups of survivors of sexual violence. Their initiatives, which we will further detail in chapter 6, are supported by the Refugee Law Project, and include awareness-raising activities, the making up of short films, of documentaries, the provision of help to other survivors and so on. As described by Edström et al. (2016), these groups can be considered as a form of "therapeutic activism", allowing survivors to retrieve agency and to act for a greater cause, by providing support to each other as well as to other survivors, but also by shedding light on the phenomenon of wartime sexual violence against men. As they become visible, survivors participating in these groups openly break a taboo, and thus demonstrate their mental and psychological strength. As shown by McClure in her work on conflict-related injuries in Northern Ireland, forming groups of survivors is an efficient strategy to gain agency and visibility (2015, 499). However, her work also shows that countering dominant narratives is a complicated task because of their hegemonic position, and that storytelling, as a classical method of victim advocacy, can be particularly tricky when what survivors want to highlight is complicated to describe or taboo. Her observations are particularly relevant with regard to the work of male survivor groups, who often have to overcome a general skepticism vis-à-vis their stories, when it is not an adamant refusal to hear them out.

It is worth mentioning that because many countries do not recognize the existence of sexual violence against men, and fuel homophobic assumptions about male survivors, men who are active in these survivors' groups prefer to call themselves human rights activists (Refugee Law Project 2013b, 12). The difficulty to ascribe a political, social or even religious or cultural meaning to male sexual victimization makes it very complicated for survivors to turn it into a mobilization resource. In cases where sexual violence against men can be explicated by a specific political or communal belonging, for instance, when sexual torture is administered as a counter-insurgency strategy, such activism should, in principle, be less complicated to organize. But when, like in the Great Lakes region of Africa, explanations remain elusive, "going public" is significantly more complicated. The fact that some still manage to organize collectively and implement support activities, especially considering the significant obstacles deriving from their refugees status and the general condemnation of homosexual acts, demonstrates their resilience and shows that destructive behavior, as well as the "compensation hypothesis" discussed above, is surely not an inevitable outcome.

4.4. LONG-TERM SOCIETAL IMPACT

The impact of wartime sexual violence against men (or against women) on post-conflict peace-building and reconciliation processes is extremely difficult to trace. In contrast with the wealth of publications researching conflict-related and especially militarized masculinities, very few studies focus on post-conflict masculinities, which are often assumed to be unproblematic since the conflict has ended or receded (Cahn and Ní Aoláin 2009). In cases where episodes of sexual violence have been sporadic and relatively small-scale, silence surrounds them and they are usually not mainstreamed in the analysis. Some cases of conflict that have been the focus of more academic attention, such as the Great Lakes region of Africa, are still largely ongoing, and we still lack the necessary distance to assess the long-term impact of large-scale sexual violence against men.

Post-Conflict Masculinities and Male Survivors

Whereas issues related to gender-based and sexual violence against women are increasingly taken into account in peace agreements and in post-conflict political arrangements, at least at the discursive level (Féron 2017), most post-conflict societies do not officially recognize the existence of male survivors of sexual violence. Of course many other concerns related to gender-based and sexual violence, such as "war babies" (Seto 2013), still have to make their way into the public debate, but issues related to male survivors are particularly shunned. As we have seen, knowledge on the topic is lacking, and in the specific post-war context, male survivors, who have not been able to defend and protect themselves not to mention the group or nation, are excluded from the national narrative (Zarkov 2001, 77). This has to be understood in relation to the fact that most post-conflict societies continue to glorify war heroes, hyper- and militarized models of masculinity, which further obscure the fate of male survivors. As explained by Ní Aoláin et al. in one of the rare publications focusing on post-conflict masculinities, "the prevalence of this kind of masculinity poses complex issues for undoing violence, for mainstreaming gender equality, and for remaking societies that have been fractured and deeply divided" (Ní Aoláin, Cahn and Haynes 2013, 130). Dominant and militarized masculinity models embed a set of values and characteristics, which proceed to include or exclude individuals, especially those seen as deviant or not masculine enough. Post-conflict political elites continue to rely strongly on these models, by which they themselves often abide. In many ways, the perpetuation of unquestioned masculinity models inherited from the conflict period explains the maintenance of high levels of violence in post-conflict settings, especially between males, as shown by Morrell in the case of South Africa (2000). There is also the belief that since post-conflict societies are facing great challenges pertaining to reconstruction, stabilization and reconciliation, they are more than ever in need of "strong men" who are able to uphold and defend national values and unity. In Burundi, for instance, right after the end of the civil war in 2006 the government decided that all citizens had a duty to participate every Saturday in community work, notably through the cleaning and maintenance of roads. Many male survivors, however, feel too weak for participating in such physical work:

> I am always tired. I feel weak. Who would need someone like me? I cannot even participate in community work on Saturdays. I feel useless. (Didace 2014, interview)

Post-conflict national narratives also heavily rely on the vision of a golden and mythical past where gender roles and relations were clear-cut and following a traditional script (Myrttinen 2003, 42–43). This is confirmed by what evidence could be collected on cases like Bosnia-Herzegovina or Croatia, where, in spite of the documented presence of numerous male survivors of sexual violence, the reconstruction of post-conflict national identities has been achieved *against* stories like those of male survivors: "The raped or castrated Croat man—in the context where rape and castration were associated with homosexuality and emasculation—would undermine construction of the Croat nation as virile and powerful" (Zarkov 2001, 80). In other words, even in cases where sexual violence against men has been widespread, post-conflict societies "cope" with the symbolic emasculation it entails by simply erasing it from national history and memory. While women's victimization is acknowledged, men are assumed to be victorious combatants who are just in need of demobilization or reintegration. By contrast, male survivors (alongside noncombatant men) are neither targeted directly or indirectly by post-conflict policies, nor invited to take up an active role in reconstruction. Similar preconceptions determine international programs supporting post-conflict reconstruction and reconciliation, which either focus on women as victims of sexual and gender-based violence, or on former combatants who need to be reintegrated. As a consequence, the suffering that such violence induces at the individual and collective levels is denied any legitimacy, generating further suffering and frustration. Such tendencies are particularly obvious in Disarmament, Demobilization and Reintegration (DDR) programs, which have so far absolutely ignored the issue of male survivors of sexual violence. Whereas, and largely thanks to feminist and women's movements and awareness campaigns, specific provisions for dealing with gender-based and sexual violence against women are now more and more frequently included in DDR provisions[9], issues related to male survivors are still totally ignored. As underscored by Eriksson Baaz and Stern, this is remarkably detrimental to post-conflict stabilization objectives, since ex-combatants who have experienced such trauma might be prone to perpetrate further violent acts if not supported (Eriksson Baaz and Stern 2010a).

In the long term, the strength of hegemonic conflict narratives that are shunning and silencing male survivors' experiences is likely to slowly fade and allow for alternative and more inclusive narratives to unfold. However, decades may need to pass before these taboo issues can be discussed openly.

Post-Conflict Societies and Sexual Violence

The legacy of conflict-related sexual violence against men also raises issues that are strikingly similar to those pertaining to sexual violence against women: since, as we have seen in the previous chapter, many of these acts were perpetrated by members of armies or armed groups, it is likely that most survivors will have lost trust in security institutions in general, and in people carrying weapons in particular. Instead of considering post-conflict (and often reformed) armies, police and justice systems as providers of security and stabilization, both female and male survivors generally display a very high level of mistrust and defiance towards these institutions:

> I don't trust soldiers. They are the same as other brigands, here or at home [in South Kivu] they steal, they pillage, they torture, they rape all the same. (Bernard 2013, interview)

Because most cases of sexual violence are not prosecuted—also due to a lack of reporting, as we will further detail in chapter 7—trust in the justice system decreases too. And when sexual violence has been perpetrated by a traditional or community leader, as is sometimes the case, trust in authority is replaced by a general defiance and feeling of bewilderment. Survivors who have not fled and resettled elsewhere might also have to meet on an everyday basis their torturers[10]. This can be paarticularly painful, especially when these perpetrators remain unprosecuted and when they hold respectable positions in the post-conflict society, which happens, for instance, in Bosnia-Herzegovina (Karabegović 2010). As a result, social structures and links are weakened, and difficult to mend, which does not bode well in the perspective of stabilization and reconciliation.

And consequences are significant at the economic level too. Many male survivors I have met have had to give up their previous job or occupation, because of the physical suffering and sometimes incapacitation entailed by sexual violence, but also because of shame and of the ostracism they face, and sometimes for fear of encountering the perpetrators again (see also Christian et al. 2011). As a result, their families experience a great loss of revenue and of social status, which has repercussions in terms of community development too. Male survivors who are not able to resume their economic activities are likely to be abandoned by their families, forcing many of them into begging and turning them into easy prey for trafficking networks. In rural areas like in the parts of North Kivu where violence has been the most intense, many male victims of sexual violence have been killed, abducted or have fled, and the others are often too young, too old or too weak to engage in significant economic activities. Of course, impediments to economic development relate to many other factors than sexual violence, but it is clear that the multi-faceted victimization that both male and female survivors of sexual violence face constitutes a major obstacle to economic recovery. The collective consequences of wartime sexual violence thus do not just affect traditional political and cultural structures, but also social and economic ones.

At the interpersonal level, sexual violence against both men and women also induces changes in gender roles and in relations within families that might have an impact on wider communities and social relations. Some wounds are likely to never heal, like when a man has been forced to rape a member of his family and/or when members of the family were forced to watch the perpetration of sexual violence on the survivor. Trans-generational transmission of trauma is also a possibility, as is a degradation of parental authority over the next generation, leading to a further unraveling of community structures.

Finally, it is worth underscoring the long-term health impact of sexual violence, not just in terms of trauma, mental illnesses and serious physical injuries, but also in terms of spread of HIV and other sexually transmitted diseases. Although I have not found any evidence of sexual violence against men being used as a deliberate tool for spreading HIV, as it has been demonstrated in cases of systematic sexual violence against women in Rwanda, for instance, (Aginam and Roupiya 2012), it is clear that many male survivors have been infected by HIV and other sexually transmitted diseases. This raises serious concerns for the already weak, underfunded and understaffed health sectors in conflict as well as post-conflict societies.

Chapter 5

The Elusiveness of Narratives on Wartime Sexual Violence Against Men

When wartime sexual violence against men is evoked in the media, it is often through a discourse of exceptionality, of novelty, as if it was a new problem that had just been discovered. It also frequently builds on a narrative of endless horror, related to some places embodying war's savagery and backwardness in Western imaginary, such as Eastern Congo, for instance: "Another growing problem: men raping men" (Gettleman 2009; see also Vandecasteele 2011). As we have seen, archaeologists, historians and anthropologists have long documented this practice, with examples from all around the world, from ancient times to contemporary warfare. So why do we seem to rediscover it each time a related story is published in a major newspaper, or broadcasted on television? A few NGOs like Médecins Sans Frontières (2009) also present some male survivors' stories now and then, but their scattered accounts are in general based on just a few personal testimonies, which contribute to presenting the issue as dramatic, but also as sporadic. In other words, cases of sexual violence against men are most of the time featured like exceptional occurrences that do not really fit in the grand narrative on wartime sexual violence. As such, they are dismissed as anecdotal, and useless for helping us making sense of the greater picture.

Narratives on international politics are woven in such a way that gender issues, and women, are most of the time made invisible, while men's and masculinities' omnipresence in international scripts is normalized and almost never critically scrutinized (Sjoberg 2013; Hutchings 2008). But discourses on wartime sexual violence constitute an exception with regards to the general invisibility of women and gender in international politics. In this area of study, femininity works as a common sense, as an implicit explanation, which is mapped against models of hegemonic, dominant, hyper-violent and militarized masculinity that put the stress on power and force as masculine traits. Such a script is not, per se, in contradiction with the recognition of the existence of male perpetrators of sexual violence against men, as it is built around associations between femininity and vulnerability, and masculinity and aggression. However, this general narrative leaves no space for acknowledging male vulnerability, especially in military settings, and for recognizing the existence of male survivors and of sexual violence against men in general. This is a major shortcoming that feminist studies have a duty to engage with since, as Detraz (2012, 11) argues, "feminist security studies concentrate on the ways world politics can contribute to the insecurity of individuals, especially individuals who are marginalized and disempowered". In that perspective, there is no doubt that more attention should be paid to male survivors of wartime sexual violence.

Fortunately, some major cracks have recently begun to appear in the rather simplistic understandings of wartime sexual violence that have been circulating during the past decades. Scholars and experts working on wartime sexual violence have started taking stock of advances in masculinity studies, highlighting diversities and hierarchies between models of masculinity and also disarticulating equations that had been previously made between men and masculinities, and women and femininities. Reports arriving from conflict zones, focusing on female survivors of sexual violence but also highlighting the plight of male survivors, have rendered the renovation and restructuring of narratives on conflict-related sexual violence even more urgent. In spite of this growing awareness though, when international documents or policies mention male survivors, it is still almost as an afterthought, and without any significant attempt to understand and analyse the phenomenon, and to come up with specifically targeted prevention and support policies.

What is puzzling is that the visibility of victims usually enhanced by a situation of conflict where both the media and the international community function as receptacles and amplifiers of testimonies of suffering, such as in the case of Eastern DRC, for instance, does not seem to be fully enacted in the case of male survivors of sexual violence. In light of these seemingly contradictory trends, this chapter explores understandings of, and narratives on, wartime sexual violence against men, as well as some of the questions they raise: Why are we seemingly paying less attention to sexual violence perpetrated against men than when it is perpetrated against women, even though there is mounting evidence of the latter? Can our understanding of sexual violence be reconciled with situations in which men are the victims and not the perpetrators, without damaging the work done by feminists to highlight the victimization of women? As we will see, this resounding silence originates in various sources. First, survivors themselves have a tendency to silence what happened to them, but so does the rest of the society, and of course the perpetrators. The international community, on the other hand, seems to alternate between recognition and denial, and struggles to find a place for male survivors in its narratives on war and sexual violence. This chapter argues that gender representations that are dominating at local, national but also international levels hinder the acknowledgement of the existence of male survivors of sexual violence, and thus obscure our understanding of the underlying mechanisms sustaining wartime sexual violence. The chapter explores what accounts for such a silencing, from representations of sexual violence where men stand as perpetrators, to patriarchal cultures associating masculinity to strength, protection and invulnerability.

5.1. THE BROKEN AND UNFINISHED NARRATIVES OF SURVIVORS

One of the first striking elements about narratives on wartime sexual violence against men is that they seldom come from survivors themselves. Admittedly, even after the conflict has ended they rarely are in a position to make themselves heard, but there is also a genuine reluctance not only to tell their stories, but also to acknowledge the gendered and sexual nature of the violence they have been victims of. This is, of course, not very surprising considering the strong taboo around sexuality that persists in many societies around the world, but it is also related to the specific post-conflict context. In post-conflict and reconstruction settings, male survivors face great difficulties voicing out what happened to them, mostly because that type of sexual violence usually does not fit grand narratives about the conflict—frequently presenting men as saviors, defenders and protectors of civilian women and children. In addition, the apparent impossibility, at least in some settings, to make sense of conflict-related sexual violence against men, to assign a political meaning to it, relegates it to the inherent savagery and folly of war, in a way neither curable nor eligible for reparation. Male survivors are thus pushed away in the limbo of the post-conflict era, as obscene and embarrassing by-products of war that do not qualify for entering the realm of the political and politicized:

> Nobody cares what happened to me. I am not a soldier, I am not a rebel, who cares what happened to me? (Jean-Claude 2011, interview)

The difficulties survivors face in coping with the physical and psychological pain also somehow sound dissonant amid discourses calling for peace and reconciliation. Post-conflict discourses enjoin everyone to move on, to let go of their resentment, to forgive and to cease dwelling on what happened. In such circumstances, their unceasing suffering simply does not fit:

I cannot forget what happened. They say it is peace now, that all Burundi's problems are solved. But my problems are still here, and I don't feel at peace. (Aimable 2010, interview)

What complicates the recognition of the suffering of male survivors, and of their victimhood, is also the fact that most of their injuries are often not visible to the naked eye, and can, therefore, be dismissed as unimportant. Nicole McClure has highlighted similar processes with victims of the troubles in Northern Ireland, showing that even though many of them are still in pain, they feel like their suffering is illegitimate and largely invisible in current narratives about the past: "The Injured are not visibly marked in any way that indicates that their injury was incurred in conflict violence. (…) There are also those whose injuries are invisible to the naked eye (psychological trauma or injuries that can be hidden from view) who have continued to maintain a seemingly normal life; they disappear simply because their injuries are assumed to be healed or nonexistent" (McClure 2015, 500).[1]

I have met survivors in both "conflict" and "post-conflict"[1] settings. They had faced various types of sexual violence and torture, like having been raped, forced to rape family members, sexually tortured with objects or with electric shocks or been mutilated. None of them spontaneously described any of these instances as sexual violence. It is as if this concept was reserved to women only. Repeatedly, people—survivors, relatives and even local medical staff—I talked to confused sexual violence against males with violence in general, or with homosexuality. According to a local source quoted in a report by OCHA[2], "Men do not use the word *rape*, which is too hard. They prefer to talk about torture, abomination". My research participants were no exception. In a sense, I had the feeling that it was less an attempt to euphemise what had happened than an indication of their own incapacity to recognize that such a thing had happened to them. The interpretation of the metaphors and paraphrases they used was made easier by parallels they made between female prisoners and themselves, or by their indignation of having been "used as if they were women" (Dionise 2011, interview). They were bewildered at having been treated in a way that they considered as contradicting with their gender, and that was "against nature".

Sexual violence seems to be even more difficult to accept and speak about when it is perpetrated by women. According to the previously quoted report on sexual violence compiled by Médecins Sans Frontières, which covers several African cases, including Burundi and Eastern DRC, such occurrences are not exceptional:

While men can be victims of sexual violence, women can also be perpetrators. Male rape survivors attending MSF clinics in Ituri reported being forced to have intercourse with female fighters or guards while in detention. Most of these assaults were committed publicly, to cause humiliation. Even if not involved directly in forced sex, women may play a role as accomplices, facilitating repeated aggression or preventing the violation from being reported. (Médecins Sans Frontières 2009, 11)

Among the survivors I have met, and who had been abused while in detention, none reported clear cases of forced intercourse with female fighters, but several mentioned the fact that other abducted women were present when they had been "humiliated", and that some female combatants had "participated in their torture" (Félicien 2010, interview).

Whether such episodes of sexual violence happen under the eyes of external witnesses or not is also obviously important for understanding the survivors' reaction—many "public" male victims of rape I know or have heard of have fled their regions of origin or committed suicide. Facing public shame, disapproval, ostracism, not to mention accusations of homosexuality or of weakness, in addition to the suffering they already have to handle often proves impossible. The fact that they were abused publicly prevents them from being in control of their own narrative, and of their own victimization. In addition to attacking (symbolically but also sometimes physically) their masculinity and their pride, the public perpetration of sexual violence ensures that survivors are also deprived of control over their own story.

But what also often prevents male survivors from sharing their stories publicly, even years after the end of the conflict, is that they think that what happened to them was so unusual, so exceptional, that nobody will believe them. Because public discourses on sexual violence focus on women as victims, many male survivors have the impression of having had to suffer an aberration. That is especially true of those who suffered episodes of sexual violence outside of detention settings, and who are not in contact with other survivors:

> I don't know of anyone else here who has suffered what I have suffered. I don't think there are many others like me. It might happen once in a while, but not often, no. Who could believe that it can happen? (Didace 2014, interview)

Thinking that they are exceptional cases, that they do not legitimately belong to any category of conflict victims, prevents them from feeling included in post-war narratives. And when they cannot find a rational explanation for what befell them, for instance, connected to conflict issues and divisions, they conclude that they must somehow be responsible for what happened, and that they had better stay silent:

It is better for me not to tell anyone about what happened. If that has happened, then it must be because God wanted to punish me for things I have done in the past. So it is better for me to accept it, to beg forgiveness and not speak about what happened. (Vincent 2014, interview)

For the very few local organizations that try to help both male and female survivors of sexual violence, men's reluctance to speak, not just to support staff but also to their own relatives, can be a major obstacle to recovery. In the capital city of Burundi, for instance, organizations like SERUKA say that only 5% of the victims they receive are men and boys, and that there is evidence of low reporting rates for male victims (SERUKA 2012, interview). But even those who make the decision to seek help find it almost impossible to talk about it to their relatives, especially to their wives: "Comment puis-je dire à ma femme qu'on a fait de moi une femme?"[3]. The fact that most international programs dealing with sexual violence during conflicts focus on women—and indeed tend to imply that only women can be victims—also leads to devastating consequences for male victims: since they think that these programs are "made for women", they do not dare come forward, and feel as if their own suffering was totally ignored, silenced, too outrageous to even be spoken about. And the equation that is made between women and victims further alienates them, because it indeed confirms what many of them are already feeling anyway: that having been raped or mutilated has "turned them into women", into "lesser men" (Jacques 2013, interview). These programs build a narrative in which men, if not perpetrators, should be protecting the victims, that is, the women. There is no room for considering the suffering of men. And if they still wish to be recognized as victims, then they will have to accept to go to facilities dedicated in priority to women, to face the added shame of being seen there[4], and they will thus be further symbolically feminized. In other words, the focus put on female victims of sexual violence furthers the suffering of male victims, by reinforcing the "de-masculinization" and "feminization" induced by what they went through.

5.2. INTERNATIONAL NARRATIVES ON WARTIME SEXUAL AND GENDER-BASED VIOLENCE

As many scholars have already observed, in international narratives about gender and conflicts, or about conflict-related sexual and gender-based violence, and especially in UNSC Resolutions dealing with women and conflicts, women are often depicted as "wars' 'others', peaceful themselves and often objecting to the war or conflict" (Sjoberg 2013, 61). They are described as forcefully displaced, pushed into prostitution or trafficking, forcefully enrolled in armed groups, etc. In short, women's actions and deeds are generally depicted as if they were outside of the conflict action and realm, or only happened to be there by accident. They are also assumed to be naturally more peaceful and less radical, and the "women and peace hypothesis"[5] is still quite popular in international arenas. UNSC Resolution 1325 (2000) underscores, for instance, "the important role of women in the prevention and resolution of conflicts and in peace-building". Women are said to be more inclined than men to think for the common good, to defend universal and humanitarian values, while men are seen as unable to move across ethnic, linguistic or religious divisions. In that perspective, women are the perfect subjects of a peaceful and reconciled world, while men embody war and politics.

In many ways, the language used in UNSC Resolutions about gender and conflicts is essentialist, as it rarely questions the categories "women" and "men", as if all women were facing the same plight, and as if all men had the same (violent) role. Femininities and masculinities are seen as unproblematic and unchangeable, and the intersectionality factor is overlooked: "women" and "men" are both assumed to be unified and homogeneous groups, in spite of the fact that conflict studies have, for instance, long shown that violence does not affect the wealthy and the poor in similar ways. Women are always associated with apolitical values, whereas men embody politics and ideology; women are assumed to be civilians, mothers, and it is their primary function as caretakers and caregivers that is underscored; a parallel hidden assumption is that men in conflict areas are either part of the military, or of armed groups. Needless to say, this representation excludes many women taking part in conflict, such as female combatants, who represent between 10% and 40% of combatants depending on the conflict zone, and it of course also overlooks the numerous men who are "just" civilians, as well as those who are victims of the conflict, like male survivors of sexual violence. In many ways these discourses ensure the reproduction of highly patriarchal values and worldviews, whereby women are seen as weaker and have to be protected in order to be able to fulfill their traditional functions, as underscored by Detraz: "A project that unquestioningly asserts an association between women and peace may actually serve to disempower women by defining them in opposition to the ideas security studies considers most crucial, specifically strategizing for and fighting in wars" (2012, 12). These discourses obviously also reinforce the association that is usually made between men and power, or men and violence.

These stereotypical narratives are never more obvious than in declarations and resolutions dealing with conflict-related sexual violence. UNSC Resolutions 1325 (2000), 1820 (2008), but also 1888 (2009), 1889 (2009), 1960 (2010), 2106 (2013), 2122 (2013) and all subsequent others seem to assume that sexual violence has universal effects on the victims; they also presuppose universal hierarchical gender relations and overlook the diversity of individual experiences. As recognized by a report published by the UN itself, "The Security Council Resolutions from 1325-2122 focus on female victims; male victims are mentioned only once, in UNSCR 2106, some thirteen years after the UNSCR 1325 was passed. As such, the Women, Peace and Security lens may have inadvertently led to adverse and exclusionary programming practices in the field" (UN 2013, 7). Suffering that is experienced at the individual level is reinterpreted, reconstructed and framed in international discourses in a way that reduces and negates the individuals' agency, and these discourses are singularly blind to the multiplicity of the survivors' experiences, and to the individuals' resiliency. UNSC Resolution 1820 (2008) is particularly representative of that type of framing. As shown by Seto (2013, 67), "Resolution 1820 treats sexual violence as a 'fixed reality' of the experience of women. It reinforces the idea that women are continuously vulnerable to the dealings of the public sphere". These discourses restrict women's and men's agency, oversimplify women's and men's experiences of conflict, and overlook the fact that many women (and men) who have been victims of sexual violence develop multiple strategies to cope with, and recover from, what they went through. They also overlook the fact that individuals who have been raped or survived different types of sexual violence have the ability to redefine their social identities after the conflict, even if this ability is constrained by various political, material, social and cultural factors (Skjelsbæk 2006, 396). Further, Otto argues (2009, 24), "the assumption in Resolution 1820 that sexual violence is always perpetrated by men against women and children promotes homophobic mythologies and stigma, making it virtually impossible for male victims to speak out, let alone join the queue of evacuees". This has obvious consequences not only in terms of access to medical and psychological support, but also in terms of asylum seeking procedures, of reparation and prosecution of perpetrators, and so on. These narratives make it very complicated for male survivors, even when they belong to particularly vulnerable categories, such as refugees, internally displaced, sexual minorities, migrant workers, or disabled, to have their plight recognized. In other words, picturing women as passive victims of sexual violence, and men as senseless perpetrators of this violence is not just inaccurate, it is also perpetuating a conflict narrative in which women have no chance to ever reach and develop any kind of agency; it also throws suspicion on all men, and prevents male survivors from being seen, heard and supported.

In these discourses, women are always depicted as being in a position of inferiority, vulnerability (Butler 2014), need and lacking, when men remain in their position of decision-makers, of power-holders, to the point that, as Charlesworth argues (2008, 358), "women have become the metaphor for vulnerable/victim in war". UNSC Resolution 1325, for instance, emphasizes the importance of taking "into account the special needs of women and girls". These statements are built on the very gendered assumption that women are submissive victims; the attention is focused on their incapability to help themselves, and this reinforces their "a-political-ness". The focus that is put on civilian women as victims of wartime sexual violence is equally problematic, because it suggests that non-civilians cannot be victimized, when in fact a large proportion of sexual violence, like, for instance, sexual torture, is committed in military settings, and especially in detention, as explained by Sivakumaran (2010, 271): "Sexual violence is committed against civilians but not against civilians alone. Much of the sexual violence that takes place against men and boys is carried out in situations of detention, against prisoners of war and members of the armed forces or armed group. It is also carried out against 'child soldiers', both boys and girls. Yet none of these forms of sexual violence is covered by SC Res 1820 with its exclusive focus on civilians".

The stress put on the vulnerability of civilian women is epitomized by the repeated association of the words "women and children": "Using words such as 'vulnerable' and 'exploitation', and continually running together the two collective nouns 'women and children' serve to associate women with children and thereby bracket the two together conceptually, constructing what Cynthia Enloe calls 'womenandchildren' (1990)" (Shepherd 2008, 41). Considering the fact that children are often depicted as devoid of agency, as in need of constant care and protection, this association between women and children raises important questions about how the international community contributes to the (symbolic, but maybe also material) disempowerment of women, and the parallel empowerment of (some) men, in zones of conflict. Furthermore, this association promotes a narrow understanding of the situation and needs of women, by putting the stress on their duties as mothers—as providers of care to their children—overlooking the fact that women might have needs totally unrelated to their status as mothers—or that they might not be mothers at all.

Crucially, narratives about conflict-related sexual violence build on "silent others", men, who are by contrast understood to be responsible for the suffering of women. UNSC Resolution 1820 (2008) states, for instance, that "women and girls are particularly targeted by the use of sexual violence, including as a tactic of war to humiliate, dominate, instill fear in, disperse and/or forcibly relocate civilian members of a community or ethnic group". The assumption that it is men who are targeting women by the use of sexual violence is implicit, overlooking the fact that, for instance, in a region like Eastern DRC, famously named the "world capital of rape", it is estimated that more than 40% of perpetrators of sexual violence against women are women themselves (Johnson et al. 2010). These discourses build on an assumed link between heterosexuality and rape (as well as on a reduced understanding of sexual violence to rape), pertaining to a strong heteronormativity which obscures the existence of wartime sexual violence against men. As a corollary, men are asked to change their behavior and stop from engaging in sexual violence (Otto 2009, 14). This once again builds on the assumption that men hold power over women, and is "congruent with existing gender narratives, which tell of 'men' as being empowered, controlling, and active, as well as aggressive" (Shepherd 2008, 40). Men are those who, by their actions, can either perpetrate these atrocities, or put an end to them. Contrary to women, they can exercise their agency, they are in control. Violence becomes the preserve of men, a defining characteristic of masculinity, a natural part of male behavior (that thus has to be controlled). While most post structuralist feminists have underscored the fact that these narratives on wartime sexual violence essentialize and "biologize" women, the same can be said about men, who are reduced to their basic instincts. The victim/perpetrator distinction is essentialized too, and (con-)fused with the woman/man division, thus further entrenching beliefs associating women with passivity and weakness, and men with agency, power and violence.

Even when the existence of wartime sexual violence against men is acknowledged, it is often interpreted as a choice that men make, a result of their agency, rather than something that is done to them. As explained by Chynoweth, Freccero and Touquet (2017, 3) in the case of sexual trafficking, "boys may be perceived as 'prostituting themselves' or 'experimenting with their sexuality' and, therefore, less in need or deserving of protection or support" (see also Dennis 2008). This reinforces stereotypes relating to masculinity, agency and strength, and hampers male survivors' access to support.

Further, in the few instances where sexual violence against men is acknowledged at the international level, it is not presented as *sexual*, but as *political*—a framing which echoes survivors' stories and refusal to use references to sex to describe what happened to them. Such is the case, for instance, of narratives on the use of torture in detention, where as we have seen in chapter 1, male sexual torture is seldom mentioned as such[6]. It is as if the choice of, say, applying electric shocks to the male genitals was accidental and not related to their sexual and gendered meaning, whereas when a female prisoner is brutalized, the focus is put on the sexual element of torture even if it made up only a small part of the suffering the female prisoner has had to go through (for detailed accounts of torture of female militants, see, for instance, MacDonald 1991). This is in line with the reasoning of Ross (2002) showing how violence against men is racialized or politicized or related to class, whereas violence against women tends to be primarily sexualized and de-politicized. Wartime sexual violence against men is thus de-sexualized, just as male bodies are de-gendered. Sexual violence against men is often referred to with the metaphorical concept of "emasculation" which puts the stress on its political consequences (weakening, loss of agency, and so on), and which somehow obscures the materiality of sexual violence against men as a practice (Ross 2002, 307–11). Conversely, discourses on sexual violence against women often focus on rape as practice, and veil some of its metaphoric and political functions, as in the case of the "weapon of war" thesis.

5.3. WARTIME SEXUAL VIOLENCE, THE INTERNATIONAL SECURITY ORDER AND THE COLONIAL TAINT

What purposes do such narratives serve? What is striking to see is that stories focusing on violence against women, as stories of vulnerable, disempowered beings, fit extremely well the objectives of international actors, especially humanitarian ones, because they are seen as apolitical, and thus more in line with humanitarian discourses. Further, as several authors have shown, the victimization of women, and the parallel invisibility of male victims, often serve to justify international intervention (e.g. protect a feminized Kuwait from a hyper-masculine Iraq in 1990, saving Afghan women from Afghan men, etc.; see Sjoberg 2013, 199), where peacekeeping forces and humanitarian organizations can play the role of the masculine protector, which is assumed to be missing in the developing world. As has already been well demonstrated elsewhere, human misery is the strongest basis for NGOs' appeals for help. But misery also serves to uphold the role of the United Nations as a protector of vulnerable women, rather than to promote women's participation as agents (Seto 2013, 67). UN discourses build on the implicit idea that peacekeeping forces can help fighting wartime sexual violence— overlooking the fact that peacekeepers have also been found responsible for such acts, both against women and girls, and against men and boys, and that peacekeepers embody a masculinity model that is not much less violent than the ones that lead to episodes of sexual violence. These narratives serve to establish and legitimize a certain international security order, which builds upon a gendered understanding of violence, but also upon a violent reproduction of gender (Shepherd 2008, 170–71). In other words, associating women with vulnerability and victimhood, and men with power, violence and agency, serves to reproduce and to legitimize international policies such as intervention in conflict zones, as well as their multiple corollaries such as violent policing and imposition of Western values, norms and rules.

Such narratives obviously carry a heavy colonial taint (Eriksson Baaz and Stern 2013). Beyond the fact that calls for "gender mainstreaming" strategies try to impose Western values and conceptions of gender roles to the rest of the world, discourses on sexual violence are similarly built upon

Western and imperialist understandings of gender identities and gender roles in the developing world. Post-colonial feminisms have already shown how representations of "woman" or "women" that masquerade as "universal" are, instead, universalizing and produced through hierarchical and intersecting power relations. Similarly, the portraying of men living in the developing world as uncivilized objects comes to justify intervention. In particular, one has to recognize that the understanding and framing of the suffering induced by sexual violence in conflict areas is tightly related to how Third World masculinities (and related Third World femininities) are viewed. This is not to say, of course, that violent conflict happens only in developing countries, but rather that our understanding of sexual violence in conflict areas is largely shaped by accounts from Eastern DRC, Uganda, Sri Lanka or the Central African Republic. Women in developing countries are usually pictured as victims of a patriarchal order, but this patriarchal order, as well as the masculine agents who support it, remains largely undescribed and unquestioned: "How are we to understand 'black men'? This is not a question that has received the attention it deserves, as the focus of gender work in under-developed world contexts and in terms of race has been insistently on women. An ironic consequence has been to silence or to render black men invisible" (Morrell and Swart 2005, 96). It is perhaps never truer than in the case of wartime sexual violence against men in the developing world. Because they do not display the right gender or ethnicity, (nonwhite) male bodies cannot be in pain. This is what Lieder shows in her Scarry-inspired work: "The body in pain [is] a specifically gendered (female), classed (lowerclass), and raced (nonwhite) 'other'" (Lieder 2015, 521). Some Western media narratives[7] also purport degrading assumptions about men of the developing world, including that they are "less civilized", more likely to be violent (Carruthers 2004; Eriksson Baaz and Stern 2013) while at the same time somehow presenting their masculinity as incomplete and lacking (Ross 2002, 318). When attention is drawn to men in conflict areas, they are usually seen as responsible for the very high levels of violence against women, as well as against other men. Consequently, men who are victims of sexual violence must certainly bear some responsibility for their own fate, if only by never questioning the highly patriarchal models valued in their societies. Such narratives explain that men are excluded (save as perpetrators, of course) from accounts on sexual violence in conflict areas; they also feed the assumption that sexual violence is a phenomenon only relevant to women and girls.

In many ways, these narratives on wartime sexual violence perpetuate postcolonial representations whereby black men cannot control their sexuality (Kapur 2002). The focus that is put on rape of women justifies Western interventionism since black men are seen as incapable of protecting "their" women and thus the West needs to step in. As explained by Elizabeth

D. Heineman (2011, 17), "Reports of sexual violence also frequently serve a larger symbolic function: to differentiate the 'civilized' from the 'uncivilized'. (…) So closely intertwined are the notions of sexual restraint and civilization that efforts to legally restrain sexual violence in war often reflects efforts to claim 'civilized' status". Men and women living in conflict zones are reduced to their sexual organs, men to their "primal" instincts, women to their sexual and reproductive health. This all fits the underdevelopment paradigm, whereby underdevelopment is associated with pathologies of crime and terrorism (Duffield 2001). In this narrative, developing countries require external help, and their civilian population—in particular women and girls—is victimized. This imagery of a defenseless population needing to be protected by Western intervention is itself consistent with a representation of patriarchal relations between the international community and States in conflict.

As a consequence, existing gender narratives whereby women are in need of protection that only (white) men can provide are strengthened. And representations of (colonized/colored) men as oversexed, strong and uncontrollable, whose behavior is characterized first and foremost by violence, come to justify interventionist and paternalistic policies. These narratives, which equate conflict zones with areas of wilderness where violence is deregulated, savage and incomprehensible, come to contradict well-established—though questionable, as we have seen—understandings of rape and sexual violence as *political* weapons of war. Because men of color are presented as exerting (and, when it is acknowledged, being victims of) sexual violence in a seemingly random and uncontrollable fashion, they are deprived of strategy and of political agency, thus legitimizing their position at the bottom of the international security order, as well as the silencing of male survivors' plight.

5.4. NATIONAL MYTHS, PATRIARCHIES AND MALE SURVIVORS

It is perhaps at the national and community levels that the silencing of wartime sexual violence against men is, so to say, the loudest. Here, social constructions of masculinity roles, attributing the most important functions to men, actively prevent any kind of recognition of their potential vulnerability. As is well known, patriarchal and nationalist cultures, especially in conflict zones, usually assign a role of protectors to men; they have to be strong and unyielding, in order to protect themselves, their family, their community, but also their nation or State (Yuval-Davis 1993). Men who have been victims of sexual violence have failed to protect themselves and are thus considered as less likely to be able to protect their family, provided that their family still accepts them. Male survivors are thus seen as failed in their masculinity; they have failed to emulate the model of hegemonic masculinity that assigns to men the most important positions within the family, as backbones of their family, community and nation. Neither men nor women—their social identity might be feminized by sexual violence, their body usually still remains identified as male by the wider society—and neither fearful defenders nor glorious-in-defeat combatants, they cannot fill any useful purpose in national narratives which glorify national heroes "as resolutely individualistic, moral, rebellious and tough" (Munn 2008, 151).

Some of the humanitarian staff I spoke with believe that raping men stems from a similar strategy to that of raping women: an ethnic cleansing one[8]. Even though such a statement should certainly be qualified, it is true that in societies where ethnicity is seen as being transmitted by males only, it is indeed a very efficient way to target specifically the bearer of ethnicity and hence destroy his own capacity to perpetuate his ethnic group. And in countries where a strong connection has been built and strengthened between nationalism, ethnic belonging and masculinity, sexual violence against men and boys specifically attacks and weakens what lies at the core of national or ethnic identity and pride. As Zarkov illustrates in the case of Croatia, wartime sexual violence against men is a powerful way to undermine the strength of a nation or of an ethnic group:

> Because the phallic power of the penis defines the virility of the nation, there can be no just retribution for its loss. So, when the male body is ethnic and male at the same time, the castration of a single man of the ethnically defined enemy is symbolic appropriation of the masculinity of the whole group. Sexual humiliation of a man from another ethnicity is, thus, a proof not only that he is a lesser man, but also that his ethnicity is a lesser ethnicity. Emasculation annihilates the power of the ethnic Other by annihilating the power of its men's masculinity. (Zarkov 2011, 78)

The violation of the male body (that is, the violation of the body of any man belonging to the national or ethnic group) is very complicated to accept from a collective perspective, because the male body symbolically epitomizes the symbiotic link that is forged between masculine strength and national or group culture. Acknowledging it would publicize the symbolic feminization and subjugation of the entire nation or ethnic group. The existence of sexual violence against men is, therefore, collectively denied or silenced, especially in contexts where national or ethnic identities are seen as weakened or threatened, which is almost always the case in conflict and post-conflict settings.

If publicly exposed, the capacity of sexual violence against men to destroy family and community linkages is striking. In most patriarchal societies (Sivakumaran 2007, 268), there is a strong belief that in contrast to women, men should be invulnerable. This belief is of course highly gendered and gendering: "Vulnerability and invulnerability are not essential features of men or women, but, rather, processes of gender formation, the effects of modes of power that have as one of their aims the production of gender differences along lines of inequality" (Butler 2014, 112). But since men embody national or communal pride, the recognition that they have been violated implies that it is the whole group that has been attacked and been made vulnerable. This is maybe what explains the extreme taboo surrounding male sexual victimization in military settings, like male sexual torture at the hands of the "enemy", for instance. Recognizing that "our soldiers" have been violated in such a way, when they stand as a bulwark against external aggression, when they are here to uphold and bolster national pride, borders on the impossible. In that way, dominant models of masculinity obliterate the possibility of certain types of male suffering, especially those that do not allow the victim to gain honor or glory. As a consequence, men who have experienced sexual abuse "are treated solely as torture survivors, and the sexual component of their suffering is virtually ignored" (Stemple 2009, 635).

If it is publicly recognized, the suffering induced by sexual violence against men expands to include the whole community, which is left humiliated, unprotected and disempowered. As a result, the communities to which they belong lose their ethnicity, but also their masculinity. The performativity of sexual violence against men turns them into communities of womanized men, of homosexuals, symbolically and psychologically deprived of any ability to regenerate and perpetuate themselves. For the concerned societies, acknowledging the existence of sexual violence against men would thus mean acknowledging that one's group is a lesser group. The only alternative to silencing is, therefore, ostracizing survivors, casting them out of the communal space, in cases where survivors have not already fled:

> I tried to speak about it to the chief of the village, but he told me not to speak about these things. These are evil things he said, better not to speak about it. So I try to forget what happened to me, and I have told nobody else. (Jean-Paul 2009, interview)

These representations are also quite obviously related to a strong heteronormativity, whereby what we can call a hegemonic heterosexuality is shaping the perception of male victimization experience. This is particularly true of male survivors who also happen to be civilian, and who are, therefore, doubly feminized (and homosexualized): "A male who is exposed to rape and sexual violence in wartime has already been feminized by virtue of having assumed noncombatant status or having been forced into it through disarming and detention/incarceration" (Jones 2006, 459). Because it exposes collective fractures, tensions and weaknesses, the vulnerability of male survivors threatens to contaminate the whole society, and should, therefore, be silenced in order to hide the immense shame they carry.

Ultimately, the wider recognition of, and response to, the suffering induced by wartime sexual violence against men is impeded at the national and community levels by the same assumptions regarding "typical" masculine values and behavior that are held at the international level. As we will explore in the next chapter, some actors in the humanitarian field also fear that acknowledging the suffering of men, or paying "too much" attention to it, will somehow distract attention from the suffering of women. But such beliefs are the result of simplistic understandings of gender relations. Actually, as I have tried to show, the silencing of male survivors' stories results in the strengthening of patriarchal discourses, and should, therefore, be considered as counterproductive by those who are fighting for women's rights. Pretending that wartime sexual violence against men does not exist, or that it is anecdotal since "women make up the vast majority of victims"[9], is playing into the hands of patriarchy. This silencing reinforces existing gender representations, and allows for the perpetuation of a masculinist gender order, where masculinity is associated with violence and power, and femininity with weakness and powerlessness. In other words, far from drawing attention to gender inequalities, and from helping to improve women's situation, this silencing is highly detrimental to feminists' objectives, because it reinforces the link between masculinity, power and invulnerability: "Perceiving men only and always as offender and never as victims of rape and other forms of sexual violence is a very specific, gendered narrative of war. In that narrative, dominant notions of masculinity merge with norms of heterosexuality and definitions of ethnicity and ultimately designate who can or cannot be named a victim of sexual violence" (Zarkov 2011, 69). In these narratives, conflict-related sexual violence, trauma and vulnerability are feminized, paradoxically resulting in a heightened vulnerability of women, and in a reluctance on the part of male victims to seek physical and mental health support.

Chapter 6

Conceptualizing and Implementing Care and Support Programs for Male Survivors

Providing support to male survivors of wartime sexual violence entails overcoming a series of major challenges, some of which are related to the narratives detailed in the previous chapter, while others pertain to material and funding obstacles. Because men have long been totally invisible as victims in international as well as national discourses about conflict-related sexual violence, the policies that have been designed and put in place to help female survivors have de facto excluded them from access to support. Further, when men appear in the equation, it has most of the time been as potential perpetrators of sexual violence—which some of them undoubtedly are—thus generating policies somehow presenting men as threats from which survivors of sexual violence have to be protected. As noted in a report published by the UN, "sexual and gender-based violence scenarios are populated by male perpetrators and female victims" (2013, 9). In many ways, the efficiency and impact of policies designed for offering support to survivors are impeded by these discourses' Manichaean structure, offering simplistic explanations and thus unable to grasp the complex causes underpinning the phenomenon they are trying to oppose. As we will see, this Manichaean and binary discursive structure is part and parcel of a humanitarian narrative that needs simple explanations to attract external support and funding.

There are, however, some indications that discourses and practices are slowly evolving, becoming more aware and more inclusive of male survivors' needs (Touquet and Gorris 2016). Over the past decade, academics, NGOs but also medical staff have started articulating strong criticism of existing programs addressing conflict-related sexual violence, especially because of their blatant oversight of male survivors (see, for instance, Carpenter 2006; Gorris 2015; Sivakumaran 2010). For the time being, however, this increased awareness has only generated fairly limited changes. In conflict settings all around the world, most humanitarian organizations, including major international ones, still focus almost exclusively—in discourse as well as in practice—on female survivors. As we will see, the setting up of support programs specifically targeting, or being inclusive of, male survivors is particularly complicated to organize in conflict areas, and not just for reasons pertaining to how gender-based violence is discursively framed. Organizing support in neighboring countries, and especially in refugee camps, constitutes an alternative but not fully satisfactory path. Support is sometimes provided in a post-conflict environment, decades after the sexual assault has taken place, as the example of Bosnian survivors' associations shows. In such circumstances, the much-needed reflection on how to set up care policies that would take stock of recent research on wartime vulnerabilities, not to mention long-term prevention policies—addressing wartime sexual violence against both men and women—looks like a very remote prospect.

The analysis framework of care outlined by Vaittinen (2015, 111) proves very useful for understanding where we currently stand with regards to support for male survivors of wartime sexual violence. According to Vaittinen, the process of care can be subdivided in four separate and interconnected phases: "The first, caring about, refers to the processes where a need of care is recognized, whereas the second phase, taking care of, refers to assuming responsibility for the other's needs. The concrete bodywork of care is then the third phase, labeled as care-giving, and the fourth and final phase is about care-receiving, which 'recognizes that the object of care will respond to the care it receives'". If we apply this framework to male survivors of conflict-related sexual violence, we see that if the need of care is increasingly recognized by major international and local actors, responsibility for providing that care is not yet entirely clear, especially as far as national institutions are concerned. As a consequence, "care-giving" is only partially implemented, and "care-receiving" is considerably impeded by the stigma and isolation still faced by male survivors. This chapter proposes to explore these multiple and overlapping discrepancies.

6.1. INTERNATIONAL SUPPORT INITIATIVES AND PROGRAMS

Over the past few years, the international community's awareness of the existence, and extent, of conflict-related sexual violence against men has been steadily growing. This evolution has been particularly noticeable within the UN, where the topic is now being taken up by various agencies, including at the highest level (Sivakumaran 2010, 262). This increased awareness has translated into a series of policy papers, such as the guidelines issued by the

UNHCR in 2012 on how to identify and support male victims of rape and other forms of sexual violence in conflict settings and displacement situations (UNHCR 2012). This publication had been preceded by other groundbreaking international reports that have been written in the wake of major wars or genocides, such as the Final Report of the UN Commission of Experts on the war in former Yugoslavia (UN 1994), which recognized the existence and extent of sexual violence and torture against men. These reports have significantly improved and enlarged UN agencies' understanding of wartime sexual violence, to the point that over the past few years the UN has spearheaded several initiatives focusing on wartime sexual violence against men, such as a specific workshop held in New York in July 2013. More recently, a UN Security Council Report published on "conflict-related sexual violence" (UN 2016) explicitly recognizes the existence of sexual and gender-based violence against men and boys, especially in detention settings (§2, p.3). Like previous UN yearly reports on conflict-related sexual violence, this document details cases of sexual violence against both men and women that occurred during the preceding year. In 2016 alone, cases of wartime sexual violence against men and boys were officially documented in Afghanistan, the Central African Republic, the Democratic Republic of the Congo, Myanmar, Sudan and Syria, among other examples.

But even at the UN level, considerable progress is still needed, especially when it comes to translating these texts into concrete plans for action. The report on the above-mentioned workshop on wartime sexual violence against men, organized by the UN in 2013, recognizes, for instance: "While the working tools of the GBV Information Management System of the UN are gender neutral, the materials provided by the UN's own Global Protection Cluster under the heading Gender Based Violence reflect a gender-exclusive approach to Sexual and Gender Based Violence" (UN 2013, 15). Most of the guidelines and concrete tools used by UN agencies for training on conflict-related sexual and gender-based violence, including reference manuals or indicators, still draw on exclusively female case studies and totally ignore the existence of male survivors.

Another major limit of changes witnessed at the UN level is that so far most of the proposed measures seem more targeted towards the prosecution of acts of sexual violence, rather than towards the provision of support to survivors, not to mention prevention measures. In the UN yearly reports on conflict-related sexual violence, for instance, measures envisaged range from training for UN peacekeepers, to the deployment of Women's Protection Advisers in Democratic Republic of the Congo and Côte d'Ivoire, and to the setting up of early warning indicators of conflict-related sexual violence to be used by UN forces in countries like South Sudan. The UN has also been providing technical support to relevant countries, through the training of envoys, mediators and mediation experts whose main task is to ensure that provisions on sexual violence are included in peace and ceasefire agreements (UN 2015, §89, p.26). The SG Report includes only one paragraph addressing the issue of support to survivors, stating the importance of ensuring "differentiated and appropriate services" for male survivors, but it remains very vague, stating responsibilities without guidelines for practical implementation (UN 2015, §100, p. 29). In the same vein, the "Guidelines for Investigating Conflict-Related Sexual and Gender-Based Violence Against Men and Boys", compiled by the Institute for International Criminal Investigations (2016), aim at helping criminal justice and human rights investigators to monitor, document and investigate wartime sexual and gender-based violence against men and boys, but do not discuss support or prevention options. A very similar initiative has been the publication in 2017 of the second edition of the "International Protocol on the Documentation and Investigation of Sexual Violence in Conflict", which now includes a full and detailed chapter on male victims (UK Foreign & Commonwealth Office 2017). The Geneva Centre for the Democratic Control of Armed Forces (DCAF) has also published a guidance note for security institutions on sexual violence against men, which adopts a broader perspective by focusing on both conflict and non-conflict settings, and by including the issue of domestic violence against men (Watson 2014).

Among all these texts mostly dedicated to prosecution measures, one document stands out, the previously mentioned UNHCR report (UNHCR 2012), which directly focuses on the provision of support to male survivors of conflict-related sexual violence. It offers guidelines for staff and other aid workers on how to identify and support male victims of rape and of other types of sexual violence in conflict and displacement situations. The report underscores the reasons for the vulnerability of refugee men and boys, and "provides guidance on how to access survivors, facilitate reporting, provide protection and deliver essential medical, legal and social services" (p. 2). It also advocates for the setting up of inclusive programs for both male and female survivors of sexual violence (p. 8), and for the creation of peer support groups (p. 13) which, as we will see, have so far constituted one of the most effective, though scattered, source of support for survivors. While this report undoubtedly signals a change in attitudes at the international level, it stops short of developing proactive strategies to prevent sexual violence against men from occurring. This is representative of the generally reactive rather than proactive attitude of the international community on conflict-related sexual violence against both women and men. What is more, it is quite complicated to assess the real impact that this report has on practices, especially since it doesn't seem to have circulated widely outside of UN agencies[1]. Most health-care professionals who are aware of the existence of the UNHCR Guidelines find them too vague to really help. Most other available guidelines or toolkits for providing medical, mental health and psychosocial support to survivors of wartime sexual violence, like those published by the World Health Organization in 2012, or by the Australian Civil-Military Centre in 2014, only mention male victims of sexual violence in passing. Similarly, the UN-led campaign "Stop Rape Now" (UN action against sexual violence in conflict) does not seem to be interested in male survivors, and is rather structured as a campaign against conflict-related sexual violence against women (Grey and Shepherd 2012). Admittedly, the UN has launched several initiatives to tackle the legacy of conflict-related sexual violence, for instance, in 2015 in Bosnia-Herzegovina, where its objectives are not just to provide access to justice and reparations, but also to improve the situation of survivors of wartime sexual violence by mapping their needs and capacities, and by trying to reduce the stigma still attached to them. However, none of these programs specifically mentions or targets male survivors, and one can also question the efficiency of such programs when they are put in place, as in the case of Bosnia-Herzegovina, more than two decades after the end of the conflict.

In the humanitarian field, several major organizations such as Physicians for Human Rights or Médecins Sans Frontières (MSF) have started to open up their programs and awareness campaigns to the plight of male survivors. For instance, in 2015 MSF launched its first comprehensive program dedicated to survivors of sexual violence in Port Harcourt in Nigeria, which includes among other initiatives an awareness campaign targeting different facilities like universities, schools and health clinics, and which organizes discussions around male sexual abuse. In July 2014 MSF also opened in Bangui (Central African Republic) a medical and psychological care service for victims of sexual violence, where male survivors are also taken care of. Similar initiatives have been implemented by the International Rescue Committee and other international NGOs like Care, which has developed in 2015 a Training Manual on "Gender Peace and Conflict" acknowledging male victimhood in situations of conflict-related gender-based violence. Resistance to this inclusion is, however, still strong among regional organizations, where men are still mostly referred to as either indirect victims (for instance, men witnessing female relatives being sexually abused) or perpetrators of sexual violence. Even though NGO staff is increasingly aware of the need to broaden their perspective and programs, the equation between women as victims, and men as perpetrators, still frames humanitarian discourses and actions:

> We know that there are men among victims too. But we work under a series of constraints, like the lack of staff training, or the fact that not all of our intervention and support procedures have been updated to mainstream male survivors'

needs, and so on. And let's be honest, I am not sure we would have the financial means to provide adequate support to male survivors, like separate facilities, for instance. (International Rescue Committee 2014, interview)

The provision of support to male survivors of wartime sexual violence is an increasingly important issue for humanitarian organizations located outside of conflict zones too, in particular for organizations supporting refugees who have been victims of sexual torture. In Lebanon, for instance, organizations like the Danish Refugee Council, International Medical Corps (IMC), UNHCR and UNRWA have established male-focused centers (UNHCR 2017a, 43). In Western countries, however, where the arrival of refugees fleeing war in the Middle East and in Afghanistan has recently attracted a lot of media attention, the general level of awareness of the occurrence and prevalence of sexual torture is still very low. There are some specialized institutions that help survivors dealing with the consequences of torture, mostly at the psychological level, like, for instance, Freedom from Torture, based in the United Kingdom, or the Centre for Torture Survivors in Finland. None of them is specifically targeting survivors of sexual torture, but this is certainly an issue they are familiar with, including when it has been perpetrated on men (Halla 2016, interview). Other major institutions such as the International Rehabilitation Council for Torture Victims, located in Denmark, have developed training programs such as the project PROTECT-ABLE[2], which aims at improving the access to psychological and medical care for asylum seekers and refugees who have been victims of torture. But stereotypes attached to who can, or cannot, be a victim of sexual violence linger on, especially with regards to asylum applications. This is particularly worrying since it has been estimated that in New York, for instance, male survivors of sexual assault make up at least 10% of asylum applications[3]. In a study conducted in 2002, Del Zotto and Jones (2002) examined thirty-six US asylum cases of women versus forty-four cases of men, and found that all but two women were asked whether or not they would face sexual danger in their country of origin, whereas none of the men were asked equivalent questions. Unfortunately, more than fifteen years afterwards, these trends seem to have remained unchanged (Halla 2016, interview).

6.2. SURVIVORS' ORGANIZATIONS AND LOCAL INITIATIVES

Progress is even slower at the level of local clinics and NGOs, which remain almost entirely focused on female survivors. Very few local organizations have included male survivors among their potential recipients, and even fewer have developed specific programs or premises dedicated to the support of male survivors. According to the study conducted by Del Zotto and Jones, at the beginning of the 2000 decade, out of more than four thousand non-governmental groups tackling conflict-related sexual violence, "only 3% mention the experiences of males at all in their programs and informational literature. About one quarter of the groups explicitly deny that male-on-male violence is a serious problem" (Del Zotto and Jones 2002). If changes in discourses have been visible over the past ten years or so, as explained by Lwambo (2013), they have so far failed to translate at the practical level. Programs addressing wartime sexual violence have sometimes been re-packaged as "gender-sensitive" as opposed to targeting women only, but they in fact still pursue a women-centered approach, whereby men (understood here as primarily military and local decision-makers) are only marginally included under the term "sensitization". As a consequence they fail to properly address men's needs, when they are not entirely ignoring them. In Burundi, for instance, where numerous cases of sexual torture against men have been documented over the past decades (see, for instance, Amnesty International 2015), organizations like Nturengaho still focus exclusively and explicitly on girls and women (Nturengaho 2012, interview). Sometimes this reluctance to offer support to male survivors can be explained by the agenda of donors who usually prioritize support to women, or by the religious background of these organizations. And, just like for international humanitarian organizations, funding is often lacking: "Many working on Gender-Based Violence against women and girls believe that funding for their work is inadequate to the need, and that extending work to include men and boys will further dilute these already inadequate resources" (UN 2013, 15).

In such a context, the emergence over the past five to ten years of structured groups of male survivors seeking to organize themselves and to provide support to other survivors constitutes a major development and a source of hope (Edström et al. 2016). These groups are rarely active in conflict areas themselves, but can be found in refugee camps located in neighboring countries, like in Uganda where, as we will see, a lot of Congolese men and women have taken refuge. These groups of survivors are also more likely to be set up in the post-conflict period, as in the case of Bosnia-Herzegovina. In many ways, male survivors' organizations are well ahead of any public initiative or program in this field, in terms of both the quality and the innovative nature of the support they provide. However, their impact is limited geographically, and their initiatives face numerous practical, legal and financial constraints. Many of these groups are located in sub-Saharan Africa, and especially in Uganda. The Makerere University–based Refugee Law Project supports several of these survivors groups, like Men of Hope and Men of Courage, both funded in 2011, and Men of Peace, funded in 2013. Their membership varies from a few dozen to more than a hundred, almost all recruited in the refugee camps scattered throughout Uganda. These survivors-led organizations share similar goals, like raising awareness of wartime sexual violence against men and its consequences, protecting male survivors, advocating for them and providing medical and psychosocial support. In addition, most of them have set up educational programs for male survivors, in order to help them become more autonomous and self-confident. These organizations liaise with donors, and some also support projects for survivors with disabilities, like, for instance, building houses. In contrast to international initiatives, they are not mainly focused on initiating the prosecution of cases of sexual violence, or on obtaining reparations for survivors, which would in any case prove particularly complicated since many African countries do not recognize sexual violence against men as an offense. In countries like Uganda, where an Anti-Homosexuality Bill was passed by Parliament in December 2013, and where some judges refuse to distinguish between consensual and nonconsensual same-sex relationships, male survivors are often assumed to be homosexual, which threatens their security. Organizing collectively can help improve survivors' psychological and material security, even though heightened security threats have sometimes been reported (see, for instance, Men of Peace Association 2014).

Some male survivors' organizations are also active in post-conflict settings, for instance, in Cambodia with the organization First Step Cambodia. There are also a lot of survivors' organizations in Bosnia-Herzegovina and in other ex-Yugoslav countries, but most of them focus primarily on female survivors. In Bosnia-Herzegovina, for example, many of these organizations are gathered under an umbrella organization called the Association of Concentration Camp Torture Survivors (ACCTS), which was established in 1997. As in many other conflict and post-conflict countries though, there is no independent structure specifically providing support for male survivors of wartime sexual violence: structures are either dedicated to former detainees, and, therefore, focus on the experience of detention in general, and not specifically on sexual violence (though some of them have specific wings for former female detainees which primarily address the consequences of sexual torture), or to female survivors of sexual violence. The latter sometimes accept male members too, like, for instance, the Naš Glas association, established in 2012, or the Association of Women-Victims of War, an NGO founded in 2003 and which has accepted male members since 2006. Like their counterparts based in Uganda, these organizations focus on capacity-building activities, and on psychological as well as material support for survivors. However, some of these organizations additionally provide legal support, for instance, by issuing certificates attesting to the situation of victims of sexual violence, which survivors need in order to apply for the status as civilian victim of war in Bosnia-Herzegovina.

Whether located in refugee camps or in post-conflict settings, the impact of the work undertaken by these survivors-led organizations is, however, severely limited, mostly for financial reasons. The general lack of public awareness on wartime sexual violence against men impedes fund-raising, and the low socioeconomic status of their members prevents them from relying on members' financial contributions. Their capacity for reaching out to other male survivors is also often very limited geographically, as many operate only within the limits of a single refugee camp, or of a municipality or region. This is particularly problematic since, as we have seen, in Africa in particular wartime sexual violence often occurs among rural and relatively isolated communities, which, therefore, have little chance to be offered any type of support. It is not uncommon to hear about (male and female) survivors of sexual violence who have died while they were being transported to the clinic or the hospital, because of geographical distance, or because of deteriorated roads (Panzi Hospital 2012, interview), not to mention those who, in the absence of any medical or psychological support, commit suicide.

In spite of these geographical limitations, the support offered to survivors-led groups by larger organizations like the Refugee Law Project or the African Centre for the Treatment and Rehabilitation of Torture Victims, also located in Uganda, is paramount. In addition to providing direct support to male survivors, these organizations cover the expenses related to many reconstructive surgery operations, and to related medical treatments, which survivor groups cannot afford. They also contribute to raising awareness on conflict-related sexual violence against men by organizing training programs targeting health services or policy makers, and they have participated in the launch of several research initiatives, such as the "South-South Institute on Sexual Violence against Men and Boys in Conflict and Displacement," whose kick-off event was organized in April 2013 in Kampala. Of course they also have their own financial constraints, and neither of these organizations can afford to cover the other related costs for male survivors, like the compensation for job loss, provision of food or housing costs, which, therefore, constitute areas where major progress is needed. However, such support is unlikely to be offered until major international humanitarian organizations active in conflict areas implement comprehensive programs specifically addressing the needs of male survivors of sexual violence.

6.3. LINGERING CHALLENGES AND OBSTACLES TO THE PROVISION OF SUPPORT

The challenges in offering support to male survivors are significant and varied, and pertain mostly to the medical, psychosocial, legal and social consequences that the experience of sexual violence entails for survivors. But since this is an issue that had until recently been almost totally ignored and silenced at the international and national levels, humanitarian organizations as well as national health-care service providers still lack insight and information on what works best (Chynoweth, Freccero and Touquet 2017). Of course the work of organizations offering support to male survivors of sexual violence does not entirely differ from what they propose to female survivors, and some inspiration can also be found in the support offered to male victims of rape in peaceful countries. However, working with male survivors of conflict-related sexual violence entails taking into account not only the context of war, but also the specific psychological and cultural situation of male survivors, which means that they will be highly unlikely to seek assistance unless they really have no other choice. In order to reach them, support organizations, therefore, don't just need to be prepared to help them, they also have to develop a proactive approach, while paying attention to confidentiality issues. This is a difficult balance to keep, since being proactive entails a danger of disclosing the identity of male survivors in cultural environments where sexual violence against men is often strongly stigmatized. There is thus a high risk of involuntarily worsening the situation of the survivor, as explained by Duroch and Schulte-Hillen: "The difficulty lies in reaching a justifiable balance between the added value medical care can have for the victim, both in the short and long term, and the exposure to the social risk that rape-related stigma involves, including the risk of the victim being ostracized" (2014, 611).

The issue of access to support programs is a complicated one, and does not just pertain to the reluctance of male survivors themselves. A number of organizational practices are hampering their access to support, in particular the fact that most relevant organizations active in conflict areas seem to be targeting female survivors only. Their brochures, leaflets or posters often picture women only, and even their names sometimes include references to women and female issues, which ostracize male survivors. This in turn leads to a lack of data and of information available on prevalence rates, mostly due to underreporting, and feeds the impression that there are very few, if any, male survivors. Such targeted branding reinforces the feelings of shame of male survivors, who thus only come forward when their injuries are life threatening, and sometimes it is too late to save them (International Rescue

Committee 2013, interview). Most other cases seem to be left unreported, and the level of reporting for wartime sexual violence against men is generally thought to be significantly lower than for women and girls (Sivakumaran 2007). This reluctance to speak about what happened is not only maintaining the level of reporting, and, therefore, of awareness, at very low levels, but it is also impeding the provision of proper support and care: "Some male survivors do not want the person they have confided in to share the information further, making referrals for additional service provisions problematic" (Refugee Law Project 2013b, 26). No wonder then that female survivors are always presented as making up the "vast majority" of victims (a highly credible assumption, but based on reported cases, and not on "actual" figures which are in any case almost impossible to gather), thus de facto dismissing the importance of the existence of male survivors. This dismissal in turn hampers the setting up of dedicated prevention and support programs: "The absent presence of masculinity and the silencing effects of the logic of 'the vast majority' in scholarly literature on war-time rape denies the materiality of the violated male body. For us, this is problematic, as without envisioning the violated male body we can neither hope to prevent its violation nor seek redress for violence committed against it" (Grey and Shepherd 2012, 122). This is what a UN report has described as a "chicken and egg situation" (UN 2013, 16), since programming is indeed often based on statistical reports.

Interestingly, the number of male victims who are reporting sexual assault seems to depend a lot on whether the clinic or hospital has the reputation to treat those issues, which also feeds a kind of vicious circle—male victims being more likely to avoid places that have a reputation of treating women only, thus reinforcing existing patterns. Conversely, when men are encouraged to seek help, for instance, through the publication of brochures mentioning the phenomenon of sexual violence against men, or quoting testimonies from men who have been victimized and who have received support, the level of reporting significantly increases, as explained by Rumbold in the case of one Kenyan hospital:

> The Gender Violence Recovery Centre in Nairobi Women's Hospital treats sexual abuse survivors of all ages and genders. The presentation of male survivors (albeit 85% 15 and under) has increased steadily over the last four years, which is attributed to increased awareness among the population (personal communication, 2006 with GVRC counsellor). The hospital conducts awareness campaigns, during which they advertise the availability of services to male survivors. Services, both medical and psychological, are broadly the same as those offered to women, with the exception of pregnancy prevention. (2008, 15)

In the same perspective, a UN report on conflict-related sexual violence against men proposes to generalize screening in order to improve the level of reporting and, therefore, raise the awareness of service providers: "Normalising the screening for everybody can prompt a change in patterns of reporting. The resultant increase in numbers requiring services will help create the pressure required for service providers to seek new resources for this area of work, and for donors to allocate new resources to it" (2013, 16). In the absence of such proactive strategies, the access of male survivors to adequate care is likely to remain very low, and restricted to the most tragic cases.

One of the most immediate consequences of the low level of reporting and general lack of awareness about conflict-related sexual violence against men is an un-preparedness of medical facilities and staff for dealing with such cases. Medical staff and health care professionals lack training with regards to detecting, identifying and tackling the injuries related to this type of violence, and many doctors in conflict areas even seem to ignore that such cases exist (Féron 2015, 37). Because most of the time services for survivors of sexual and gender-based violence are located in gynecology departments, many male survivors are referred to them, but medical staff in these departments are not trained and prepared to take care of the psychological and physical suffering induced by sexual violence on males. The amount of knowledge and training about how to deal with survivors of violence and torture is very low, and often limited to extremely general guidelines like the 2004 Istanbul Protocol (UNHCR 2004). Even in services where male survivors are treated, the medical staff frequently works under the assumption that their needs (apart from fistulas and unwanted pregnancies following rape) are entirely similar to those of female survivors, which is untrue. For instance, they display different kinds of physical injuries, have different psychological needs and do not necessarily relate to what happened to them in exactly the same way—for example, in terms of questioning their gender identity. A UN report highlights these shortcomings:

> In most contexts, medical, social and humanitarian workers have no training in working with male survivors, and are thus ill-equipped to identify or respond to the specificities of such cases. Clinics, particularly within emergency settings, have neither the protocols, medication, supplies, nor the trained staff needed for adequate clinical management (…). The spaces within which they work are often not safe or conducive for male survivors; in some situations male survivors are referred to gynecological units, to their own discomfort and that of the women for whom these units are intended. Information, Education and Communication (IEC) materials such as posters and pamphlets giving information to male survivors are almost non-existent. (UN 2013, 15)

Some male survivors also find it difficult to speak to female service providers (UNHCR 2017a, 43), who often are in majority in departments offering support to sexual violence survivors, which is sometimes interpreted as an indication of the need to set up separate units to accommodate them. However, as explained by Le Pape (2012, 4), there is no agreement among health-care professionals about whether separate support units for male survivors are a good option or not. Some argue that separate units for male and for female victims are indispensable for avoiding re-traumatizing female survivors, and for creating "safe spaces" for them; from the perspective of male survivors, having separate services is less likely to reinforce the confusion they frequently feel about their gender identity. It also helps to avoid "feminizing" them a second time—by treating them in units that are mostly treating women, after the feminizing nature of sexual violence itself. On the other hand, others argue that offering joint services would effectively fight stereotypes associated with sexual violence, for instance, by demonstrating that vulnerability is not a quality attached to the female body, and also by countering the idea that all men are violent and aggressive. For the time being, the solution that is most frequently adopted by hospitals and clinics operating in conflict zones is that of joint services, but more because of a lack of resources than because of a deliberate choice:

> We try to do as much as we can with what we have, and we don't have much. (Panzi Hospital 2012, interview)

In any case, it looks indispensable to develop ways to provide support to male survivors without further damaging their self-image and further "feminizing" them—just as it is crucial to unpack the link that is constantly made, consciously as well as unconsciously, between female bodies, femininity, victimhood and vulnerability. This link is detrimental to both male and female survivors, as it traps them, and the staff supporting them, in pre-determined roles that also assign to them a specific social positioning. This conceptual nexus might be quite complicated to entangle, though. This is what Vaittinen explains:

> To write about the vulnerable body is to write about a deeply feminized field of discourse where two effeminate realms of life come together: the body and vulnerability. In the Cartesian mind/body dualism(s) that dominates modern political thinking, the mind tends to be associated with masculine forms of autonomous, rational and public (political) life; whereas the body is linked with femininity, irrationality and the private (apolitical) life (…). This means that when a person—regardless of sex—is perceived as vulnerable, s/he is simultaneously coded as effeminate. (2015, 103)

Such representations dominate most humanitarian narratives and interventions, and also underpin practices of care well beyond the specialized field of support to survivors of sexual violence. However, in this case in particular, it seems particularly important to carefully review and adapt discourses, facilities and protocols to the specific needs of male survivors, in order to avoid deepening, instead of mending, the psychological scars left by sexual violence.

This requires, among other imperatives, taking stock of the knowledge accumulated on masculinities, and mainstreaming it in support programs. Helping male survivors cannot be efficiently done without acknowledging the specific challenges that this type of violence entails in contexts where conceptions of masculinity render the sexual brutalization of men unthinkable. In a very interesting paper adopting precisely that perspective, Russell et al. (2011, 5) list a series of messages that public information campaigns on conflict-related sexual violence against men should focus on, such as "You are not alone", "It was not your fault" or "Men who have experienced sexual violence need the support of their families and communities", which could admittedly be applied to female survivors too. However, they also add a series of messages that specifically address masculinity models and try to dissociate masculinity from concepts such as violence or invulnerability. The objective is to help male survivors cope with what happened to them, and to help them make sense of their experience, such as: "You do not need to question your sexuality", especially for dismissing the confusion that survivors feel at having been involuntarily aroused during an assault; or, crucially, "The experience of sexual violence does not make you 'less of a man'", which underscores the fact that a man can be vulnerable, and that not all masculinity models are linked to aggression and violence.

One of the other main difficulties with the provision of adequate care lies in the need to offer holistic support not just targeting male survivors' physical pain, but also providing often much-needed psychological support, as well as proposing community-based options for promoting reintegration and for fighting stigma and segregation. Supporting survivors' families might also be needed, especially in order to compensate for the survivors' loss of financial resources, and to help them deal with potential tensions within the family itself. In some cases, involving community leaders, and raising awareness at the local level on cases of sexual violence against men, in order especially to dissociate them from homosexuality, might also be necessary, though, as noted above, public disclosure of acts of sexual violence entails a risk of further discrimination against survivors. Support has, in other words, to be multifaceted and multilevel. The UNHCR Guidelines on "Working with men and boys survivors of sexual and gender-based violence in forced displacement" (2012, 10) have adopted such a holistic perspective and list, for instance, beyond medical treatment, mental and social health issues, livelihood support and legal protection as major survivors' needs. Similarly, Dr. Chris Dolan, the director of the Refugee Law Project that has spearheaded several support initiatives in this field, underscores the importance of a series of key challenges like "medical and psychosocial service provision, legal redress (both immediate, and in terms of transitional justice measures after a conflict is over), survivor organization (particularly to recover lost voice, lost livelihoods and lost respect in their communities), and dealing with community shaming so that the community can once again become a source of support to survivors rather than the driver of stigmatization" (Refugee Law Project 2013b, 10–11).

Addressing these challenges undoubtedly represents a considerable and daunting task, in a context where most health systems in conflict-affected countries are underfunded and understaffed. When they are still operating, hospitals and clinics located in conflict areas struggle to cope with the number of patients, and often prioritize those who present the most serious diseases and injuries, and also those whom they think they can really help. Because of the lack of awareness and training in how to deal with sexual violence against men, and because humanitarian assistance also tends to prioritize female survivors, male survivors are often left in limbo. And even in the few instances when their physical injuries are taken care of, the widespread understanding of health as absence of disease, overlooking the psychosocial aspects of relief, prevents the other dimensions of their suffering from being addressed and alleviated. If, as we have seen, survivors-led organizations existing in some countries like Uganda provide psychological support, the deep social impact that sexual violence can have on male survivors seems much more complicated to handle, especially in terms of lost livelihoods and work incapacity. So far, these difficulties have not been addressed in support programs, even by the largest humanitarian organizations: "Although it is recognized in work with women survivors that livelihoods are an important component of recovery and protection from further violence, livelihood programs for male survivors which recognize that they may have particular physical limitations during their recovery process, have yet to be established" (UN 2013, 16). Alleviating that type of suffering lies well beyond the competences and expertise of medical services, but it does not seem to be tackled by any other public or private institution or initiative either. The great majority of male survivors of wartime sexual violence have thus access to scattered and limited support, if at all, notably because many of them live far away from urban centers where medical, psychological and social help is more readily available.

Last but certainly not least, the development and setting up of adequate support programs for male survivors of wartime sexual violence will not be fully achieved if they are still viewed as competing with existing services for female survivors. For numerous humanitarian actors, speaking about the need to support male survivors of sexual violence amounts to somehow undermining policies and programs designed to fight rape and other types of sexual and gender-based violence against women during wartime, by demonstrating that women are not the only victims—and might even also be perpetrators—of sexual violence. For instance, a UNHCR worker interviewed by Charli Carpenter argued: "I recognize our discourse is a bit outdated. But it's very difficult because as soon as you stop talking about women, women are forgotten. Men want to see what they will gain out of this gender business, so you have to be strategic" (Carpenter 2006, 99). It is true that the recognition of the scope and severity of sexual violence against women during conflict times is relatively recent, and arguably still fragile, but such discourses feed competition between categories of victims, which is useless, not to mention indecent, even in a context where funds are limited. These discourses also overlook the deep and complex connections that exist between patterns of sexual violence against men and against women, and they have tragic consequences on practices (Oosterhoff et al. 2004, 68).

The clear dichotomy that is established between male perpetrators and female victims lies at the very core of many humanitarian narratives, which feeds on gendered representations to garner support, and funding. Because there is an expectation that women will be victimized and in need of support, it is much easier to undertake fund-raising activities for helping them than supporting male survivors, who fall outside of normal interpretative schemes (Solangon and Patel 2012, 424). In a context where funding is scarce and difficult to come by, the weight of these representations has to be reckoned with. Many funding agencies demand that their contributions are used for helping women and girls, and them only, as recognized during a workshop organized by the UN: "Donors create funds to address sexual and gender-based violence, but specify that the intervention must work with women and girls, or, at best, women and children" (UN 2013, 9). The trend towards a "commercialization of rape" of women (Eriksson Baaz and Stern 2013, 96–106) in DRC and in other conflict areas, whereby rape has become a lucrative issue for various local, national and international actors, also explains the reluctance to acknowledge the existence of other types of victims.

6.4. CONTEXTUALIZING AND PREVENTING WARTIME SEXUAL VIOLENCE AGAINST MEN

At a more general level, what seems to limit the efficiency of the approaches that are currently developed in order to address wartime sexual violence against men is the fact that they fail to acknowledge and factor in the context in which this type of violence is perpetrated. As has been amply documented, during conflicts both men and women are victimized in multiple, gendered ways that are also often interrelated. Organizations that focus exclusively on sexual violence and hence neglect other types of violence that are perpetrated during conflict times, and to which sexual violence is tightly connected, run the real risk of coming up with unsuitable answers. As we have explored in chapter 2, conflict-related sexual violence does not happen in a vacuum, and has to be put in the context of the other experiences of war that the person has had and that are paramount for making sense of sexual violence itself. If support programs for male victims centralize the experience of sexual violence and thus signal it as the worst that can ever happen to any man, they run the risk of replicating the flaws of support programs for female victims. The idea that some male survivors might not think that this is the worst that happened to them, and that they might actually draw agency from their victimization, should not be overlooked.

Taking the broader context of conflict and violence into account is also essential for helping survivors overcome their trauma. As with every person who has been victim of any form of torture or violence (McClure 2015), male survivors of wartime sexual violence strive to understand why this has happened to them. Of course, they are often aware of the specific conditions as well as of the more general factors (such as belonging to a certain ethnic group, supporting an opposition movement, and so on) that increase their vulnerability. But whether sexual violence is seemingly committed in a "random" fashion, or can be explained by the specific religious, political or ethnic belonging of the victim, it ultimately only makes sense in the broader context of the war situation and of the spread of uncontrolled violence. Wartime sexual and gender-based violence is tightly connected to other forms of violence, and is a highly multicausal phenomenon linked, among other factors, to specific gender roles and images in the relevant society, but also to impunity, poverty and so on. What is more, the other experiences of violence that survivors have faced often make it more difficult for them to recover from the physical and psychological trauma entailed by sexual violence. Having been forced to leave their country or region of origin, having lost several or all members of their family, having witnessed atrocities, for instance, all dramatically hamper their capacity to deal with, and recover from, the suffering induced by sexual violence:

> It would not be that bad if I still had my family. But I have lost everything, I have lost everyone. It is very difficult to be in pain, on the top of everything else. (Didace 2014, interview)

What complicates the contextualization of sexual violence is the fact that it has, especially when it is committed against women, become a stand-alone category, as if it was all that mattered about what happened to women during war, to the point that, as we have seen in the previous chapter, sexual violence has come to epitomize women's experience of war. In many ways, most male survivors of conflict-related violence are in the exact opposite situation: up to now, everything *but* their sexual victimization matters in their experience of war. As a consequence, neither male nor female survivors can own their experience of sexual violence, men because it is unspeakable, or because it is "anecdotalized", and women because it becomes larger than them, it is categorized, standardized and "relocated to a place (the imaginary body of a colossus) where it is no longer recognizable or interpretable", as Scarry (1985, 71) aptly describes. For female survivors, this standardization impedes the narration of individual stories or experiences that would not fit the pre-established model. For male survivors, this pre-established model disregards, minimizes or even negates the possibility of the occurrence of sexual violence, when it does not try to requalify it in order to fit traditional conflict narratives. In both cases, contextualization becomes impossible.

What current support programs at local, national and international levels also lack is an emphasis on longer-term prevention. Admittedly, programs addressing conflict-related sexual violence against women have just started developing prevention strategies, focusing on education, awareness-raising activities and on associating men "as central agents of change"[4]. It is, therefore, no surprise that support programs for male survivors, which are still in their infancy, have not yet worked much on the issue of prevention. But since wartime sexual violence against women and against men are both tightly related to how masculinities are built in times of war, and in particular to models of militarized and dominant masculinities, it would be worth considering the implementation of prevention programs addressing all types of wartime sexual violence in a holistic way. This would necessitate acknowledging and better understanding the core relationship between conceptions of masculinity and the conduct of war, while taking into account the fact that male and female survivors have specific needs in terms of protection.

In other words, the study of relevant conflict factors and features, and of masculinity models, is a key aspect that has to be mainstreamed in responses and support offered to male and female survivors, as well as in prevention policies. Masculinity models are important not only because they largely explicate why wartime sexual violence against both men and women occurs, but also because they determine how male survivors react to their victimization: for instance, whether they will question their gender identity, how much they will put the blame on themselves rather than on perpetrators, whether they will feel guilty when they seek help, or whether they think that they should be able to cope with the suffering and the trauma on their own. Similarly, masculinity models help to understand specific patterns of sexual violence against men, for instance, against new recruits in military groups, against political opponents in detention, against some specific ethnic or religious groups and so on. They also suggest that some individuals are more likely than others to become perpetrators. In that sense it seems impossible to design, and much less implement, prevention policies until we factor in these contextual variables—conflict features and masculinity models, among others—which will help us gain a better understanding, for each conflict situation, of why men are targeted by sexual violence, and which categories of men are more vulnerable.

This also entails thinking about the way gender intersects with other variables to produce specific vulnerabilities—for instance, how men and women belonging to a specific ethnic or religious group are more likely to be targeted, or how geographic location, poverty, age, displacement and sexual orientation can heighten the vulnerability of men and women in different ways. Without this systematic screening and analysis, sexual violence against men will continue to look like a random (and, therefore, inexplicable) phenomenon, and prevention will remain wishful thinking. Similarly, responses to sexual violence against women will stay trapped in the "rape as a weapon of war" paradigm, which does not provide much detailed analytical tools, and which overlooks the relations between patterns of sexual violence and the wider structures of power in society, between but also within groups (Kirby 2012). As Dolan explains, such intersectional analysis cannot be conducted without institutionalizing data collection and processing:

> Alongside a default assumption that anyone could be a victim until proven otherwise, therefore, there must be a consistent concern with establishing relevant data that allows context-specific and evidence-based interventions. (…) Documentation is not a matter of stand-alone research projects, as these are neither desirable nor particularly feasible in many crisis situations. What is required instead is to ensure that in the routine collection of data (registration data, food distribution lists, clinic attendance, health screening, etc.), the right questions are asked and the resultant data are subjected to a gender analysis. (2014b, 498)

Several obstacles stand in the way of such an approach, though. There are, of course, funding issues, as setting up comprehensive prevention programs would require significant financial resources, and the building and strengthening of an expertise that is still largely nascent, even when it comes to sexual violence against women. What is more, as we have seen, programming in the field of sexual violence is still too often done in terms of either/or, as if including male survivors in the overall picture would somehow undermine the hard-won advances in the fight against sexual and gender-based violence against women. This is particularly true of prevention activities, as explained by Sivakumaran (2010, 268): "When it is at the level of heightening awareness and responsiveness, the language is inclusive—all civilians, including women and children. However, as the provision goes on, and when the matter shifts to the more onerous prevention of sexual violence, the objects of protection are exclusively women and girls". More generally, preventive policies are notoriously difficult to implement in conflict settings, where they are seen as too complicated to design and set up, expensive, and where their efficiency is difficult to demonstrate (Ackermann 2003). Harnessing support for prevention on the part of the policy-making community, but also of donors, is, however, imperative if we want to significantly reduce the suffering induced by wartime sexual violence against both men and women.

Several researchers have explored avenues for preventing wartime sexual violence, like, for instance, the PRIO report compiled by Nordås (2013). Drawing on cases of conflict where wartime sexual violence is absent or has decreased, Nordås outlines several avenues for prevention, like "changing norms—including changing how survivors are perceived and treated in their communities", "creating safer spaces—including improving infrastructure and reporting practices", "improving reporting—including protection of witnesses", "ending impunity" and "assuring accountability". One of the limits of these proposals is that they do not really address the root causes of sexual violence against both men and women, in particular masculinity models, as well as the enabling role played by the conflict context—often entailing, among other things, a breakdown of law and order. These proposals also fail to take into account the fact that a significant proportion of acts of sexual violence are perpetrated by non-State actors whose accountability is almost impossible to ensure. By focusing mostly on how survivors and perpetrators are treated after the fact, the hope that lies at the core of these proposals is that these norms and knowledge will gradually have an impact on practices. Like many other reports written on the issue, which seem more interested in punitive options than in genuine prevention, this PRIO report assumes that by changing the way survivors are treated, by trying to end impunity and by ensuring accountability through the strengthening of commanders' responsibility for acts committed by their troops, the reasons that push perpetrators to commit sexual violence will disappear. Undoubtedly, as we will explore in the next chapter, impunity is a crucial factor, and military leadership certainly has a role to play too. As Wood (2009) has shown in the case of the Liberation Tigers of Tamil Eelam (LTTE) in Sri Lanka, the enforcement of strict rules and discipline by the military hierarchy, even in a non-State military group, can play a role in the absence, or decreasing occurrence, of wartime sexual violence. But as Kirby (2011, 813–14) has pointed at, all depends on whether you think that the occurrence of wartime sexual violence results from a military strategic choice, or from a lack of discipline within military ranks: "In the latter example, efforts to strengthen and train militaries in conflict zones will decrease rape. In the former, such efforts will only increase the effectiveness of the masculinized war machine".

In another PRIO policy brief on "Preventing Perpetrators" dealing with sexual violence against both women and men, Skjelsbæk (2013) adopts a different approach, taking stock of the role played by cultural factors and by militarized masculinities in the perpetration of wartime sexual violence. She argues for a three-tier approach: encouraging research on perpetrators (individual focus), holding military leaders responsible (group focus) and fostering military cultures in which perpetrators of sexual violence are exposed and condemned (cultural focus). Even if these proposals again largely ignore perpetrators who do not belong to the military, the recognition that sexual violence can be triggered by individual, group-level and cultural factors, separately or jointly, sounds very promising.

Chapter 7

Prosecuting Wartime Sexual Violence Against Men

Up to a recent period, wartime sexual violence against women or men was very rarely prosecuted, and many observers used to consider it as a harrowing, but inevitable, corollary of war. For instance, only a handful of the numerous and well documented episodes of sexual violence against women that occurred during World War II were prosecuted during the Nuremberg and the Tokyo trials, or during any other major trial that followed. And when they were condemned, these acts were charged as "ill treatment", "persecution" or "other inhumane acts", thus overlooking the sexual nature of the offenses. Over the past few years, however, more and more cases of conflict-related sexual violence against women have been taken up and charged as such by both international and national courts. Yet, when it comes to sexual violence against men, progress is much less obvious. As Manivannan (2014, 646) notes, with regard to the prosecution of wartime sexual violence "many of the problems faced by male victims can be considered particularly egregious manifestations of the issues involved in addressing sexual violence against women".

The International Criminal Tribunal for the former Yugoslavia (ICTY) established in 1993 was the first international tribunal to prosecute cases of wartime sexual violence against both men and women. The International Criminal Tribunal for Rwanda (ICTR) established a year later in 1994 has been prosecuting cases of conflict-related sexual violence too, but to date has not charged anyone with committing rape or sexual assault against men, despite its well documented occurrence during the genocide. In parallel, several national and ad hoc tribunals, courts and commissions have been set up in various post-conflict countries like Bosnia-Herzegovina, Cambodia and Sierra Leone, and have attempted to tackle the issue, with mixed results. Prosecuting perpetrators and providing justice to survivors is paramount in order to give a sense of justice to survivors, to break the cycle of impunity and also possibly to prevent further cases of sexual violence by acting as a deterrent. Many challenges lie upon the way though, notably related to the existence of a fragmented legal and institutional framework for prosecution, to underreporting by survivors, to the difficulties in apprehending suspects and so on.

7.1. ACCOUNTABILITY AND IMPUNITY ISSUES

The way wartime sexual violence against men is perpetrated dramatically complicates the allocation of responsibility. Many of the cases that have so far been documented are extremely complex, involving, for instance, male prisoners forced to rape others, or to bite off their testicles, as in the Omarska Camp in Bosnia-Herzegovina, for instance, (Bassiouni 1994). The fact that wartime sexual violence against men, especially rape, is often committed collectively, thus diluting responsibility both in terms of initiation and of actual perpetration, also entails accountability issues. In addition, some of my interviews suggest that cases where perpetrators have been victimized in the past, or where victims (are forced to) become perpetrators, are not uncommon. How are we to judge these cases? Should we hold prisoners accountable for what they have done to other prisoners, or should we consider that they had no choice and that the only ones who should be condemned are the ones who ordered them to perform those acts? But then shouldn't we also take into account the peer pressure factor in the perpetration of sexual violence by members of armed groups? New recruits, for instance, are likely to be under specific collective pressure, since the perpetration of sexual violence is often seen as a proof of loyalty and commitment to the group. As Price explains (2001, 224) in the case of sexual violence committed during the break-up of former Yugoslavia, "It is important not to dismiss the very real, immediate physical threat under which some perpetrators felt themselves to be. Surrounded by armed men drunk on alcohol, testosterone, and triumphant nationalism, men who knew that their worst excesses would be ignored (if not condoned) by their political and military masters, it is perhaps understandable that some men raped out of fear for their lives". Conversely and as we have seen in chapter 3, there is ample evidence of cases where members of armed groups and armies, including new recruits, refused to commit those acts, in spite of peer pressure. Most perpetrators—save, perhaps, prisoners whose only alternative is likely to be death—seem to have a choice, even if this is a limited and costly one.

What is more, the fact that most perpetrators seem to be perfectly aware that perpetrating sexual violence against both men and women is forbidden by their hierarchies if not by law, and that many of them judge it morally reprehensible[1], suggests that they should be held fully accountable, even in cases where group pressure is high. Some of the perpetrators I have interviewed perfectly knew that their acts were illegal and could someday be prosecuted:

> It was wrong what I did. It was against the law, and against the laws of God and nature. I will pay for it one day, maybe if they set up this Reconciliation Commission they are talking about. (Joseph 2013, interview)[2]

At the same time, some obviously thought that prosecution was unlikely:

> Of course it was wrong, we knew it was forbidden to do such things [sexual violence against both men and women], our commanders had told us so, many times. But everybody was doing it. So what can they do to us now? Put us all in prison? Execute us all? (Serge 2010, interview)

Some of my research participants even seemed to think that they were somehow above the law, and, therefore, could not be held accountable:

> We have a conflict here. You can't expect us to respect the rules. It is those who are the most powerful who impose their rule. (Richard 2009, interview)

This underscores the lack of signaling effects of previous or current cases of prosecution of wartime sexual violence, because there have so far been too few of them, and because they are more likely to take place in the post-conflict phase, thus after the peak of violence: "In part, there is a lack of evidence on signaling effects—for the obvious reason that there have been very few cases of wartime rape that have ended up in trials and subsequent punishment. Also, when there have been such trials, they have occurred after a conflict has ended, and can, therefore, only affect other ongoing conflicts or future conflict behavior" (Nordås 2013, 3).

Accountability can also be a problematic issue when soldiers, armed combatants or police officers use sexual torture as part of routine interrogation procedures. Can, for instance, a criminal tribunal accept the excuse, or mitigating fact, of following orders or an established procedure? The so-called "superior orders" defense, according to which a member of the armed forces or a civilian cannot be held responsible for actions that were ordered by a superior military officer or a public official, has been at the core of several court cases since World War I, with various outcomes. In the specific case of acts of wartime sexual violence against men though, the ICTY has rejected such plea and has often charged the person ordering and the person perpetrating such acts in the same way. As observed by Askin, in the "Miljković and others, 'Bosanski Šamac' case", "the individual directly responsible for the sexual violence and the superior who failed to prevent, stop, or punish him were charged under exactly the same articles and sub-articles" (1999, 118).

But even if perpetrators can be held accountable, prosecution is often impeded by a series of additional issues, in particular related to under-reporting. Victims are more likely to relate cases of sexual violence that they have witnessed than the one(s) that they have experienced. And, as we have seen, when they speak about what happened to them, they often do so by qualifying it as torture, beatings, abomination and so on. Because of the strong taboo related to that type of violence, many victims do not describe, and perhaps perceive, what happened to them as sexual violence. For instance, they very rarely use words like "rape" or "castration" (Manivannan 2014, 651). Unfortunately, and as underscored by Leiby (2012), the fact that male survivors rarely speak directly about the sexual violence that they have endured can only reinforce existing stereotypes that many officers conducting the interrogation or gathering testimonies are holding. In other words, the fact that survivors often remain silent about their sexual victimization only comes to confirm the idea that they cannot be sexually victimized. These stereotypes, as well as a lack of training on these issues, in turn prevent police investigators and judges from looking for, and from recognizing cases of sexual violence against men. Existing interrogation procedures with regard to sexual violence, even in the frame of investigations conducted during a conflict or after, therefore, usually focus exclusively on cases of sexual violence against women. And many male survivors, if not specifically asked, will never really disclose what happened, which means that a large number of sexual assault cases might never be uncovered.

In addition, many male survivors refuse to testify in front of a court, either because of shame, or because of a fear of reprisal (Karabegović 2010). The OSCE report on criminal proceedings before the courts of the Federation of Bosnia and Herzegovina, for instance, lists a series of cases where male victims did not even want criminal proceedings to begin, or stopped cooperating with the prosecution when they realized that the investigators had information about the sexual violence they survived, and some of them even retracted their declarations (OSCE 2015, 39–40). In those cases, only eyewitness testimonies were presented, which sometimes led to an abandoning of the charges, or a significant weakening of the cases: "In the case of Monika Karan-Ilić, the male victim of alleged sexual violence refused to testify before the court. The prosecutor read the most relevant parts of his investigative statement and the victim-witness only confirmed. The defense was not in a position to cross-examine this witness, as the witness stated that he did not feel well, did not remember what he was saying at the time, and did not want to recall the alleged event" (OSCE 2015, 40). Of course, similar issues exist in cases related to (wartime) sexual violence against women, and it raises the important question, not yet satisfactorily addressed by international and national courts, of how to best organize the collection of testimonies in such sensitive cases. What makes the reporting and subsequent prosecution of such crimes difficult is also the fact that in many countries where homosexuality is penalized, survivors run the risk of being accused of having engaged in (illegal) homosexual acts. This would have both penal and social consequences for the survivor, since he would run the risk of being condemned to pay a heavy fine or even to be jailed, and he would also have to bear the stigma, and related ostracism, of being labeled homosexual in sometimes very homophobic societies. In other words, reporting these acts would mean, for male victims, becoming visible either as "women" ("womanized" men) or as homosexual.

Because most of these cases of violence are not reported, criminal justice systems have so far not really taken the matter as seriously as they should, and perpetrators are not prosecuted and condemned for these acts. This feeds a sense of impunity, itself creating a climate in which sexual torture of men can become more widespread. Of course, impunity does not just apply to sexual violence, but unfortunately to most acts committed by armed forces and armed groups during recent wars. And it is particularly significant in ongoing conflicts, such as in Eastern Congo. In that sense, impunity with regard to cases of conflict-related sexual violence against men is not an exception, but it is further enhanced by a set of factors. Beyond all the causes that we have already mentioned, impunity can be the result of a lack of political will, of inaction or even of corruption of the relevant State or international institutions (Van Katwyk 2010). Impunity can also derive from a cultural reluctance to prosecute sexual and gender-based violence, or from the absence of a specific legislation prohibiting sexual violence against men. Population displacement, often following phases of open violence, also complicates the access of survivors to justice, and to any compensation system.

In addition, impunity with regard to acts committed during conflicts is favored by the difficulties associated with the collection of physical evidence to support the testimony, especially if the trial occurs years later, in the post-conflict stage. These difficulties are particularly salient in cases of sexual violence against both men and women, because sexual violence does not always leave visible physical scars and traces. However, the case of Bosnia-Herzegovina shows that in spite of all these obstacles, impunity is not an inevitability. Not only did political will at the national and international levels exist, but several Bosnian courts have also "affirmed that corroboration of a victim's evidence concerning sexual violence [was] not required" (OSCE 2015, 21), thus facilitating prosecution. All in all, courts and tribunals in Bosnia-Herzegovina have prosecuted numerous cases involving wartime sexual violence crimes, equivalent to approximately 20% of all wartime cases that were prosecuted. However, even in Bosnia-Herzegovina the victims' access to compensation remains complicated. The Bosnian "Law on Civilian Victims of War" was introduced in 2006 to offer monetary compensation for male and female survivors of conflict-related sexual violence, but to date very few individuals have been recognized as "legally approved" survivors, and have, therefore, been able to receive compensation. Applicants to the "legally approved" survivor's status have to show their medical documentation from the time the assault was committed, or to have at least two witnesses ready to give testimony in front of the tribunal. Either condition is extremely difficult to meet, years after the end of the conflict, and considering the circumstances in which most sexual violence acts were committed. Another option for survivors is to seek compensation through civil cases, but these are often expensive and cumbersome procedures[3]. Cases will likely take years to be resolved, thus further delaying closure for survivors.

But even as a perfectible example of how conflict-related sexual violence against both men and women can be prosecuted, Bosnia-Herzegovina stands as an exception. In most other cases, impunity with regard to wartime violence is the norm, especially when sexual violence has been perpetrated by senior military officers. In the case of the DRC, for instance, very few soldiers or combatants have been convicted for acts of sexual violence (all committed against women and girls) by national courts, and all of them were lower-ranking soldiers. This is what explains a report compiled by Human Rights Watch in 2009:

> No senior military figure has been prosecuted for sexual crimes; the criminal responsibility of senior officials, including their command responsibility, is rarely the subject of investigations by military prosecutors. The most senior officer convicted of crimes of sexual violence in the Kivus has been a captain— no major, lieutenant colonel, colonel, or general has been prosecuted. Military commanders continue to be powerful figures who are treated as untouchable by political and military leaders; brigade commanders in particular are often given free reign. (Human Rights Watch 2009, 6)

When needed, many military commanders also protect their soldiers, including by obstructing the course of justice, which renders the prosecution of wartime sexual violence almost impossible even when it is committed by lower-ranking soldiers. The situation is similar in Burundi, where up to now very few cases of sexual violence against women have been prosecuted, let alone against men.

What makes the situation particularly complex to handle is that both the Burundian and the Congolese armies, like many other armies around the world, have integrated combatants with serious human rights abuse records, notably via DDR processes. This has contributed to a climate of impunity whereby State security forces are almost never held accountable, to the dismay of many survivors:

> [Speaking about soldiers and members of armed groups]
> They could do whatever they wanted to us, and what could we do? We could not go and complain to them afterwards, they would have laughed at us, or worse. So where were we supposed to go and complain? And now they are parading around, on their armed vehicles, and saying that they are keeping the peace. (Jacques 2013, interview)

Special laws or state of emergency situations, which allow security forces to override citizens' and prisoners' basic human rights, further complicate the prosecution of cases of sexual torture. In some countries, like in Sri Lanka, for instance, this has undoubtedly hampered investigations for past and more recent cases of sexual violence exerted by State institutions (Sooka 2014, 66).

In cases where conflict-related sexual violence is committed by non-State actors, prosecution is impeded by other factors, such as the weakening or even disappearance of traditional authorities like the Bashingantahe in Burundi, for instance, which used to settle local conflicts, and whose authority has been challenged during the conflict (Naniwe-Kaburahe 2008). Such a process also feeds impunity in Eastern Congo, as explained by Eriksson Baaz: "After the outbreak of the war, these traditional systems have disintegrated and been replaced by total impunity at all levels, surely also contributing to the normalization of sexual violence in the communities" (2009, 503). In parallel, criminal justice systems at the national level do not take the matter seriously, either because they want to concentrate on what they see as more pressing issues, or because, as we will explore in the next section, sexual violence against men is not considered as a crime. It is also worth underscoring the fact that conflict-affected countries are often trapped in a vicious cycle, whereby the maintenance of high levels of violence weakens judicial systems, which in turn feeds impunity and violence. This adds to the survivors' despair, disillusionment and loneliness:

> These men will never be judged for what they did to me and to others. I hope they will, but deep inside me I know that they won't. Who would judge them anyway? And who would believe me, rather than them? (Bernard 2013, interview)

7.2. GENDER BIASES AND THE (ABSENCE OF) PENALIZATION OF SEXUAL VIOLENCE AGAINST MEN

In countries where cases related to wartime sexual violence are prosecuted, other challenges appear, mostly relating to how sexual violence is defined, and to whether or not this definition is gender-inclusive and takes sexual violence against men into account. A UN report, for instance, lists a number of countries where cases of conflict-related sexual violence against men have been numerous and well documented, but where prosecution is or was impossible because of restrictive definitions of sexual violence. This is, for instance, the case in Colombia, where men were for the first time included as potential victims of sexual violence in the 2012 draft law on "access to justice for victims of sexual violence" (UN 2013, 18). This is not an isolated case. According to Dolan (2014a, 6) who surveyed 189 countries, in 2014 a total of 63 countries, representing almost two-thirds of the world's population, still recognized only female victims of rape. Some countries, like the DRC, have recently adopted more inclusive laws, but so far Congolese courts have only prosecuted cases of sexual violence against women, and as shown by Kippenberg (2005), justice has scarcely been delivered in cases of conflict-related female rape anyway.

But even in cases where assault against men is not explicitly excluded from definitions of sexual violence, restricted understandings of sexual violence, for instance, limited to rape, seriously impede prosecution by excluding the most common types of wartime sexual violence against men, such as partial or total castration, or traumas to the genitals. For instance, the Criminal Code of the Socialist Federal Republic of Yugoslavia (1976), which has served as one of the basis for trials after the end of the conflict in Bosnia-Herzegovina, does not explicitly proscribe the full range of sexual violence recognized under international law. It only explicitly proscribes forced prostitution and rape (OSCE 2015, 18), and does not penalize crimes against humanity but only war crimes—thus not allowing for the prosecution of sexual violence against civilians under the heading of crimes against humanity. This means that as far as national courts in Bosnia-Herzegovina were concerned, wartime sexual violence could only be prosecuted as torture or inhuman treatment, which made a great difference for survivors since it overlooked the sexual nature of the act. Similar restrictions were at play in Peru, where in spite of a rather broad definition of sexual violence, the Truth and Reconciliation Commission only investigated cases of rape, and thus overlooked most cases of conflict-related sexual violence (Leiby 2012, 343). In Colombia, both NGOs and government databases for human rights violations have classified conflict-related sexual violence against men, especially when committed by

State security forces, as "torture", thus silencing its sexual nature (Quijano and Kelly 2012, 482).

Further, empirical evidence points to the existence of a strong gender bias with regard to how the definition of rape is applied during national and local trials. In several cases in Bosnia-Herzegovina, for instance, local courts have been using different definitional elements according to the gender of the victim, as underscored by a report compiled by the OSCE: "While the issue of consent and whether the victim could resist were considered by the courts in several cases involving female victims, these issues were not raised in the cases of Milanović or Minić et al., which involved male victims" (2015, 32). This gender bias has even led to a different labeling of cases of sexual violence when victims were men, such as in the Minić et al. case, where the Bijeljina District Court qualified forced fellatio as an "outrage upon [prisoners'] personal dignity" and as an "inhuman treatment", when it had, in cases where victims had been female, been recognized as rape. This gendered reading and application of the definition of sexual violence strengthen existing gender stereotypes, whereby men can never be victims, thus reinforcing the equation between, on the one hand, male bodies and (sexual) invulnerability and, on the other hand, female bodies and (sexual) vulnerability.

There is also some evidence that the way sexual violence is sanctioned depends not just on the gender of the victim, but also on the gender of the judges, as King and Greening have observed in the case of the former Yugoslavia: "Once women are present in institutions and command increased authority, different benefits transfer to their gender constituency. This entrepreneurial effect may be present for men as well. Male judges sanction male sexual violence more severely than do female jurists, and perhaps both men and women identify with the victim's gender status" (2007, 1066). If this observation is confirmed in other conflict and post-conflict settings, ensuring a greater diversity among judges in terms of gender identity should undoubtedly become a priority.

Another major challenge impeding the prosecution of cases of wartime sexual violence against men pertains to the criminalization, in a number of countries, of same-sex sexual acts, regardless of whether the behavior is consensual or not (UN 2013, 16). Such legislations make it very complicated, if not impossible, for male survivors to seek justice and reparation[4]. According to the survey of 189 countries compiled by Dolan (2014a, 6), 70 States criminalize men who report sexual abuse. Some of these countries, like Uganda, for instance, are in a post-conflict stage and/or host numerous refugees, a large proportion of which have been victim of wartime sexual violence. The Penal Code in Uganda not only excludes men from its definition of rape, but also condemns, in its Article 145 dedicated to "unnatural offences", homosexual acts, which are made an offense punishable by a life sentence. This definition that applies to both consensual and non-consensual acts, de facto criminalizes male survivors of both wartime and peacetime sexual violence (Refugee Law Project 2013a). Needless to say, reporting and prosecuting sexual violence against men becomes impossible, as survivors risk being accused of homosexuality, and thus arrest, if they speak about what happened to them.

The case of Uganda is not isolated. In many countries, especially in Africa, where homosexuality is severely penalized legally but also socially[5], confusing sexual violence against men with homosexuality is very common. Added to the lack of awareness and training for judges, prosecutors and police investigators, such representations and legal provisions come to "prove" that sexual violence against men does not exist, or that if it does, it is not a problem worth addressing. The fact that International Criminal Law and International Humanitarian Law, as we will see in the next section, are more progressive on this issue leads to a somewhat paradoxical situation, described by Lewis: "Due to the criminalization of male-male sexual behavior in some countries, victims of male-male sexual violence in those countries enjoy, perversely, greater legal protection in wartime than they do in peacetime" (2009/2010, 17).

7.3. PROMISES AND LIMITS OF INTERNATIONAL LAW

Acts of sexual violence committed during war can be prosecuted via various international legal instruments. Three main frameworks can apply. First is International Criminal Law, which addresses the criminal responsibility of individuals for international crimes, like genocide, war crimes and crimes against humanity; International Criminal Law has rapidly developed since the Nuremberg and Tokyo trials, with the creation, during the 1990s, of the International Criminal Tribunal for the former Yugoslavia (ICTY) and the International Criminal Tribunal for Rwanda (ICTR) by the United Nations Security Council, and more recently, the International Criminal Court (ICC) in 2002. The second framework is International Humanitarian Law, whose main objective is to regulate the conduct of war, and to limit the effects of armed conflict on those who are not or no longer participating in the conflict. It is notably based on various conventions like the Geneva and the Hague Conventions, as well as on other international treaties and protocols. The third framework is International Human Rights Law, based on the Universal Declaration of Human Rights as well as on a series of International Human Rights Treaties, and which seeks to promote human rights and human dignity all around the world. International Human Rights Law applies mostly in times of peace, but remains applicable in times of war.

If, as we will further explore below, both International Criminal Law and International Humanitarian Law have adopted a gender-neutral approach with regard to conflict-related sexual violence, it is not the case of International Human Rights Law, which is mostly based on the CEDAW (Convention on the Elimination of all Forms of Discrimination Against Women, entered into force in 1981). No International Human Rights instrument explicitly addresses sexual violence against men or male sexual abuse, and International Humans Rights Law generally uses female-specific language on sexual violence; it is, therefore, largely unsuitable to address (wartime) sexual violence against men, and to raise awareness about it. Even when they belong to the most vulnerable categories, men seem to be excluded from the protection offered by International Human Rights Law to victims of sexual violence, as explained by Stemple:

> Men with characteristics that make them particularly vulnerable to violence are consistently excluded from human rights instruments. Sub groups of at-risk men, such as refugees, the internally displaced, migrant workers, disabled men, or men who are vulnerable to sexual violence because of their membership in a particular racial or ethnic group during armed conflict are excluded. Human rights instruments that do address the vulnerability of these groups to sexual violence address only the vulnerability of women. (2009, 624)

By contrast, International Criminal Law and International Humanitarian Law offer a multiplicity of options to address the issue of wartime sexual violence against men, as exemplified by the work of the ICTY, the ICTR and in the Rome statute of the International Criminal Court. Together, these institutions offer the most comprehensive and efficient framework for prosecuting these cases, and have convincingly used various existing human rights treaties and conventions, regarding, for instance, freedom from torture and degrading treatment, rights to life, personal security and physical security and so on. The ICTR and the ICTY in particular were even the first to consider that wartime rape, against both men and women, should be judged as a crime against humanity (Zawati 2007, 27). Before that, the various international war tribunals, especially those set up after World War II, had excluded rape from crimes against humanity. Further, these institutions have introduced the use of gender-neutral definitions of wartime rape, the Trial Chamber 1 of the ICTR even making clear references to male victims of sexual violence in the Akayesu case (1998): "Rape and sexual violence certainly constitute infliction of a serious bodily and mental harm on the victim and are even, according to the Chamber, one of the worst ways to inflict harm on the victim as he or she suffers both bodily and mental harm" (quoted in Obote-Odora 2005, 137). Even if the Office of the Prosecutor of the ICTR eventually did not charge anyone with rape against men, this was undoubtedly a landmark ruling.

But the ICTY had proven to be even more progressive on these matters, and can be considered as a pioneer in defining sexual violence in an inclusive manner, and in prosecuting wartime sexual violence against men (Gorris 2015, 413). In 1997, in the first decision it issued, so in the first international war crimes trial since Nuremberg and Tokyo, the ICTY found Duško Tadić, a former Bosnian Serb Democratic Party's local board president, guilty of cruel treatment (violation of the laws and customs of war) and inhumane acts (crime against humanity) for the part he played in acts of sexual violence against men, in particular male sexual assault and mutilation (King and Greening 2007, 1056). In appeal two years later, in a judgement based on International Humanitarian Law principles and in particular on the Geneva Conventions, the Appeals Chambers confirmed the previous judgement and sentenced Tadić to twenty years' imprisonment: "Through his presence, Duško Tadić aided and encouraged the group of men actively taking part in the assault. Of particular concern here is the cruelty and humiliation inflicted on the victim and the other detainees". The ICTY subsequently examined other cases of wartime sexual violence against men. In *Prosecutor v. Milošević*, for instance, the prosecutor charged acts of forced fellatio, forced incest and gang rape of men as persecution as a crime against humanity, and in *Prosecutor v. Češić*, Češić was convicted of humiliating and degrading treatment as a violation of the laws or customs of war and of rape as a crime against humanity for having forced, at gunpoint, two Muslim brothers detained at Luka camp to perform fellatio on each other. It is worth underscoring here that if the ICTY and the ICTR prosecute wartime rape as a specific type of sexual violence, they also allow the prosecution other types of sexual violence against men such as castration under other categories, such as "torture".

Other courts and tribunals, such as the Special Court for Sierra Leone, set up in 2002 by the government of Sierra Leone and the United Nations and whose aim is to prosecute crimes that occurred during the civil war in Sierra Leone, have followed suit. In *Prosecutor v. Sesay*, Kallon and Gbao, for instance, the Special Court for Sierra Leone charged the accused of sexual offenses against both men and women with outrages upon personal dignity as war crimes, and recognized that both men and women can be victims of rape. The Rome statute of the International Criminal Court, adopted in 1998 and entered into force in 2002, synthesizes these advances, notably in its article 7(1)(g): "The Rome Statute expanded the expressly enumerated sexual violence crimes in International Criminal Law, by adding sexual slavery, enforced prostitution, forced pregnancy, enforced sterilization and other forms of Sexual Violence of equivalent gravity to the list of war crimes and crimes against humanity. It acknowledged that sexual violence can be committed against men and women, and also included coercion as an element in the crime" (UN 2013, 17). This means that these offenses may henceforth be considered as crimes against humanity, whether they are committed against women or against men. The Rome statute of the ICC even goes a step further than the ICTR or the ICTY, as underscored in a working paper published by the Refugee Law Project: "Unlike the ICTR and ICTY, which prohibited persecution as a crime against humanity when committed on the basis of religion, politics and/or race, the Rome Statute also prohibited persecution as a crime against humanity based on gender" (2013a, 23). Conflict-related sexual violence against both men and women may thus be prosecuted, depending on the precise circumstances, as an act of genocide, a war crime or a crime against humanity. Of course some conditions have to be met for an act of sexual violence to be prosecuted by the ICC or by another UN international criminal tribunal: "To constitute a crime under international criminal law, sexual violence must have a sufficient nexus to a genocide, to a widespread or systematic attack against a civilian population (for crimes against humanity), or to an armed conflict (for war crimes)" (Lewis 2009/2010, 16). Among other conditions, the accused must be a national of a country who has ratified the Rome statute[6], or the crime must have taken place on the territory of one of the State parties. In addition, as "a court of last resort" (ibid.), the ICC can only prosecute cases that national or local courts are unwilling or unable to deal with.

However, judgements by the ICC, the ICTR, the ICTY or the Special Court for Sierra Leone demonstrate that these progressive and gender-neutral definitions of wartime sexual violence are not always applied, or not consistently, even by international criminal tribunals (Sivakumaran 2010, 272). In many cases, conflict-related sexual violence against men is mentioned but characterized as torture or inhumane treatment instead of sexual violence, which reinforces the idea that men are not concerned by the phenomenon of wartime sexual violence. Gender biases identified at the local and national levels are thus present at the level of international criminal justice too. One archetypical example of this is the case of *Prosecutor v. Kenyatta*, prosecuted by the ICC, which in 2012 classified crimes of forced circumcision and sexual mutilation under the category of "other inhumane acts". As explained by the Refugee Law Project (2013a, 31–32), the decision not to charge forced circumcision as sexual violence but as an "inhumane act" is consistent with previous decisions taken by international criminal courts, in particular the ICTY, which has only once charged rape of men as crime against humanity—in the previously quoted *Prosecutor v. Češić* case. This classification entails a refusal to consider the sexual nature of these acts, and gives the impression that they are less important than rape or forced prostitution, or other types of sexual violence that are primarily associated with female victims.

In other words, "sexual violence against men appears to be treated differently from sexual violence against women" (ibid., 32). This trend has been confirmed in another recent ICC decision concerning the trial of the Lord's Resistance Army commander Dominic Ongwen. In February 2018, the legal representatives for victims in this trial sought leave to present additional evidence on cases of sexual violence against men and boys, which had not been included in the initial charges. In March 2018 the ICC Trial Chamber IX rejected this request, stating that this was not "appropriate and necessary for the determination of the truth", and that instances of sexual violence against men and boys are in any case "consequences of the crimes charged and their results are, therefore, part of the harm suffered by the victims"[7].

In other instances, acts of sexual violence against men are mentioned and characterized as sexual violence, but not condemned as such, or not condemned at all, as in the cases of *Prosecutor v. Muhimana*, or of *Prosecutor v. Bagosora*, judged by the ICTR:

> A Trial Chamber of the ICTR recalled that several witnesses had seen that a certain Kabanda's "private parts had been severed" and that his genitals had been hung on a spike. However, in its findings, the Trial Chamber simply referred to the killing of Kabanda and no more. Similarly, in Bagosora, the Trial Chamber found Bagosora guilty of other inhumane acts in respect of inter alia "the stripping of female refugees at the Saint Josephite Centre". Yet the summary of the relevant witness' anticipated testimony annexed to the Prosecution's Pre-Trial Brief, and reproduced in the Trial Judgement, specifically states that [s]ome of the victims were naked, men and women. (Sivakumaran 2010: 274)

Actually, even if it has recognized that rape and sexual violence can be committed against both men and women, the ICTR has never charged anyone with committing rape or sexual assault against men, in spite of supporting empirical evidence. Similar observations have been made with regard to the Special Court of Sierra Leone, which in some cases took note of episodes of sexual violence against both men and women, but only prosecuted those concerning women (Oosterveld 2011, 71). Even some judgements handed down by the ICTY followed a similar pattern, as noted by Manivannan (2014, 663): "At the ICTY, only sixteen out of seventy-seven sexual violence indictments included charges of sexual violence involving male victims, of which seven led to convictions. An additional three cases that strongly indicated sexual violence against only male victims did not even lead to indictments for sex crimes". It thus seems that conflict-related sexual violence against men is still, up to now, considered by international criminal tribunals as less severe than when it is committed against women.

In addition, some perpetrators seem to be excluded from the sphere of application of International Criminal Law. As explained by Zawati (2007, 35–37), countries like the United States that have not ratified the Rome statute have taken steps in order to protect their military and police personnel, particularly after the scandals of Abu Ghraib and Guantánamo Bay. The highly controversial US Military Commissions Act of 2006 (MCA), for instance, has rendered the Geneva Conventions and related treaties unenforceable in court in civil cases involving the US government or its agents. Until the adoption of the MCA, all US military and police personnel could be prosecuted for any violation of article 3 of the Geneva Conventions (notably prohibiting murder, mutilation, torture, cruel, humiliating and degrading treatment and so on). The MCA changed this rule, so that only "grave breaches" of article 3 could be prosecuted. This means that US military and police personnel who perpetrate torture, mutilation, rape, sexual assault, abuse and other inhumane treatment in war situations can no longer be punished under US law. This is particularly worrying, considering the empirical evidence pointing at the (past) use of sexual torture on prisoners by US officers, and considering the presence of US security forces in many conflict areas all around the world. According to the Center for Constitutional Rights, the MCA also exempts "certain US officials who have implemented or had command responsibility for coercive interrogation techniques from war crimes prosecutions" (2010, 5–6), which adds a further layer of unaccountability.

In the past, and in reaction to the adoption of the Rome statute of the ICC, the United States had already made an attempt to protect its troops stationed in Afghanistan, by pushing for the adoption of the UN Security Council Resolution 1487. This resolution, eventually adopted on 12 June 2003, granted a (renewable) one-year immunity from prosecution by the ICC to UN peacekeeping troops originating from countries that were not party to the ICC. However, following the Abu Ghraib scandal in 2004, the Security Council refused to renew the exemption. Described by Zawati (2007, 35–37) as "the promotion of the culture of impunity by an international organization", this episode highlights the limits and shortcomings of recent advances in International Criminal Law.

It would, however, be inopportune to dismiss the significant progress made by international law with regard to the prosecution of wartime sexual violence against men. Even if the legal framework that has been built by the ICTY and ICC, among other institutions, is not fully enforced yet, there is good reason to assume that it will increasingly be used both at the international, and at the national levels. The Rome statute of the ICC in particular has been hailed as a source of hope for the prosecution of cases of wartime sexual violence at the international, but also at the domestic level (UN 2013, 19). The domestication of the Rome statute has, to date, been undertaken by sixty-four countries, which have enacted legislation containing either complementarity or cooperation provisions, or both, into their domestic law. Thirty-four additional countries have started adapting their legislation. As Chris Dolan explains, the Rome statute of the ICC is "leading the way in establishing international response to the scourge of sexual violence" (Dolan 2014a, 6). As such, it could be not only further strengthened, but also used as a source for a reform of national legislations. International law could serve, among other purposes, to promote gender-neutral definitions of sexual violence[8], to redefine sexual violence to account for abuse of power and eliminate consent as a barrier to accountability (as the absence of consent is always difficult to prove) and to increase the levels of reporting of sexual violence against men, which are in many countries very low due to fear of criminal prosecution for homosexuality (Refugee Law Project 2013a, 57–63). Even the women-specific instruments used by International Human Rights Law could, with little effort, be reworked to include men as potential victims (Lewis 2009/2010, 20).

Changes are on the way. For instance, during the trial of Jean-Pierre Bemba at the ICC that started in 2010 and which led to his acquittal in 2018, the court referred to a gender-neutral definition of sexual violence, as outlined in the article 7(3) of the Rome statute. Further, in its "Policy Paper on Sexual and Gender-Based Crimes" published in June 2014, the ICC has systematically included men and boys in its definitions of sexual and gender-based violence, which it had previously failed to do.

Some authors like Manivannan (2014) also suggest that transitional justice mechanisms should be used more systematically in addition to international war crimes tribunals to improve the access to justice and reparations of male survivors of sexual violence. It is, however, unclear what effects these trials might have on survivors, especially when they entail giving testimony in front of a court. Is revealing really healing, as the slogan of the South African Truth and Reconciliation Commission went? In the case of the 2007/2008 post-electoral violence in Kenya, for example, statements from men who had been sexually assaulted were received and examined by the Truth, Justice and Reconciliation Commission (TJRC) established in 2008 by the Kenyan government. These cases were, however, not prosecuted, either because certain types of gender-based and sexual violence were excluded by the Penal Code, or because of a lack or poor quality of evidence (ICTJ 2014). The TJRC simply took note of the statements and referred male survivors for medical and psychological support at health services. To date, the Kenyan government has not implemented the TJRC recommendations regarding the setting up of a reparations program for survivors of sexual violence, or the creation of Gender Violence Recovery Centers for providing medical and psychological support to survivors. Previously, the truth commissions established in Timor

Leste, Sierra Leone or South Africa have paid attention to female victims of sexual violence, but did not pay attention to male victims (ICTJ 2016).

Many truth seeking and reparations mechanisms of transitional justice are set up years after the end of a conflict, so that the collection of credible evidence regarding sexual assaults is extremely complicated, and that the support it might offer to survivors comes very (too?) late. And in the absence of a systematic domestication of the advances brought forward by International Criminal Law, many instances of conflict-related sexual violence are likely to remain unpunished. In Burundi, for instance, the Commission Vérité et Réconciliation that had been foreseen in the Arusha Agreement of 2000 only became operational in March 2016, and the Special Tribunal for prosecuting war crimes seems all but forgotten. This does not bode well for victims of conflict-related sexual violence, especially since Burundi also decided to leave the ICC in 2017. In the absence of broader awareness-raising campaigns on the scope and severity of wartime sexual violence against both men and women, and without a better understanding of masculinities in post-conflict societies (Hamber 2016), it seems that the capacity of transitional justice to bring healing and a sense of closure to survivors will remain limited. They will continue to be seen as collateral, and thus not central, victims of the conflict, and to face stigmatization and even rejection.

Conclusion

The examples and stories discussed throughout this book show that wartime sexual violence against men is not a corollary of war, but that it is intrinsically intertwined with larger political and military struggles. Its occurrence and main features are not just related to the characteristics and strength of militarized actors, but also to the much broader structural violence of intersecting gender, ethnic, religious, socio-economic, and so on, hierarchies. As such, it does not simply happen because of a lack of military discipline, by chance or on the contrary as the result of some carefully devised military strategy. In other words, it cannot be fully captured if just understood as a "weapon of war", or conversely as an "opportunistic" type of violence. It is deeply embedded in the patriarchal values that sustain conflict processes themselves. It produces, at the same time that it is produced by, a violent and heteronormative patriarchal (dis)order.

As conflicts and wars induce tensions and insecurities about who controls the political, social and economic resources, the performance of strong and powerful masculinity models becomes an asset in the competition between and within warring groups. So by simultaneously allowing perpetrators to question the masculinity, authority and agency of victims, and to reinforce their own influence and societal/political position, sexual violence against men can play an important role in these struggles. In that sense, the perpetration of sexual violence against men tells us as much about gendered, ethnic, racial, political and socio-economic hierarchies and tensions as it does about military strategies, or lack thereof.

However, the effectiveness of sexual violence against men, and the consequences it has on survivors as well as on perpetrators, are related to broader social, cultural and gender norms, and are, therefore, by no means constant across time, societies and cultures. The empirical data collected for this book, in particular regarding survivors' and perpetrators' experiences and narratives, is thus not meant to be representative of all existing configurations. Much remains to be explored, in terms of conflict settings, of historical variations, of consequences on survivors and their families and of impact on societies in the long term. Nevertheless, what the collected data notably shows is that the way wartime sexual violence against men is understood and framed has implications on how survivors can cope with it. When survivors are able to revert the stigma, by exposing sexual violence for what it is—an act that is feminizing and subjugating only insofar as we believe in its performativity—spaces of resilience and of resistance can open up.

Wartime sexual violence is rarely granted the attention it deserves, and international narratives about conflicts, and related policies, almost always fail to grasp how symptomatic and meaningful such violence is. The patriarchal and heteronormative values underpinning conflict-related sexual violence simultaneously endeavor to silence or downplay it, either by picturing it as a sort of "natural" side effect of fighting, when women are targeted, or by rendering it so shameful and exceptional that victims and bystanders alike stay silent about it, when men are targeted. Admittedly, and thanks to the work done over the past decades by feminists in the policy, humanitarian and academic fields, numerous international, national and local initiatives have been launched in order to address and try to prevent wartime sexual violence against women. They have also helped to raise awareness on situations where, following the "rape as a weapon of war" argument, sexual violence has been used as a war strategy—even if, as we have seen, this analysis grid is far from being entirely satisfactory. Yet the work to raise awareness on the existence and magnitude of wartime sexual violence against other groups of people, such as men and boys, but also LGBTQI individuals, remains to be done, as an important step towards a truly encompassing understanding of sexual violence. Until this is done, until we stop speaking about wartime sexual violence as if it was necessarily perpetrated by (heterosexual) men on (heterosexual) women, our understanding of the phenomenon will remain limited.

In that perspective, empirical data needs to be collected in a more systematic fashion in order to further explore how the type of conflict and of conflict setting influences how and when wartime sexual violence is perpetrated, and the profiles of victims and of perpetrators. Cases of conflicts where sexual violence against men (and women) is not committed at all, or at least not at all by some conflict actors, deserve more attention too, as they could provide indications for the setting up of prevention programs. It would also be useful to collect data on whether the use of sexual violence evolves (in both qualitative and quantitative terms) during the course of a conflict. Similarly, paying more attention to variations in models and expressions of masculinity can help us to understand not only what types of violence are perpetrated and who are the victims and the perpetrators, but also how survivors react and try to cope with the experience of sexual violence. In the same manner, models of masculinities and femininities could be used to frame support policies for all victims, whatever their gender and sexual orientation, and to better map the impact of sexual violence on survivors' lives, and on the communities to which they belong. Further, the multiple linkages and interplay between conflict-related sexual violence against individuals belonging to different "categories" (men, women, LGBTQI individuals, refugees, members of minority groups, etc.) have yet to be unpacked. Beyond demonstrating that they are embedded in the very same patriarchal principles, research could document how they might feed each other, for instance, whether a high prevalence of sexual violence against women is always accompanied by high rates of sexual violence against men, whether they are likely to occur at the same conflict stages, etc. Empirical data also ought to be gathered on perpetrators' profiles, since, as we have seen in the case of Eastern DRC, there seems to be some differences in who perpetrates sexual violence against men, and against women. At the same time, the fact that there are apparently some cases where victims are not really differentiated by their gender, and where both male and female prisoners are submitted to the same kind of sexual torture, calls for further investigation. How to reconcile these configurations with other cases where women are systematically targeted for rape, while men are much more likely to be subjected to other forms of (sexualized) torture? Answering all of these questions requires a significantly increased academic engagement with the field and with local actors on the ground.

Even more importantly, it is urgent to take stock of recent advances in feminist studies, and to start considering that rather than the sex of the victim or even of the perpetrator, one should take seriously the performativity of sexual violence, for both perpetrators and victims. That the victim is a man or a woman is less important than the meaning that sexual violence intends to convey, that is a super/subordination relation which is also related to broader—e.g. economic, political, racial, caste, cultural—relations of power. "Queering" theoretical approaches to conflict-related sexual violence by going beyond the gender binary is crucial to avoid reproducing the limits and shortcomings of previous theoretical models. In other words, an "add men and stir" recipe is unlikely to provide satisfactory answers. Of course, this has to be done carefully so that attention and funding do not drift away from female survivors. But a drastic change in how we frame and understand wartime sexual violence is needed, and long overdue.

Unveiling the super/subordination relations conveyed through sexual violence, regardless of who the victims or the perpetrators are, has important consequences in both research and policy terms, notably because it influences the way survivors of sexual violence are able to cope with what happened to them. Support offered to survivors has to take stock not just of the sexual or even gendered dimensions of sexual violence, but also of how it is interconnected to other types of violence, be they physical, structural or symbolic. Survivors' recovery is indeed, as we have seen, impeded by the fact that they often belong to otherwise dominated social or cultural groups—which also partly explains why women are particularly vulnerable to sexual violence.

Thus, rather than to analyse wartime sexual violence as a separate category of violence perpetrated during conflicts, it seems that we need to pay more attention to how it is embedded within larger political, economic, social, cultural and military struggles. It also makes sense with regard to survivors' experiences: sexual violence is part of a much wider continuum of conflict-related violence, and it is almost always perpetrated alongside other forms of violence. The fact that sexual violence is not necessarily what survivors recall the most of their experience of war, and that they almost always mention other types of violence that they have been victims of, is very telling in that respect. When survivors are able to relate their experience of sexual violence to other types of discrimination and structural violence they have faced, as in the case of political opponents tortured because of their opinions or militancy, it increases their chances to be able to cope with it. In other words, connecting gender-based violence to other dimensions of social power opens up spaces of resilience and resistance to the practice of sexual violence, and to its effects. One major task of research is, therefore, to unveil and unpack these connections, so that prevention policies, but also support programs, can be built around them.

Accounting for the context in which wartime sexual violence is perpetrated is paramount, whether it has been committed against men, against women, or against individuals targeted because of their sexual orientation or their ethnic, religious or political belonging. One should be wary of overstating the importance of sexual victimization in the war experience, at the expense of other types of suffering. As has been observed by many feminist scholars, when it comes to speaking about women's experiences of conflict, sexual violence almost always comes to the fore, pushing into oblivion other non-sexual types of violence, such as beatings, but also displacement, increased poverty, forced recruitment, etc. One of the consequences of this focus put on sexual violence, among all potential forms of violence, is what we could call the "biologization" of women, that is, the assumption that what is the most important about/to women, is their reproductive and sexual health. This incredibly patriarchal and heteronormative representation of women veils the multiple other discriminations they are victim of, and allows gendered inequalities to reproduce themselves.

In parallel, as we have seen, the fact that wartime sexual violence against men hasn't received much attention yet means that a certain vision of masculinity as invulnerable and as the backbone of the national, ethnic or religious group can be preserved. In other words, the hyper-visibility of the sexual brutalization of women vs. the silencing of the sexual brutalization of men are two sides of the same patriarchal and heteronormative coin. Unveiling and highlighting this is a major feminist task, which demands to treat wartime sexual violence, whatever the gender and sexual orientation of its victims, as part of a much broader experience of war, and as related to wider societal relations of power.

Notes

INTRODUCTION

1. The expression has been become popular since the UN Security Council Resolution 1820 (2008) on Women and Peace and Security noted that "women and girls are particularly targeted by the use of sexual violence, including as a tactic of war to humiliate, dominate, instill fear in, disperse and/or forcibly relocate civilian members of a community or ethnic group".

2. The other two main differences with what we know of peacetime or non-conflict-related childhood sexual abuse pertain to the public nature of wartime sexual violence, whereas non-conflict-related childhood sexual abuse is usually perpetrated in secrecy, and to the fact that perpetrators of non-conflict-related childhood sexual abuse are often relatives and in a position of trust vis-à-vis the victim, in opposition to perpetrators of wartime sexual violence, who are often unknown or enemies to the victim (UN 2013, 14–15).

3. The expression was used in 2010 by Margot Wallstrom, the UN's special representative on sexual violence in conflict, after her return from the Congo.

4. These figures only include interviews during which the topic of wartime sexual violence against men came up and was discussed.

5. Worth mentioning also is the fact that the consent process was oral rather than written, mostly because a significant portion of my informants in Africa were not literate.

6. I have been assisted by local male and female interpreters. It is difficult for me to assess the impact of the interpreter's gender on the interviewing process, considering the sensitive nature of the information that was discussed. My feeling is that there is no "better" gender for interviewing male survivors or perpetrators of sexual violence, as some interviewees seemed at times to feel more relaxed with male interpreters, while some others were apparently more comfortable around women.

7. Homosexuality has been banned in Burundi since 2009. Those found guilty of engaging in consensual same-sex relations risk imprisonment of two to three years and a fine of fifty thousand to one hundred thousand Burundian francs.

CHAPTER 1

1. Especially in the United States with the 2012 documentary film called *The Invisible War* about sexual assault in the US military, which has received several awards, and in France with the publication in February 2014 of the book *La Guerre Invisible*, which tackles the same issue of sexual violence within the French Army.
2. Of course, such types of violence can, and indeed do often, include sexual violence, but this is almost never discussed.
3. See, for instance, https://www.newscientist.com/article/dn14522-sexual-abuse-of-male-soldiers-common-in-liberian-war/. Accessed 2 May 2018.
4. The doctor mentioned that none of the other male victims had reported to the hospital, which is a good indication of the very low level of reporting of such acts.
5. Interestingly, Johnson et al. registered a percentage of 41.1% of female perpetrators of sexual violence against women, another indication that the victim/female, perpetrator/male distinction is both empirically and analytically incorrect.
6. It was also the case of 73.9% of female survivors.
7. Beatings of the genitals are, for instance, more likely to be reported than cases of rape, which are much more stigmatizing for survivors. As observed by Feldman (1991, 128) in the case of Northern Ireland, such beatings were reported almost casually by survivors, as if they were not something to be particularly upset about. The follow up question is of course: are these beatings making up a large percentage of cases of sexual torture in detention because they are more common, or because other instances of sexual violence are less reported?

CHAPTER 2

1. As we will explore further, the extreme displays of violence, transgression and breaking of taboos entailed in the perpetration of sexual violence against men are not likely to gain broad social acceptance.
2. They might not always manage to do so though, among other reasons because as they transgress taboos around sexual violence against men, they run the risk of never securing broad societal acceptance in the post-conflict society, not to mention the risk of being prosecuted for their war crimes, as the example of the ICTY suggests (please also refer to chapter 7).
3. This is not to imply that non-State actors do not perpetrate sexual violence. Among other examples, recent cases involving FARC military leaders have, for instance, been revealed. In many asymmetrical conflict settings such as Sri Lanka,

however, the State has been much more likely to commit such crimes than non-State actors (see, for instance, Wood 2009).

4. The expression "bad apples" has often been used to describe the way the US administration had tried to dismiss cases of (sexual) torture committed in Abu Ghraib and Guantánamo. Donald Rumsfeld, then US Secretary of Defense, had, for instance, declared in a hearing before the Senate Armed Services Committee: "It's important for the American people and the world to know that while these terrible acts were perpetrated by a small number of US military, they were also brought to light by the honorable and responsible actions of other military personnel" (7 May 2004).

5. See, for instance, the study led by Johnson et al. (2010) in Eastern Congo, where 82% of perpetrators of male sexual violence were combatants (78% in the case of female sexual violence).

6. Please refer to chapter 3 for some examples.

7. It should first be noted that, as the work of Frank Barrett (1996) on the US Navy has demonstrated, there is not one but several constructions of military masculinity. It is also quite clear that the masculinity "model" of those who perpetrated atrocities in Abu Ghraib or Guantánamo was never celebrated as an example for other soldiers to emulate (Sjoberg and Gentry 2007, 58–87), and can, therefore, not be called "hegemonic".

8. Interestingly enough, I had not mentioned the Unites States or "America", but made a general reference to the international community.

9. To date there has, for instance, never been any mention, in any UN Security Council Resolution dealing with sexual violence in conflict zones, of the fact that women themselves could be perpetrators. In other words, men are always considered as perpetrators "by default".

CHAPTER 3

1. Because of my interviewing strategy, I almost never knew in advance whether the person I was meeting was a survivor, a perpetrator, both or neither. So the same security measures were applied for each interview.

2. The death penalty sentence was, however, not always carried out, notably because most cases were not reported. One former FNL female combatant I spoke with told me she had been raped by one fellow combatant but never reported the rape because she thought death penalty "was a bit too harsh a punition" (Violette 2011, interview).

3. The report on "Investigation of Intelligence Activities at Abu Ghraib" published in 2004 states, for instance, page 4: "Most, though not all, of the violent or sexual abuses occurred separately from scheduled interrogations and did not focus on persons held for intelligence purposes. No policy, directive or doctrine directly or indirectly caused violent or sexual abuse. In these cases, Soldiers knew they were violating the approved techniques and procedures. Confusion about what interrogation techniques were authorized resulted from the proliferation of guidance and information from other theaters of operation; individual interrogator experiences in

other theaters; and, the failure to distinguish between interrogation operations in other theaters and Iraq". The report is available at: http://www.globalsecurity.org/intell/library/reports/2004/intell-abu-ghraib_ar15-6.pdf (checked on 25 April 2018).

4. See also Sooka, 2014, who quotes several male survivors of sexual violence in the hands of Sri Lankan militaries, whose torturers were drunk.

5. In the Johnson et al. study on wartime sexual violence in Eastern DRC, for instance, only 2% of male survivors said perpetrators were "non-combatant strangers", vs. 14.4% immediate or extended family members and 85.9% combatants (2010: 557).

6. "We called them like this because they had to stay there without moving" (Déo 2011, interview).

7. According to the study conducted by Johnson et al. (2010) in Eastern DRC, 10% of perpetrators of wartime sexual violence against men are women.

8. Survivors of sexual violence seem to attract much more academic interest and media attention than perpetrators.

9. This is not to say, of course, that sexual violence against women is acceptable either legally or morally, but rather that in the discourses of most of the combatants I spoke with, sexually abusing women was considered as neither exceptional nor "against nature".

CHAPTER 4

1. Similar patterns might of course occur in cases of widespread sexual violence against women.

2. I have notably used some data produced by male survivors' groups, and available on the Refugee Law Project's website, http://www.refugeelawproject.org/.

3. This is consistent with survivors' narratives in many other settings, for instance, in Bosnia-Herzegovina. See, for instance, Karabegović (2010).

4. Maybe worth mentioning also is that being a woman in her forties, unmarried and without children, I embodied a social exception verging on the side of cultural transgression in this region of the world.

5. Aimable, for instance, told me that he had stopped going outside to meet other men and share beers with them, and that he preferred staying at home where he felt "safer" (interviewed in Bubanza Province, Burundi, 18 April 2010).

6. "Cutting" is an expression that was used during the Rwandan genocide, meaning being killed with a machete.

7. For instance, a survey by Johns Hopkins University, in cooperation with the Refugee Law Project in Uganda, surveyed 447 male refugees (99% from Congo) and found that 38.5% had experienced sexual violence at some point of their life (Dolan 2014a).

8. A minority of survivors I interviewed were on the contrary quite agitated and vocal.

9. Examples include the Agreement on DDR between the Government of Uganda and the Lord's Resistance Army (2008) and the Darfur Peace Agreement (2006). For more details, see "Guidance for Mediators. Addressing Conflict-Related Sexual

Violence in Ceasefire and Peace Agreements." New York: UN/DPA, Policy and Mediation Division, 2012.

10. Which of course also happens for survivors of other types of violence, including after genocide. See, for instance, Hatzfeld (2010), exploring the everyday interactions between *"rescapés"* and *"génocidaires"* in post-genocide Rwanda.

CHAPTER 5

1. Quotation marks are used to underscore the great fluidity and porosity of this conflict/post-conflict distinction, as the situation in Burundi at the time of writing, for instance, illustrates.

2. http://www.irinnews.org/Report/93399/DRC-UGANDA-Male-sexual-abuse-survivors-living-on-the-margins, checked on 27 April 2018.

3. Which can be translated as: "How can I say to my wife that they have turned me into a woman?" I have left the quote in French, as "femme" means both "wife" and "woman" in French, which makes this statement even more striking. Male survivor quoted by SERUKA's director, Bujumbura, Burundi, 25 April 2012.

4. During my visits in facilities of support organizations for victims of sexual violence, or hospital services dedicated to gynecology and sexual violence-related surgery, I have been struck by the absence of men. The only visible ones were either doctors and surgeons, or cleaning and maintenance staff.

5. Which could be read as follows: "the *very stereotype* portraying women as more peace oriented than men—regardless of its validity—may grant women with an increased capability of waging or promoting peace, through their higher ability to elicit support for peace proposals" (Maoz 2009, 520).

6. There are of course exceptions, like the Guantánamo/Abu Ghraib cases, but I would argue that the media focus on the sexual torture of Iraqi prisoners by female officers was not primarily produced by the sexual nature of these acts, but by the gender of their perpetrators. And, needless to say, the other (nonsexual) dimensions of torture used on Iraqi prisoners have been receiving ample media attention too.

7. "News" about events related to sorcery, sexual perversion or cannibalism in Africa are extremely common in Western media. An example among a million others, a BBC report called "CAR Cannibal: Why I Ate Man's Leg", 13 January 2014. http://www.bbc.com/news/world-africa-25708024 (checked 30 April 2018).

8. This was mentioned to me by an interviewee from the International Rescue Committee (Bujumbura, Burundi, 12 May 2012) as well as by another working for Caritas International (Goma, North Kivu, DRC, 03 May 2009).

9. This is a statement often heard and read, even in discourses otherwise acknowledging the important victimization of men. My point here is absolutely not to deny that across the world women and girls are the first targets of wartime sexual violence. However, because it is also known that men are a lot less likely to report acts of sexual violence, and because recent research has shown that in certain conflict areas the proportion of affected men and boys was more than half that of women and girls (see, for instance, Johnson et al. 2010), we also have to admit that it is impossible to say how large exactly that majority is.

CHAPTER 6

1. Apart from the staff working with UN agencies and in particular with the UNHCR, almost none of the medical staff I have interviewed, be it in conflict zones or in Western countries receiving applications for asylum from people victims of sexual torture, had heard about these guidelines.
2. PROTECT-ABLE Project (checked on 30 April 2018): http://protect-able.eu/.
3. The Bellevue/New York University Program for Survivors of Torture in New York City has compiled 204 cases of sexual assault out of a total of 2,019 male asylum seekers or refugees since 1996 (Anderson 2015).
4. See, for instance, the Wababa Project developed by Heal Africa (checked on 30 April 2018): https://healafrica.org/nehemiah-initiative/.

CHAPTER 7

1. Néhémie (interviewed in Goma, North Kivu, DRC, 3 May 2009), for instance, described it as "pure evil".
2. He was referring to the Burundian Commission Vérité et Réconciliation (Truth and Reconciliation Commission, CVR), which was finally established, after many years of debate, in May 2014.
3. And there are also concerns, regarding these civil cases, over who will pay in case perpetrators cannot or do not want to pay.
4. Of course, it also creates issues for female survivors of sexual violence perpetrated by women.
5. To the point that some of my Master students at the UNESCO Chair in Peaceful Resolution of Conflicts at the Université Nationale du Burundi told me during one of my courses in 2014 that "homosexuality doesn't exist in Burundi".
6. To date, 123 countries have ratified or accepted the Rome statute, among which are 34 African States, 19 Asia-Pacific States, 18 Eastern European States, 27 Latin America and Caribbean States and 25 Western European and other States.
7. Trial Chamber IX, "Public Redacted Version of Decision on the Legal Representatives for Victims Requests to Present Evidence and Views and Concerns and related requests" ICC-02/04-01/15-1199-Red, 6 March 2018. The full decision can be accessed at: https://www.icc-cpi.int/Pages/record.aspx?docNo=ICC-02/04-01/15-1199-Red (checked on 30 April 2018).
8. The Rome statute includes, for instance, a very detailed list of sexual violence crimes, of which both men and women can be victim, such as enforced sterilization, which is defined as the deprivation of "biological reproductive capacity" and can thus encompass common male experiences of wartime sexual violence like castration, genital beatings and so on (see Manivannan 2014, 662).

Bibliography

Ackermann, Alice. "The Idea and Practice of Conflict Prevention." *Journal of Peace Research* 40, no. 3 (2003): 339–47.
Adhiambo, Onyango Monica, and Karen Hampanda. "Social Constructions of Masculinity and Male Survivors of Wartime Sexual Violence: an Analytical Review." *International Journal of Sexual Health* 23, no. 4 (2011): 237–47.
Agger, Inger. "Sexual Torture of Political Prisoners: An Overview." *Journal of Traumatic Stress* 2, no. 3 (July 1989): 305–18.
Aginam, Obijiofor, and Martin R. Rupiya, eds. *HIV/AIDS and the Security Sector in Africa*. Tokyo: UNU Press, 2012.
Ahuka, O. L., Kasereka, M. C., and J. Rominjo. "Fistula and Traumatic Genital Injury from Sexual Violence in a Conflict Setting in Eastern Congo: Case Studies." *Reproductive Health Matters* 16, no. 31 (2008): 132–41.
Alison, Miranda. "Wartime Sexual Violence: Women's Human Rights and Questions of Masculinity." *Review of International Studies* 33 (2007): 75–90.
All Survivors Project. *Legacies and Lessons. Sexual Violence against Men and Boys in Sri Lanka and in Bosnia & Herzegovina*. Los Angeles: UCLA, 2017.
Amir, Menachem. *Patterns in Forcible Rape*. Chicago: University of Chicago Press, 1971.
Amnesty International. *"I Wanted to Die." Syria's Torture Survivors Speak Out*. London: Amnesty International, March 2012.
Amnesty International. *"Just Tell Me What to Confess To," Torture and Other Ill-Treatment by Burundi's Police and Intelligence Service since April 2015*. London: Amnesty International, August 2015.
Anand, Dibyesh. "Anxious Sexualities: Masculinity, Nationalism and Violence." *British Journal of Politics and International Relations* 9, no. 2 (2007): 257–69.
Anderson, Pauline. "Male Sexual Assault Victims at Particularly High PTSD Risk." *Save*, May 19, 2015. http://www.saveservices.org/2015/05/male-sexual-assault-victims-at-particularly-high-ptsd-risk/.

Anderson, Ronald E. *Human Suffering and Quality of Life, Conceptualizing Stories and Statistics*. New York: Springer, 2014.

Askin, Kelly D. "Sexual Violence in Decisions and Indictments of the Yugoslav and Rwandan Tribunals: Current Status." *The American Journal of International Law* 93, no. 1 (January 1999): 97–123.

Barker, Gary, and Christine Ricardo. "Young Men and the Construction of Masculinity in Sub-Saharan Africa: Implications for HIV/AIDS, Conflict, and Violence." *Social Development Papers, Conflict Prevention & Reconstruction*, paper no. 26, June 2005.

Barrett, Frank J. "The Organizational Construction of Hegemonic Masculinity: The Case of the US Navy." *Gender, Work and Organization* 3, no. 3 (1996): 129–42.

Bassiouni, Cherif. "Final Report of the United Nations Commission of Experts established pursuant to Security Council Resolution 780 (1992)." S/1994/674/Add.2 (Vol. 1 and 5) December, 28 1994.

Baum, Steven K. *The Psychology of Genocide. Perpetrators, Bystanders, and Rescuers*. New York: Cambridge University Press, 2008.

Beasley, Chris. "Mind the Gap." *Australian Feminist Studies* 28, no. 75 (2013): 108–24.

Belkin, Aaron, and Carver Terrell. "Militarized Masculinities and the Erasure of Violence." *International Feminist Journal of Politics* 14, no. 4 (2012): 558–67.

Betancourt, Theresa S., Borisova, Ivelina I., de la Soudière, Marie, and John Williamson. "Sierra Leone's Child Soldiers: War Exposures and Mental Health Problems by Gender." *Journal of Adolescent Health* 49, no. 1 (July 2011): 21–28.

Björkdahl, Annika, and Johanna Mannergren Selimovic. "Feminist Ethnographic Research: Excavating Narratives of Wartime Rape." In *Ethnographic Peace Research, Approaches and Tensions*, 43–64. Basingstoke: Palgrave Macmillan, 2018.

Bjørnlund, Matthias. "'A Fate Worse Than Dying': Sexual Violence during the Armenian Genocide." In *Brutality and Desire: War and Sexuality in Europe's Twentieth Century*, edited by Dagmar Herzog, 16–58. Basingstoke: Palgrave Macmillan, 2011.

Bracewell, Wendy. "Rape in Kosovo: Masculinity and Serbian Nationalism." *Nations and Nationalism* 6, no. 4 (2000): 563–90.

Brodeur, Jean-Paul. *Violence and Racial Prejudice in the Context of Peacekeeping. A Study Prepared for the Commission of Inquiry into the Deployment of Canadian Forces to Somalia*. Ottawa: Minister of Public Works and Government Services, 1997.

Browning, Christopher. *Ordinary Men: Reserve Police Battalion 101 and the Final Solution in Poland*. New York: HarperPerennial, 1993.

Brownmiller, Susan. *Against Our Will: Men, Women and Rape*. New York: Ballentine Books, 1975.

Buss, Doris E. "Rethinking 'Rape as a Weapon of War'." *Feminist Legal Studies* 17 (2009): 145–63.

Butler, Christopher K., Gluch, Tali, and Neil J. Mitchell. "Security Forces and Sexual Violence. A Cross-National Analysis of a Principal-Agent Argument." *Journal of Peace Research* 44, no. 6 (2007): 669–87.

Butler, Judith. *Gender Trouble, Feminism and the Subversion of Identity.* New York: Routledge, 1990.
Butler, Judith. "Sexual Politics, Torture, and Secular Times." *The British Journal of Sociology* 59, no. 1 (2008): 1–23.
Butler, Judith. "Bodily Vulnerability, Coalitions, and Street Politics." *Critical Studies* 37, no. 1 (September 2014): 99–119.
Byrne, Bridget. "Towards a Gendered Understanding of Conflict." *IDS Bullettin*, July 1996: 31–40.
Cahn, Naomi, and Fionnuala Ní Aoláin. "Hirsh Lecture: Gender, Masculinities, and Transition in Conflicted Societies." *New England Law Review* 44 (2009): 19p.
Card, Claudia. "Rape as a Weapon of War." *Hypatia* 11, no. 4 (1996): 5–18.
Carlson, Eric Stener. "Sexual Assault on Men in War." *The Lancet* 349 (1997): 129.
Carlson, Eric Stener. "The Hidden Prevalence of Male Sexual Assault during War Observations on Blunt Trauma to the Male Genitals." *British Journal of Criminology* 46 (2006): 16–25.
Carpenter, R. Charli "Recognizing Gender-Based Violence against Civilian Men and Boys in Conflict Situations." *Security Dialogue* 37, no. 1 (2006): 83–103.
Carruthers, Susan L. "Tribalism and Tribulation. Media Cnstructions of 'African Savagery' and 'Western Humanitarianism' in the 1990s." In *Reporting War, Journalism in Wartime*, edited by Stuart Allan and Barbie Zelizer, 155–73. London: Routledge, 2004.
Center for Constitutional Rights. "Military Commissions Act of 2006: A Summary of the Law." New York, January 11, 2010.
Chang, Irish. *The Rape of Nanking.* Harmondsworth: Penguin, 1997.
Charlesworth, Hilary. "Are Women Peaceful? Reflections on the Role of Women in Peace-Building." *Feminist Legal Studies* 16, no. 3 (2008): 347–61.
Chodorow, Nancy J. "The Enemy Outside: Thoughts on the Psychodynamics of Extreme Violence with Special Attention to Men and Masculinity." In *Masculinity Studies and Feminist Theory. New Directions*, edited by Judith Kegan Gardiner, 235–60. New York: Columbia University Press, 2002.
Christian, M., Safari, O., Ramazani, P., Burnham, G., and N. Glass. "Sexual and Gender Based Violence against Men in the Democratic Republic of Congo: Effects on Survivors, Their Families and the Community." *Medicine, Conflict and Survival* 27, no. 4 (2011): 227–46.
Chynoweth, Sarah K., Freccero, Julie, and Heleen Touquet. "Sexual Violence against Men and Boys in Conflict and Forced Displacement: Implications for the Health Sector." *Reproductive Health Matters*, 2017. doi: 10.1080/09688080.2017.1401895.
Clark, Janine N. "A Crime of Identity: Rape and Its Neglected Victims." *Journal of Human Rights* 13, no. 2 (2014): 146–69.
Cockburn, Cynthia. "The Continuum of Violence. A Gender Perspective on War and Peace." In *Sites of Violence. Gender and Conflict Zones*, edited by Wenona M. Giles and Jennifer Hyndman, 24–44. Berkeley and Los Angeles: University of California Press, 2004a.

Cockburn, Cynthia. *The Line. Women, Partition and the Gender Order in Cyprus.* London: Zed Books, 2004b.

Cohen, Dara Kay. "Explaining Rape during Civil War: Cross-National Evidence (1980–2009)." *American Political Science Review* 107, no. 3 (2013): 461–77.

Cohen, Dara Kay, Hoover Green, Amelia, and Elisabeth Jean Wood. "Wartime Sexual Violence. Misconceptions, Implications, and Ways Forward." *United States Institute of Peace*, Special Report 323, February 2013.

Collins, Randall. *Violence: A Microsociological Theory.* Princeton and Oxford: Princeton University Press, 2008.

Connell, R. W. *Gender and Power.* Cambridge and Oxford: Polity Press and Blackwell Publishers, 1987.

Connell, R. W. *Masculinities.* Cambridge, MA: Polity, 1995.

Connell, R. W. "Arms and the Man: Using the New Research on Masculinity to Understand Violence and Promote Peace in the Contemporary World." In *Male Roles, Masculinities and Violence. A Culture of Peace Perspective*, edited by Ingeborg Breines, R. W. Connell and Ingrid Eide, 21–33. Paris: Presses Universitaires de France and UNESCO Publishing, 2000.

Connell, R. W. "Globalization, Imperialism and Masculinities." In *Handbook of Studies on Men & Masculinities,* edited by Michael S. Kimmel, Jeff Hearn and R. W. Connell, 71–89. London, New Delhi, Thousand Oaks: Sage, 2005.

Connell, R. W., and James W. Messerschmidt. "Hegemonic Masculinity: Rethinking the Concept." *Gender and Society* 19, no. 6 (2005): 829–59.

Conway, Daniel. "The Masculine State in Crisis. State Response to War Resistance in Apartheid South Africa." *Men and Masculinities* 10, no. 4 (2008): 422–39.

Cornwall, Andrea. "Gendered Identities and Gender Ambiguity among Travestis in Salvador, Brazil." in *Dislocating Masculinity, Comparative Ethnographies*, edited by Andrea Cornwall and Nancy Lindisfarne, 111–32. London and New York: Routledge, 1994.

Cornwall, Andrea, and Nancy Lindisfarne. "Dislocating Masculinity, Gender, Power and Anthropology." In *Dislocating Masculinity, Comparative Ethnographies*, edited by Andrea Cornwall and Nancy Lindisfarne, 11–47. London and New York: Routledge, 1994.

Coulter, Chris. "Female Fighters in the Sierra Leone War: Challenging the Assumptions." *Feminist Review* 88 (2008): 54–73.

Daley, Patricia O. *Gender and Genocide in Burundi. The Search for Spaces of Peace in the Great Lakes Region.* Bloomington: Indiana University Press, 2008.

Dauphinée, Elizabeth. *The Ethics of Researching War. Looking for Bosnia.* Manchester and New York: Manchester University Press, 2007.

de Brouwer, Anne-Marie, Ku, Charlotte, Romkens, Renée, and Larissa van den Herik, eds. *Sexual Violence as an International Crime; Interdisciplinary Approaches.* Cambridge, Antwerp, Portland: Intersentia, 2005.

Del Zotto, A., and Adam Jones. "Male-on-Male Sexual Violence in Wartime: Human Rights' Last Taboo?" Paper presented to the Annual Convention of the International Studies Association (ISA), New Orleans, LA, March 23–27, 2002. http://adamjones.freeservers.com/malerape.htm.

Dennis, J. P. "Women Are Victims, Men Make Choices: The Invisibility of Men and Boys in the Global Sex Ttrade." *Gender Issues* 25 (2008): 11–25.
Department of Defense. *Sexual Assault Prevention and Response, Department of Defense Annual Report on Sexual Assault in the Military*. Vol. 1. Washington, 2012. http://www.sapr.mil/public/docs/reports/FY12_DoD_SAPRO_Annual_Report_on_Sexual_Assault-VOLUME_ONE.pdf.
Deschamps, Marie, Jallow, Hassan B., and Yasmin Sooka. "Taking Action on Sexual Exploitation and Abuse by Peacekeepers. Report of an Independent Review on Sexual Exploitation and Abuse by International Peacekeeping Forces in the Central African Republic." New York: United Nations, December 17, 2015.
Detraz, Nicole. *International Security and Gender*. Cambridge: Polity, 2012.
Dodd, Vikram. "Torture by the Book. The Pattern of Abuse of Iraqi Prisoners Follows Established CIA Interrogation Techniques." *The Guardian*, May 6, 2004.
Dolan, Chris. "War Is Not Yet Over. Community Perceptions of Sexual Violence and Its Underpinnings in Eastern DRC." *International Alert*, November 2010.
Dolan, Chris. "Into the Mainstream: Addressing Sexual Violence against Men and Boys in Conflict, A briefing paper prepared for the workshop held at the Overseas Development Institute." London, May 14, 2014a.
Dolan, Chris. "Letting Go of the Gender Binary: Charting New Pathways for Humanitarian Interventions on Gender-based Violence." *International Review of the Red Cross* 96, no. 894 (2014b): 485–501.
Dowd, Nancy E. *The Man Question, Male Subordination and Privilege*. New York: New York University Press, 2010.
Dudink, Stefan, Hagemann, Karen, and John Tosh, eds. *Masculinities in Politics and War. Gendering Modern History*. Manchester: Manchester University Press, 2004.
Duffield, Mark. *Global Governance and the New Wars: The Merging of Development and Security*. London: Zed Books, 2001.
Dumas, M. "Viols au Congo: Le jour où ils ont fait de moi une femme." *Rue 89*, August 2, 2011.
Duroch, Françoise, McRae, Melissa, and Rebecca F. Grais. "Description and Consequences of Sexual Violence in Ituri Province, Democratic Republic of Congo." *International Health and Human Rights* 11, no. 5 (2011).
Duroch, Françoise, and Catrin Schulte-Hillen. "Care for Victims of Sexual Violence, An Organization Pushed to Its Limits: The Case of Médecins Sans Frontières." *International Review of the Red Cross* 96, no. 894 (2014): 601–24.
Eager, Paige Whaley. *From Freedom Fighters to Terrorist. Women and Political Violence*. Aldershot: Ashgate, 2008.
Edström, Jerker, Dolan, Chris, Shahrokh, Thea, and David Onen. "Therapeutic Activism: Men of Hope Refugee Association Uganda Breaking the Silence over Male Rape in Conflict-related Sexual Violence." *Institute of Development Studies*, Evidence Report no. 182, March 2016.
Enloe, Cynthia. *Does Khaki Become You? The Militarization of Women's Lives*. New York: South End Press, 1983.
Enloe, Cynthia. *The Morning After. Sexual Politics at the End of the Cold War*. Berkeley: University of California Press, 1993.

Enloe, Cynthia. *Maneuvers: The International Politics of Militarising Women's Lives.* Berkeley and Los Angeles: University of California Press, 2000.

Eriksson Baaz, Maria. "Why Do Soldiers Rape? Masculinity, Violence, and Sexuality in the Armed Forces in the Congo (DRC)." *International Studies Quarterly* 53 (2009): 495–518.

Eriksson Baaz, Maria, and Maria Stern. "Understanding and Addressing Conflict-Related Sexual Violence. Lessons Learned from the Democratic Republic of Congo." *The Nordic Africa Institute*, Policy Notes, 3, 2010a.

Eriksson Baaz, Maria, and Maria Stern. "The Complexity of Violence. A Critical Analysis of Sexual Violence in the Democratic Republic of Congo (DRC)." *SIDA Working Paper on Gender Based Violence*, May 2010b.

Eriksson Baaz, Maria, and Maria Stern. *Sexual Violence as a Weapon of War? Perceptions, Prescriptions, Problem in the Congo and Beyond.* London: Zed Books, 2013.

Faligot, Roger. *Guerre Spéciale en Europe: Le Laboratoire Irlandais.* Paris: Flammarion, 1992.

Fanon, Franz. *The Wretched of the Earth.* New York: Grove Press, 1963.

Feldman, Allen. *Formations of Violence. The Narrative of the Body and Political Terror in Northern Ireland.* Chicago: The University of Chicago Press, 1991.

Féron, Élise. "How Can the Dividends of Conflict Be Perpetuated: The Paths to Reconversion Taken by Northern Irish Paramilitaries." *International Social Science Journal* 191 (March 2007): 225–39.

Féron, Élise. "Suffering in Silence? The Silencing of Sexual Violence Against Men in War Torn Countries." In *World Suffering and Quality of Life*, edited by Ron Anderson, 31–44. New York: Springer, 2015.

Féron, Élise. "Gender and Peace Negotiations: Why Gendering Peace Negotiations Multiplies Opportunities for Reconciliation." In *Negotiating Reconciliation in Peacemaking: Quandaries of Relationship Building*, edited by Mark Anstey and Valérie Rosoux, 93–109. New York: Springer, 2017.

Féron, Élise, and Michel Hastings. "The New Hundred Years Wars." *International Social Science Journal* 177 (September 2003): 490–500.

Ford, Nathan, Mills, Edward J., Rony, Zachariah, and Ross Upshur. "Ethics of Conducting Research in Conflict Settings." *Conflict and Health* 3, no. 7 (2009). doi:10.1186/1752-1505-3-7

Gettleman, Jeffrey. "Symbol of Unhealed Congo: Male Rape Victims." *New York Times*, August 5, 2009.

Gibbings, Sheri Lynn. "No Angry Women at the United Nations: Political Dreams and the Cultural Politics of United Nations Security Council Resolution 1325." *International Feminist Journal of Politics* 13, no. 4 (2011): 522–38.

Giles, Wenona Mary, and Jennifer Hyndman. *Sites of Violence: Gender and Conflict Zones.* Berkeley: University of California Press, 2004.

Goldstein, Joshua S. *War and Gender. How Gender Shapes the War System and Vice Versa.* Cambridge: Cambridge University Press, 2004.

Gorris, E. A. P. "Invisible Victims? Where Are Male Victims of Conflict-Related Sexual Violence in International Law and Policy?" *European Journal of Women's Studies* 22, no. 4 (2015): 412–27.

Gottschall, Jonathan. "Explaining Wartime Rape." *The Journal of Sex Research* 41, no. 2 (2004): 129–36.

Grey, R., and L. J. Shepherd. "Stop Rape Now?": Masculinity, Responsibility, and Conflict-related Sexual Violence." *Men and Masculinities* 16, no. 1 (2012): 115–35.

Hamber, Brandon. "There Is a Crack in Everything: Problematising Masculinities, Peacebuilding and Transitional Justice." *Human Rights Review* 17 (2016): 9–34.

Hatzfeld, Jean. *Machete Season: The Killers in Rwanda Speak*. New York: Farrar, Straus and Giroux, 2005.

Hatzfeld, Jean. *The Antelope's Strategy: Living in Rwanda after the Genocide*. New York: Picador, 2010.

Hawkesworth, Mary. *Globalization and Feminist Activism*. Lanham: Rowman & Littlefield Publishers, 2006.

Hearn, Jeff, Andersson, Kjerstin, and Malcolm Cowburn. "Background Paper on Guidelines for Researchers on Doing Research with Perpetrators of Sexual Violence." Linköping: Sexual Violence Research Initiative, and The Global Forum for Health Research, November 2007.

Heineman, Elizabeth D. *Sexual Violence in Conflict Zones, from the Ancient World to the Era of Human Rights*. Philadelphia: University of Pennsylvania Press, 2011.

Higate, Paul. "Peacekeepers, Masculinities, and Sexual Exploitation." *Men and Masculinities* 10, no. 1 (2007): 99–119.

Hooper, Charlotte. *Manly States. Masculinities, International Relations, and Gender Politics*. New York: Columbia University Press, 2001.

Houge, Anette Bringedal. "Subversive Victims? The (non)Reporting of Sexual Violence against Male Victims During the War in Bosnia-Herzegovina." *Nordicom Review* 29, no. 1 (2008): 63–78.

Hugman, Richard, Pittaway, Eileen, and Linda Bartolomei. "When 'Do No Harm' Is Not Enough: The Ethics of Research with Refugees and Other Vulnerable Groups." *British Journal of Social Work* 41, no. 7 (2011): 1271–87.

Human Rights Watch. "Soldiers Who Rape, Commanders Who Condone. Sexual Violence and Military Reform in the Democratic Republic of Congo." New York, July 2009.

Human Rights Watch. "Syria: Sexual Assault in Detention." June 15, 2012.

Human Rights Watch. "'We Will Teach You a Lesson', Sexual Violence against Tamils by Sri Lankan Security Forces." New York, February 26, 2013.

Hutchings, Kimberly. "Cognitive Short Cuts." In *Rethinking the Man Question, Sex, Gender and Violence in International Relations*, edited by Jane L. Parpart and Marysia Zalewski, 23–46. London: Zed Books, 2008.

ICTJ. "The Accountability Gap on Sexual Violence in Kenya: Reforms and Initiatives Since the Post-Election Crisis." New York: ICTJ Briefing, April 2014.

ICTJ. "When No One Calls It Rape. Addressing Sexual Violence Against Men and Boys in Transitional Contexts." New York: ICTJ, December 2016.

Institute for International Criminal Investigations. "Guidelines for Investigating Conflict-Related Sexual and Gender-Based Violence Against Men and Boys," Den Haag: IICI, 2016.
IRIN. "DRC-Uganda: Luzolo, 'He Abused Me. The Pain was Awful'." August 2, 2011.
IRIN. "Health: Rape as a 'Weapon of War' Against Men." October 13, 2011.
Johnson, K., Asher, J., Rosborough, S., et al. "Association of Combatant Status and Sexual Violence with Health and Mental Health Outcomes in Postconflict Liberia." *JAMA* 300, no. 6, (August 2008): 676–90.
Johnson, Kirsten et al. "Association of Sexual Violence and Human Rights Violations with Physical and Mental Health in Territories of the Eastern Democratic Republic of the Congo." *JAMA* 304, no. 5 (August 4, 2010): 553–62.
Jones, Adam. "Straight as a Rule. Heteronormativity, Gendercide, and the Noncombatant Male." *Men and Masculinities* 8, no. 4 (April 2006): 451–69.
Kapur, Ratna. "The Tragedy of Victimization Rhetoric: Resurrecting the 'Native' Subject in International/Post-Colonial Feminist Legal Politics." *Harvard Human Rights Journal*: 15 (2002): 1–37.
Karabegović, Dženana. "Bosnia: Struggle to Overcome Male Rape Taboo." *Institute for War and Peace Reporting*, April 16, 2010.
King, Diane E., and Lindia Stone. "Lineal Masculinity: Gendered Memory with Patriliny." *American Ethnologist* 37, no. 2 (2010): 323–36.
King, Kimi Lynn, and Megan Greening. "Gender Justice or Just Gender? The Role of Gender in Sexual Assault Decisions at the International Criminal Tribunal for the Former Yugoslavia." *Social Science Quarterly* 88, no. 5 (December 2007): 1049–71.
Kippenberg, Juliane. "Seeking Justice: The Prosecution of Sexual Violence in the Congo War." *Human Rights Watch*, March 17, 2005.
Kirby, Paul. "How Is Rape a Weapon of War? Feminist International Relations, Modes of Critical Explanation and the Study of Wartime Sexual Violence." *European Journal of International Relations* 19, no. 4 (2012): 797–821.
Klarreich, Kathie. *United Nations in Haiti: When Protectors Turn Predators*. Washington: 100 Reporters, January 12, 2015.
Kleinman, Arthur. "The Violences of Everyday Life. The Multiple Forms and Dynamics of Social Violence." In *Violence and Subjectivity*, edited by Veena Das, Arthur Kleinman, Mamphela Ramphele and Pamela Reynolds, 226–41. Berkeley: University of California Press, 2000.
Krishnaswamy, Revathi. *Effeminism: The Economy of Colonial Desire*. Ann Arbor: University of Michigan Press, 1998.
Kristoff, Nicholas. "Genocide in Slow Motion." *New York Review of Books* 52, no. 2 (2006).
Krug, Etienne G., Dahlberg, Linda L., Mercy, James A., Zwi, Anthony B. and Lozano Rafael, eds. *World Report on Violence and Health*, Geneva: World Health Organization, 2002.
Le Pape, Marc. "Suite à 'Viols en temps de guerre: les hommes aussi'." Paris: Centre de Réflexion sur l'Action et les Savoirs Humanitaires, Papers, January 23, 2012.

Leatherman, Janie. *Sexual Violence and Armed Conflict*. Cambridge: Polity Press, 2011.
Leiby, Michele. "The Promise and Peril of Primary Documents: Documenting Wartime Sexual Violence in El Salvador and Peru." In *Understanding and Proving International Sex Crimes*, edited by Morten Bergsmo, Alf Butenschø Skre and Elisabeth J. Wood, 315–66. Beijing: Torkel Opsahl Academic EPublisher, 2012.
Leiby, Michele L. "Wartime Sexual Violence in Guatemala and Peru." *International Studies Quarterly* 53, no. 2 (2009): 445–68.
Lentin, Ronit. "Introduction: (En)Gendering Genocides." In *Gender and Catastrophe*, edited by Lentin Ronit, 2–17. London: Zed Books, 1997.
Lewis, Dustin A. "Unrecognized Victims: Sexual Violence Against Men in Conflict Settings under International Law." *Wisconsin International Law Journal* 27, no. 1 (2009/2010): 1–49.
Lieder, K. Frances. "*Lights Out* and an Ethics of Spectatorship, or Can the Subaltern Scream?" *Peace and Change, A Journal of Peace Research* 40, no. 4 (October 2015): 517–38.
Loncar, Mladen, Henigsberg, Neven, and Pero Hrabac. "Mental Health Consequences in Men Exposed to Sexual Abuse During the War in Croatia and Bosnia." *Journal of Interpersonal Violence* 25, no. 2 (2010): 191–203.
Lunde, Inge, Rasmussen, Ole Vedel, Lindholm, Jorgen, and Gorm Wagner. "Gonadal and Sexual Functions in Tortured Greek Men." *Danish Medical Bulletin* 27, no. 5 (November 1980): 243–45.
Lwambo, Desiree. "'Before the War, I Was a Man': Men and Masculinities in Eastern DR Congo." *Gender and Development* 21, no. 1, (March 2013): 47–66.
MacDonald, Eileen. *Shoot the Women First*. New York: Random House, 1991.
MacKenzie, Megan. "Securitizing Sex? Towards a Theory of the Utility of Wartime Sexual Violence." *International Feminist Journal of Politics* 12, no. 2 (2010): 202–21.
Manivannan, Anjali. "Seeking Justice for Male Victims of Sexual Violence in Armed Conflict." *International Law and Politics* 46 (2014): 635–79.
Maoz, Ifat. "The Women and Peace Hypothesis? The Effect of Opponent Negotiators' Gender on the Evaluation of the Compromise Solutions in the Israeli-Palestinian Conflict." *International Negotiation* 14 (2009): 519–36.
Mayer, Tamar, ed. *Gender Ironies of Nationalism: Sexing the Nation*. London: Routledge, 2000.
McClure, Nicole R. "Injured Bodies, Silenced Voices: Reclaiming Personal Trauma and the Narration of Pain in Northern Ireland." *Peace and Change, A Journal of Peace Research* 40, no. 4 (October 2015): 497–516.
McGuffin, John. *The Guineapigs*. London: Penguin Books, 1974.
Mechanic, Eli. "Why Gender Still Matters: Sexual Violence and the Need to Confront Militarized Masculinities." *Insights*, Partnerships Africa Canada, December 2004.
Médecins Sans Frontières. *Shattered Lives. Immediate Medical Care Vital for Sexual Violence Victims*. Brussels, March 2009.
Meger, Sara. *Rape Loot Pillage, The Political Economy of Sexual Violence in Armed Conflict*. Oxford: Oxford University Press, 2016.

Men of Peace Association. *Together We Can, 2014 Activity Report*. Kampala, 2014. http://www.refugeelawproject.org/files/others/Men_of_Peace_2014_report.pdf.

Mervyn, Christian, Safari, Octave, Ramazani, Paul, Burnham, Gilbert, and Nancy Glass. "Sexual and Gender Based Violence against Men in the Democratic Republic of Congo: Effects on Survivors, Their Families and the Community." *Medicine, Conflict and Survival* 27, no. 4 (2011): 227–46.

Messerschmidt, James W. *Masculinity and Crime: Critique and Reconceptualization of Theory*. Lanham: Rowman and Littlefield, 1993.

Misra, Amalendu. *The Landscape of Silence. Sexual Violence Against Men in War*. London: Hurst, 2015.

Moolman, Benita. "The Reproduction of an 'Ideal' Masculinity through Gang Rape on the Cape Flats: Understanding Some Issues and Challenges for Effective Redress." *Agenda, Contemporary Activism*, 60 (2004): 109–24.

Morrell, Robert. "South African Men in the Post-Apartheid Era: Responses, Dangers and Opportunities." In *Male Roles, Masculinities and Violence. A Culture of Peace Perspective*, edited by Ingeborg Breines, R. W. Connell and Ingrid Eide, 107–115. Paris: Presses Universitaires de France and UNESCO Publishing, 2000.

Morrell, Robert, and Sandra Swart. "Men in the Third World. Post-Colonial Perspectives on Masculinity." In *Handbook of Studies on Men & Masculinities*, edited by Michael S. Kimmel, Jeff Hearn and R. W. Connell, 90–113. London, New Delhi, Thousand Oaks: Sage, 2005.

Mullins, Christopher W. "'He Would Kill Me with His Penis': Genocidal Rape in Rwanda as a State Crime." *Critical Criminology: An International Journal* 17, no. 1 (2009): doi: 10.1007/s10612-008-9067-3.

Munn, Jamie. "National Myths and the Creation of Heroes." In *Rethinking the Man Question, Sex, Gender and Violence in International Relations*, edited by Jane L. Parpart and Marysia Zalewski, 143–61. London: Zed Books, 2008.

Murray, Raymond, and Dennis Faul. *The Hooded Men: British Torture in Ireland, August, October 1971* (1st edition 1974). Dublin: Wordwell Books, 2016.

Myrttinen, Henri. "Disarming Masculinities." *Disarmament Forum*, 4 (2003): 37–46.

Myrttinen, Henri. "Sexual Violence Has Many Victims, Both Male and Female. We Need to Support Them All." *The Guardian*, April 2, 2014.

Nagel, Joane. "Masculinity and Nationalism: Gender and Sexuality in the Making of Nations." *Ethnic and Racial Studies* 21, no. 2 (1998): 242–69.

Naniwe-Kaburahe, Assumpta. "The Institution of Bashingantahe in Burundi." In *Traditional Justice and Reconciliation after Violent Conflict. Learning from African Experiences*, edited by Luc Huyse and Mark Salter, 149–80. Stockholm: International Institute for Democracy and Electoral Assistance, 2008.

Ní Aoláin, Fionnuala, Cahn, Naomi, and Dina Haynes. "Gender, Masculinities and Transition in Conflicted Societies." In *Exploring Masculinities. Feminist Legal Theory Reflections*, edited by Martha Albertson Fineman and Michael Thomson, 127–44. Farnham: Ashgate, 2013.

Nizich, Ivana. "Violations of the Rules of War by Bosnian Croat and Muslim Forces in Bosnia-Herzegovina." *Hastings Women's Law Journal* 5, no. 1 (1994): 25–52.

Nordås, Ragnhild. "Preventing Conflict-Related Sexual Violence." Oslo: PRIO Policy Brief 2, 2013.
Nusair, Isis. "Gendered, Racialized, and Sexualized Torture at Abu Ghraib." In *Feminism and War: Confronting US Imperialism*, edited by Robin L Riley, Chandra Talpade Mohanty and Minnie Bruce Pratt, 179–93. London: Zed Books, 2008.
Obote-Odora, Alex. "Rape and Sexual Violence in International Law: ICTR Contribution." *New England Journal of International and Comparative Law* 12, no. 1 (2005): 135–59.
Okot, A. C., Amony, I., and G. Otim. *Suffering in Silence: A Study of Sexual and Gender Based Violence (SGBV) In Pabbo Camp, Gulu District, Northern Uganda.* New York: UNICEF, District Sub-Working Group on SGBV, 2005.
Oloya, Opiyo. *Child to Soldier: Stories from Joseph Kony's Lord's Resistance Army.* Toronto: University of Toronto Press, 2013.
Oosterhoff, Pauline, Zwanikken, Prisca, and Evert Ketting. "Sexual Torture of Men in Croatia and Other Conflict Situations: An Open Secret." *Reproductive Health Matters* 12, no. 23 (2004): 68–77.
Oosterveld, Valerie. "The Gender Jurisprudence of the Special Court for Sierra Leone: Progress in the Revolutionary United Front Judgments." *Cornell International Law Journals* 44 (2011): 49–74.
OSCE. "Combating Impunity for Conflict-Related Sexual Violence in Bosnia and Herzegovina: Progress and Challenges. An Analysis of Criminal Proceedings Before the Courts of the Federation of Bosnia and Herzegovina, Republika Srpska and Brčko District BiH Between 2004 and 2014." Vienna: OSCE, July 13, 2015.
Otto, Dianne. "The Exile of Inclusion: Reflections on Gender Issues in International Law over the Last Decade." *Melbourne Journal of International Law* 10, no. 1 (2009): 11–26.
Owens, Patricia. "Torture, Sex and Military Orientalism." *Third World Quarterly* 31, no. 7 (2010): 1041–56.
Paige, Karen, and Jeffrey Paige. *The Politics of Reproductive Ritual.* Berkeley: University of California Press, 1981.
Partis-Jennings, Hannah. "The (in)Security of Gender in Afghanistan's Peacebuilding Project: Hybridity and Affect." *International Feminist Journal of Politics* 19, no. 4 (2017): 411–25.
Peel, M., Mahtani, A., Hinshelwood, G., and D. Forrest. "The Sexual Abuse of Men in Detention in Sri Lanka." *The Lancet* 355, (June 10, 2000): 2069–70.
Peel, Michael, ed. *Rape as a Method of Torture.* London: Medical Foundation for the Care of Victims of Torture, 2004.
Perlin, Jan. "The Guatemalan Historical Clarification Commission Finds Genocide." *ILSA Journal of International and Comparative Law* 6 (2000): 389–413.
Price, Lisa S. "Finding the Man in the Soldier-Rapist: Some Reflections on Comprehension and Accountability." *Women's Studies International Forum* 24, no. 2 (2001): 211–27.
Puar, Jasbir K. "Abu Ghraib: Arguing against Exceptionalism." *Feminist Studies* 30, no. 2 (2004): 522–34.

Punamaki, Raija-Leena. "Experiences of Torture, Means of Coping, and Levels of Symptoms among Palestinian Political Prisoners." *Journal of Palestine Studies* 17, no. 4 (1988): 81–96.

Quijano, Alejandra Azuero, and Jocelyn Kelly. "A Tale of Two Conflicts: an Unexpected Reading of Sexual Violence in Conflict through the Cases of Colombia and Democratic Republic of the Congo." In *Understanding and Proving International Sex Crimes*, edited by Morten Bergsmo, Alf Butenschø Skre and Elisabeth J. Wood, 437–93. Beijing: Torkel Opsahl Academic EPublisher, 2012.

Quijano, Aníbal. "Coloniality and Modernity/Rationality." *Cultural Studies* 21, no. 2–3 (2007): 168–78.

Razack, Sherene. "Outwhiting the White Guys: Men of Colour and Peacekeeping Violence." *UMKC Law Review* 71 (2002): 331–54.

Razack, Sherene. "How Is White Supremacy Embodied? Sexualized Racial Violence at Abu Ghraib." *Canadian Journal of Women and the Law* 17, no. 2 (2005): 343: 63.

Refugee Law Project. "Promoting Accountability for Conflict-Related Sexual Violence Against Men: A Comparative Legal Analysis of International and Domestic Laws Relating to IDP and Refugee Men in Uganda." Kampala: Refugee Law Project, Working Paper no. 24, July 2013a.

Refugee Law Project. *Report on the 1st South-South Institute on Sexual Violence Against Men and Boys in Conflict and Displacement*. Kampala: Refugee Law Project, April 8–12, 2013b. http://refugeelawproject.org/files/others/SSI_2013_report.pdf.

Refugee Law Project. "Male Survivors of Sexual Violence in Kampala Demand for Better Services." Kampala: Refugee Law Project, 2014.

Robinson, Sally. "Pedagogy of the Opaque: Teaching Masculinity Studies." In *Masculinity Studies and Feminist Theory. New Directions*, edited by Judith Kegan Gardiner, 141–60. New York: Columbia University Press, 2002.

Ross, Marlon B. (2002) "Race, Rape, Castration: Feminist Theories of Sexual Violence and Masculine Strategies of Black Protest." In *Masculinity Studies and Feminist Theory. New Directions*, edited by Judith Kegan Gardiner, 305–43. New York: Columbia University Press, 2002.

Rumbold, Victoria. *Sexual and Gender-Based Violence in Africa: Literature Review*. New York: Population Council, 2008.

Russell, Wynne, et al. "Care and Support of Male Survivors of Conflict-Related Sexual Violence: Background Paper." Pretoria: Sexual Violence Research Initiative, Briefing Paper 02/2011.

Sabo, Don. "The Study of Masculinities and Men's Health: An Overview." In *Handbook of Studies on Men & Masculinities,* edited by Michael S. Kimmel, Jeff Hearn and R. W. Connell, 326–52. London, New Delhi, Thousand Oaks: Sage, 2005.

Scarce, Michael. *Male on Male Rape. The Hidden Toll of Stigma and Shame*. Cambridge, MA: Perseus Publishing, 1997.

Scarry, Elaine. *The Body in Pain: The Making and Unmaking of the World*. Oxford: Oxford University Press, 1985.

Schwartz, Stephen. "Rape as a Weapon of War in the Former Yugoslavia." *Hastings Women's Law Journal* 5, no. 1 (1994): 69–88.

Seidler, V. J. *Young Men and Masculinities. Global Cultures and Intimate Lives.* London: Zed Books, 2006.
Seifert, Ruth. "War and Rape: A Preliminary Analysis." In *Mass Rape: The War Against Women in Bosnia-Herzegovina*, edited by Alexandra Stiglmayer, 54–72. Lincoln and London, University of Nebraska Press, 1993.
Sengupta, Shuddhabrata. "Kashmir's Abu Ghraib." In *Until My Freedom Has Come: The New Intifada in Kashmir*, edited by Sanjay Kak, 71–85. New Delhi: Penguin Books, 2011.
Seto, Donna. *No Place for a War Baby, The Global Politics of Children Born of Wartime Sexual Violence.* Farnham: Ashgate, 2013.
Shepherd, Laura. *Gender, Violence and Security: Discourse as Practice.* New York: Zed Books, 2008.
Silberschmidt, Margrethe. "Disempowerment of Men in Rural and Urban East Africa: Implications for Male Identity and Sexual Behavior." *World Development* 29, no. 4 (2001): 657–71.
Silent Scream (Nečujni Krik). Directed by Mirna Buljugić, Erna Mačkić and Dragana Erjavec. Sarajevo, Bosnia and Herzegovina: Balkan Investigative Reporting Network, 2014. Documentary.
Sivakumaran, Sandesh. "Male/Male Rape and the "Taint" of Homosexuality." *Human Rights Quarterly* 27, no. 4 (November 2005): 1274–1306.
Sivakumaran, Sandesh. "Sexual Violence against Men in Armed Conflict." *European Journal of International Law* 18, no. 2 (2007): 253–76.
Sivakumaran, Sandesh. "Lost in Translation: UN Responses to Sexual Violence against Men and Boys in Situations of Armed Conflict." *International Review of the Red Cross* 92, no. 877 (March 2010): 259–77.
Sjoberg, Laura. *Gendering Global Conflict, Toward a Feminist Theory of War.* New York: Columbia University Press, 2013.
Sjoberg, Laura. *Women as Wartime Rapists. Beyond Sensation and Stereotyping.* New York: New York University Press, 2016.
Sjoberg, Laura, and Caron E. Gentry. *Mothers, Monsters, Whores: Women's Violence in Global Politics.* London: Zed Books, 2007.
Skjelsbaek, Inger. "Sexual Violence and War: Mapping Out a Complex Relationship." *European Journal of International Relations* 7, no. 2 (2001a): 211–37.
Skjelsbæk, Inger. "SexualVviolence in Times of War: A New Challenge for Peace Operations?" *International Peacekeeping* 8, no. 2 (2001b): 69–84.
Skjelsbæk, Inger. "Victim and Survivor: Narrated Social Identities of Women Who Experienced Rape During the War in Bosnia-Herzegovina." *Feminism & Psychology* 16 (2006): 373–403.
Skjelsbæk, Inger. "Preventing Perpetrators. How to Go from Protection to Prevention of Sexual Violence in War?" Oslo: PRIO, Policy Brief, 03, 2013.
Skjelsbæk, Inger. "The Military Perpetrator. A Narrative Analysis of Sentencing Judgments on Sexual Violence Offenders at the International Criminal Tribunal for the Former Yugoslavia (ICTY)." *Journal of Social and Political Psychology* 3, no. 1 (2015). doi:10.5964/jspp.v3i1.273.

Solangon, Sarah, and Preeti Patel. "Sexual Violence Against Men in Countries Affected by Armed Conflict." *Conflict, Security & Development* 12, no. 4 (2012): 417–42.

Sooka, Yasmin. *An Unfinished War: Torture and Sexual Violence in Sri Lanka 2009–2014*. Sri Lanka: The Bar Human Rights Committee of England and Wales (BHRC) and The International Truth & Justice Project, 2014.

Stemple, Lara. "Male Rape and Human Rights." *Hastings Law Journal* 60 (2009): 605–45.

Stiglmayer, Alexandra, ed. *Mass Rape: The War Against Women in Bosnia-Herzegovina*. Lincoln and London: University of Nebraska Press, 1993.

Studzinsky, Silke. "Neglected Crimes: The Challenge of Raising Sexual and Gender-Based Crimes before the Extraordinary Chambers in the Courts of Cambodia." In *Gender in Transitional Justice*, edited by Susanne Buckley-Zistel and Ruth Stanley, 88–112. Basingstoke, UK, and New York: Palgrave Macmillan, 2012.

Swaine, Aisling. *Conflict-Related Violence Against Women—Transforming Transition*. Cambridge: Cambridge University Press, 2018.

Thomas, Calvin. "Reenfleshing the Bright Boys; or, How Male Bodies Matter to Feminist Theory." In *Masculinity Studies and Feminist Theory. New Directions*, edited by Judith Kegan Gardiner, 60–89. New York: Columbia University Press, 2002.

Touquet, Heleen, and Ellen Gorris. "Out of the Shadows? The Inclusion of Men and Boys in Conceptualizations of Wartime Sexual Violence." *Reproductive Health Matters* 47 (2016). doi: 10.1016/j.rhm.2016.04.007.

Trexler, Richard C. *Sex and Conquest: Gendered Violence, Political Order and the European Conquest of the Americas*. Ithaca, NY: Cornell University Press, 1995.

UK Foreign & Commonwealth Office. "International Protocol on the Documentation and Investigation of Sexual Violence in Conflict. Best Practice on the Documentation of Sexual Violence as a Crime or Violation of International Law." London: Foreign & Commonwealth Office, 2017. https://assets.publishing.service.gov.uk/government/uploads/system/uploads/attachment_data/file/598335/International_Protocol_2017_2nd_Edition.pdf.

UN. "Final Report of the Commission of Experts Established Pursuant to Security Council Resolution 780 (1992)." New York: United Nations, 1994. http://www.icty.org/x/file/About/OTP/un_commission_of_experts_report1994_en.pdf.

UN. "Report of Workshop on Sexual Violence against Men and Boys in Conflict Situations." New York: United Nations, Special Representative of the Secretary General on Sexual Violence in Conflict, July 25–26, 2013.

UN. "Conflict-Related Sexual Violence." New York: United Nations, 2016. http://www.un.org/en/events/elimination-of-sexual-violence-in-conflict/pdf/1494280398.pdf.

UN. "Conflict-Related Sexual Violence." New York: United Nations, 2015. http://www.securitycouncilreport.org/atf/cf/%7B65BFCF9B-6D27-4E9C-8CD3-CF6E4FF96FF9%7D/s_2015_203.pdf.

UNHCR. "Istanbul Protocol. Manual on the Effective Investigation and Documentation of Torture and Other Cruel, Inhuman or Degrading Treatment or Punishment."

Geneva: UNHCR, 2004. http://www.ohchr.org/Documents/Publications/training8Rev1en.pdf.
UNHCR. "Working with Men and Boy Survivors of Sexual and Gender-Based Violence in Forced Displacement." Geneva: UNHCR, 2012. http://www.refworld.org/cgi-bin/texis/vtx/rwmain?docid=5006aa262.
UNHCR. "'We Kept It in Our Heart': Sexual Violence against Men and Boys in the Syria Crisis." Geneva: UNHCR, October, 2017a.
UNHCR. "Conflict-Related Sexual Violence in Ukraine, 14 March 2014 to 31 January 2017." Geneva: UNHCR, February, 2017b.
UNSC Resolution 1325 (2000) available from http://www.un.org/en/ga/search/view_doc.asp?symbol=S/RES/1325(2000).
UNSC Resolution 1820 (2008) available from http://www.un.org/en/ga/search/view_doc.asp?symbol=S/RES/1820(2008).
UNSC Resolution 1888 (2009) available from http://www.un.org/en/ga/search/view_doc.asp?symbol=S/RES/1888(2009).
UNSC Resolution 1889 (2009) available from http://www.un.org/en/ga/search/view_doc.asp?symbol=S/RES/1889(2009).
UNSC Resolution 1960 (2010) available from http://www.un.org/en/ga/search/view_doc.asp?symbol=S/RES/1960(2010).
UNSC Resolution 2106 (2013) available from http://www.un.org/en/ga/search/view_doc.asp?symbol=S/RES/2106(2013).
UNSC Resolution 2122 (2013) available from http://www.un.org/en/ga/search/view_doc.asp?symbol=S/RES/2122(2013).
Vaittinen, Tiina. "The Power of the Vulnerable Body." *International Feminist Journal of Politics* 17, no. 1 (2015): 100–118.
Van Katwyk, Sasha. "The Fight over Impunity. How Political Forces are Misdirecting the Efforts to Establish Accountability in Africa." *The Atlantic International Studies Journal*, 6, (Spring 2010).
Vandecasteele, Mylène. "Congo: maintenant les hommes se font violer aussi." *L'Express*, August 9, 2011.
Vojdik, Valorie K. "Sexual Violence against Men and Women in War: A Masculinities Approach." *Nevada Law Journal* 14 (2014): 923–52.
Waller, James E. *Becoming Evil: How Ordinary People Commit Genocide and Mass Killing*. New York: Oxford University Press, 2002.
Watson, Callum. *Preventing and Responding to Sexual and Domestic Violence against Men: A Guidance Note for Security Sector Institutions*. Geneva: DCAF, 2014.
Watts, Charlotte, and Cathy Zimmerman. "Violence against Women: Global Scope and Magnitude." *The Lancet* 359 (April 6, 2002): 1232–37.
Weeks, Jeffrey. *Sexuality and Its Discontents: Meanings, Myths and Modern Sexualities*. New York: Routledge, 1985.
Weishut, Daniel J. N. "Sexual Torture of Palestinian Men by Israeli Authorities." *Reproductive Health Matters* 23, no. 46 (2015): 71–84.
Wendoh, Senorina, and Tina Wallace. "Rethinking Gender Mainstreaming in African NGOs and Communities." *Gender and Development* 13, no. 2 (2005): 70–79.

Whitworth, Sandra. "Militarized Masculinity and Post-Traumatic Stress Disorder." In *Rethinking the Man Question. Sex, Gender and Violence in International Relations*, edited by Jane L. Parpart and Marysia Zalewski, 109–26. London: Zed Books, 2008.

Williams, Walter L. *The Spirit and the Flesh: Sexual Diversity in American Indian Culture*. Boston: Beacon Press, 1986.

Wood, Elisabeth Jean. "The Ethical Challenges of Field Research in Conflict Zones." *Qualitative Sociology* 29, no. 3 (2006): 373–86.

Wood, Elisabeth Jean. "Armed Groups and Sexual Violence: When Is Wartime Rape Rare?" *Politics and Society* 37, no. 1 (2009): 131–62.

World Health Organization (WHO). *Global and Regional Estimates of Violence Against Women: Prevalence and Health Effects of Intimate Partner Violence and Non-Partner Sexual Violence*. Geneva: World Health Organization, Department of Reproductive Health and Research, 2013.

Yuval-Davis, Nira. "Gender and Nation." *Ethnic and Racial Studies* 16, no. 4 (1993): 621–32.

Yuval-Davis, Nira. *Gender and Nation*. London: Sage, 1997.

Zarkov, Dubravka. "The Body of the Other Man: Sexual Violence and the Construction of Masculinity, Sexuality and Ethnicity in the Croatian Media." In *Victims, Perpetrators or Actors? Gender, Armed Conflict and Political Violence*, edited by Caroline O. N. Moser and Fiona C. Clark, 69–82. London Zed Books, 2001.

Zawati, Hilmi M. "Impunity or Immunity: Wartime Male Rape and Sexual Torture as a Crime against Humanity." *Torture* 17, no. 1 (2007): 27–47.

List of quoted interviews

Aimable, Bubanza Province, Burundi, 18 April 2010.
Alexis, Bujumbura, Burundi, 20 April 2013.
Béatrice, Bujumbura, 3 May 2011.
Bernard, Bujumbura, Burundi, 21 April 2013.
Caritas International, Goma, North Kivu, DRC, 3 May 2009.
Claire, Bujumbura, Burundi, 9 May 2012.
Déo, Bujumbura, Burundi, 4 May 2011.
Didace, Bujumbura, Burundi, 22 May 2014.
Dionise, Bujumbura, Burundi, 3 May 2011.
Elias, Bukavu, South Kivu, 17 May 2014.
Fabiola, Goma, North Kivu, DRC, 30 April 2009.
Félicien, Bubanza Province, Burundi, 18 April 2010.
FOMULAC Hospital, Doctor, Katana, South Kivu, DRC, 29 April 2012.
Halla Tapio, Psychiatrist, Clinic for Immigrants at the Tampere City Mental Health Services, Finland, 24 February 2016.
International Rescue Committee, Staff, Bujumbura, 21 April 2013.
International Rescue Committee, Staff, Bujumbura, Burundi, 12 May 2012.
International Rescue Committee, Staff, Buvavu, South Kivu, DRC, 24 May 2014.
Jacques, Bujumbura, Burundi, 21 April 2013.
Jean Bosco, Bukavu, South Kivu, 6 May 2009.

Jean-Baptiste, Bujumbura, Burundi, 5 May 2011.
Jean-Claude, Bujumbura, Burundi, 4 May 2011.
Jean-Paul, Goma, North Kivu, DRC, 1 May 2009.
Jim, Belfast, Northern Ireland, 17 February 2006.
Joseph, Bujumbura, Burundi, 19 April 2013.
Kieran, Belfast, Northern Ireland, 5 November 2005.
Laurent, Bukavu, South Kivu, DRC, 17 May 2014.
Léonard, Bukavu, South Kivu, DRC, 17 May 2014.
Néhémie, Goma, North Kivu, DRC, 3 May 2009.
Nina, Bujumbura, Burundi, 18 April 2013.
Nturengaho, Director, Bujumbura, Burundi, 24 April 2012.
Panzi Hospital, Doctor, Bukavu, South Kivu, DRC, 30 April 2012.
Pascal, Bujumbura, Burundi, 20 April 2013.
Pat, Belfast, Northern Ireland, 30 March 2006.
René, Bukavu, South Kivu, DRC, 18 May 2014.
Richard, Goma, North Kivu, DRC, 3 May 2009.
Serge, Bubanza Province, Burundi, 18 April 2010.
SERUKA, Director, Bujumbura, Burundi, 25 April 2012.
Vincent, Bukavu, South Kivu, 18 May 2014.
Violette, Bubanza Province, Burundi, 15 April 2011.
Willy, Bukavu, South Kivu, 6 May 2009.

Index

Abu Ghraib, 8–9, 26–27, 29–30, 54, 55–56, 64–65, 69, 73–74, 167
Adhiambo, Onyango Monica, 101
Afghanistan, 9–10, 24–25, 58–59, 70–71, 132–133, 136, 167
African Centre for the Treatment and Rehabilitation of Torture Victims, 139
alcohol, 77, 85, 86, 101, 154
Algeria, 24–25, 28–29, 55–56
Alison, Miranda, 18–19
Amnesty International, 26–27
Anderson, Ronald E., 94
anti-terrorism, 6–7, 26, 27–28, 29, 47, 48
Argentina, 24–25
Armenia, 23–24, 28, 32, 68
Askin, Kelly D., 155–156
Association of Concentration Camp Torture Survivors, 138–139
Association of Women – Victims of War, 138–139
asymmetrical conflicts, 17, 53–54
asylum, 7, 8–9, 121–122, 136
Australian Civil-Military Centre, 134–135
Aztec, 22–23

Barker, Gary, 65, 70–71, 73–74
Bassiouni Report, 85
Belgium, 55–56
Belkin, Aaron, 52–53
Berdache, 32–33, 37–38
Bjørnlund, Matthias, 28, 68
bonding, 19–20, 30–31, 52, 66–67, 81, 92–93
Bosnia-Herzegovina, 8–10, 17, 19–20, 24, 27–28, 29, 32, 50, 68, 75–76, 76–77, 91–92, 112–113, 134–135, 137–139, 153–154, 156–158, 160–161
Britain. *See* United Kingdom
Browning, Christopher, 86
Burundi, 8–13, 24–25, 30, 32–34, 50–51, 61, 63, 64–65, 66–67, 69–70, 72–73, 76–77, 78, 91–92, 93, 98, 100, 103, 104, 105–106, 111–112, 118, 120, 136–137, 158, 159, 169
bush wives (men turned into), 41–42, 79, 81, 101–102, 107
Buss, Doris E., 19–20, 41
Butler, Christopher K., 64–65
Butler, Judith, 5, 36–37, 55–56, 98

Cambodia, 23–24, 138–139, 153–154
Card, Claudia, 19–20, 48–49

Care (NGO), 135
castration, 7, 21, 22–24, 26, 27–28, 29, 31, 32, 33–34, 35, 40–41, 42, 44–45, 47–48, 48–49, 54–55, 64–65, 84, 95–96, 98, 99, 104, 105, 112–113, 128, 156, 160–161, 164, 166
CEDAW. *See* Convention on the Elimination of all Forms of Discrimination Against Women
Central African Republic, 24–25, 50, 53–54, 56–57, 69, 125–126, 132–133, 135
Centre for Constitutional Rights, 167
Centre for Torture Survivors, 136
Charlesworth, Hilary, 122–123
child soldiers, 7, 24–25, 97, 122–123
Chile, 1–2, 24–25
Chodorow, Nancy J., 46
Chynoweth, Sarah K., 124
civil war, 24, 27
Clark, Janine N., 98–99
Cockburn, Cynthia, 46
Cohen, Dara Key, 65, 66–67, 81, 86–87
Collins, Randall, 84
Colombia, 24–25, 160–161
colonialism, 54–59, 71, 73–74, 125–127
Commission Vérité et Réconciliation, Burundi, 155, 169
compensation hypothesis, 73–74, 107, 108–109, 110
Congo. *See* Democratic Republic of the Congo
Connell, Raewyn, 5, 54–55, 57
constructivism, 18–19
Convention on the Elimination of all Forms of Discrimination Against Women (CEDAW), 163
Cornwall, Andrea, 37
Côte d'Ivoire, 133–134
Coulter, Chris, 69–70
counterinsurgency. *See* insurgency
Croatia, 9–10, 24, 31, 112–113, 128

Danish Refugee Council, 136
Darfur, 32
Del Zotto, Augusta, 22–23, 136–137
Democratic Republic of the Congo, 1–3, 8–10, 12–13, 17, 19–20, 22, 24–25, 27–28, 30–31, 31–32, 32–33, 50–51, 53–54, 55–56, 61–62, 63, 64–65, 69–70, 72–73, 75–76, 76–77, 78, 85, 91–92, 93–94, 98, 100, 103, 104, 106, 115, 116–117, 118, 123–124, 125–126, 132–133, 133–134, 146, 157, 158, 159, 160, 172–173
Detraz, Nicole, 3–4, 115–116, 121
displacement, 11, 26, 29–30, 39–40, 71, 103, 106, 120–121, 121–122, 123–124, 134–135, 157, 163, 174
Dolan, Chris, 20, 144–145, 149, 160, 161–162, 167–168
domestic/intimate partner violence, 7, 30–31, 68–69, 108–109, 133–134
Dowd, Nancy, 54–55
drugs, drug abuse, 77, 85, 101
Duroch, Françoise, 31–32, 140

Edström, Jerker, 109–110
El Salvador, 1–2, 9–10, 24–25, 26
endogamic violence, 4, 35–36, 52–53
Enloe, Cynthia, 8, 32, 39–40, 84, 123
Eriksson Baaz, Maria, 19–20, 73, 76, 83, 84, 85, 112–113, 159
essentialism, 18–19, 121, 123–124, 174
ethnic cleansing, 18, 29, 44–45, 128
ethnic conflict, 6–7, 13–14, 24, 27–28, 29–30, 42, 46–47, 47–48
ethnicity, 1, 3, 4, 5–6, 17, 18–19, 26, 27–30, 32, 35–36, 39, 42, 43–47, 50–51, 104, 105, 120–121, 123–124, 125–126, 128–129, 130, 147, 148–149, 163, 171, 174–175

Faligot, Roger, 74
Fanon, Franz, 57, 73–74
Feldman, Allen, 104

feminization, 1, 3–6, 18–19, 22–23, 29, 35–42, 44–50, 51, 52–56, 59, 73, 78, 97–98, 99, 101–102, 107, 108–109, 120, 127–130, 143, 171–172
First Step Cambodia, 138–139
forced actions:
  circumcision, 22–23, 26, 165–166
  bestiality, 26, 32, 40
  fellatio, 24, 26, 161, 164
  incest, 25–26, 31, 40, 53–54, 65–66, 95–96, 114, 118, 164
  masturbation, 26–27
  nudity, 26–27, 29, 31, 34, 47–48, 54, 65–66, 81
  recruitment, 19–20, 30, 39–40, 61–62, 63–64, 66–67, 72, 80–81, 120–121, 174
former Soviet Union, 24–25
former Yugoslavia, 2–3, 24, 73, 85, 132–133, 138–139, 154, 161
France, French Army, 55–56, 56–57, 69
fraternity group, 45, 50–51
Freccero, Julie, 124
Freedom From Torture, 31–32, 136

gender performativity, 5, 36–37, 38, 40, 41–42, 49–50, 52–56, 59, 74–75, 78, 101–102, 108–109, 129, 171–172, 173
Geneva Centre for the Democratic Control of Armed Forces, 133–134
Geneva Conventions, 47–48, 162, 164, 167
genitals, beating of, 7, 21–22, 26–27, 29, 31, 33–34, 41–42, 44–45, 47–48, 65–66, 104–105, 160–161. *See also* castration
genocide, 8–9, 12–13, 23–24, 27, 28, 29–30, 32, 41, 42, 43, 46, 48–49, 65–66, 68, 75–76, 86, 91–92, 105, 153–154, 162, 164–165
Goldstein, Joshua S., 68, 99
Great Lakes region of Africa, 8–11, 12–15, 25–26, 31, 41–42, 43, 52–53, 72, 80–81, 84–85, 91–92, 93, 95–96, 105, 110, 111
Greece, 1–2, 22–23, 24–25, 32–33
Greening, Megan, 161
Guantánamo, 8–9, 26–27, 29–30, 55–56, 64–65, 73–74, 167
Guatemala, 24–25
guerrilla, 27

Hague Conventions, 162
Haiti, 69
Hampanda, Karen, 101
Hatzfeld, Jean, 86
hegemonic masculinity, 5, 37–38, 40–41, 45, 51, 55–57, 71, 72, 73–74, 88, 115–116, 127–128
Heineman, Elizabeth D., 126–127
heterosexual norms, 3, 13–14, 18–19, 22–23, 36–37, 38, 40, 44–45, 48, 50, 51, 54, 71, 76, 78, 98–99, 123–124, 129–130, 171, 172, 174–175
Higate, Paul, 56–57
Holocaust, 86
homosexuality, homophobia, 12–13, 22–23, 29–30, 35, 43–44, 44–45, 50–51, 55–56, 78, 98–99, 102, 106–107, 110, 112–113, 118, 119, 121–122, 129–130, 137–138, 144–145, 156–157, 161–162, 167–168. *See also* LGBTQI, sexual minorities
Houge, Anette Bringedal, 2–3
Human Rights Watch, 158

ICTR. *See* International Criminal Tribunal for Rwanda
impunity, 15–16, 49–50, 56–57, 83, 113, 147, 150–151, 153–154, 157–158, 159, 167
Institute for International Criminal Investigations, 133–134
insurgency, 6–7, 13–14, 47, 48, 110
International Criminal Court, 15–16, 162, 163–168, 169

International Criminal Tribunal for Rwanda (ICTR), 15–16, 153–154, 162, 163–166
International Criminal Tribunal for the former Yugoslavia (ITCY), 15–16, 76–77, 153–154, 155–156, 162, 163–166, 167–168
International Medical Corps, 136
International Rehabilitation Council for Torture Victims, 136
International Rescue Committee, 25–26, 135
intersectionality, 1–2, 4, 5–6, 18–19, 29–30, 39, 103, 121, 125–126, 149, 171, 174
interstate conflict, 24, 27
intervention, 3–4, 6–7, 13–14, 53–57, 125–127
Iran, 24–25
Iraq, 8–9, 26–27, 55–56, 58, 64–65, 68, 70–71
Israel, 24–25, 55–56, 64–65, 69, 76–77
Istanbul Protocol, 142
ITCY. *See* International Criminal Tribunal for the former Yugoslavia

Jones, Adam, 22–23, 38, 136–137

Kashmir, 24–25, 29–30
Kenya, 24–25, 55–56, 141, 168
King, Kimi Lynn, 161
Kippenberg, Juliane, 160
Kirby, Paul, 19, 150–151
Kosovo, 24, 44
Kuwait, 24–25

Leatherman, Janie, 51
Lebanon, 136
Leiby, Michele, 156
Le Pape, Marc, 143
Lewis, Dustin A., 162

LGBTQI, sexual minorities, 29–30, 46–47, 91–92, 121–122, 172–173. *See also* homosexuality, homophobia
Liberia, 17, 24–25, 64–65, 97
Libya, 8–9
Lieder, Frances K., 125–126
Lindisfarne, Nancy, 37
looting, 18, 19–20, 32, 84, 87
lynching, 54–55

MacKenzie, Megan, 19–20, 43
Manchouria, 53–54
Manivannan, Anjali, 153, 166, 168
McClure, Nicole R., 109–110, 118
McGuffin, John, 74
Médecins Sans Frontières, 12–13, 115, 118, 135
Men of Courage, 137–138
Men of Hope, 137–138
Men of Peace, 137–138
mental health, 8–9, 75, 94, 96–97, 106–107, 114, 130, 134–135, 144–145
Mervyn, Christian, 31–32
Mesoamerica, 22–23
Messerschmidt, James W., 5, 73, 108–109
militarization, militarized masculinity, 6, 14, 18–19, 27–28, 30–31, 39–41, 50–52, 54–57, 59, 61–62, 68–69, 69–70, 70–71, 72, 75, 83, 88, 98, 99, 111–112, 115–116, 148, 151
Moolman, Benita, 82
Morrell, Robert, 111–112
Mullins, Christopher W., 32
mutilation, 7, 17, 21–22, 24, 26, 27–28, 31, 32, 33–34, 35, 40, 44–45, 79, 105–106, 118, 120, 164, 165–166, 167
Myanmar, 132–133
Myrttinen, Henri, 27

Nanking, 23–24, 68
Naš Glas, 138–139

Native American peoples, 22–23, 32–33
Ní Aoláin, Fionnuala, 111–112
Nigeria, 28–29, 135
Nordås, Ragnhild, 150–151
North Kivu, 8–9, 57, 113–114
Northern Ireland, 8–11, 12–13, 15, 64–65, 68, 74, 91–92, 92–93, 104, 109–110, 118
Nturengaho, 136–137
Nuremberg Trials, 153, 162, 164
Nusair, Isis, 55–56

Oloya, Opiyo, 52
OSCE, 156–157, 161
Owens, Patricia, 55–56, 58–59

Palestine, 24–25, 29–30, 64–65, 76–77
Panzi Hospital, 8, 12–13, 25–26, 96
patriarchy, 5, 13–14, 15, 18–19, 19–20, 22–23, 36, 38–39, 42, 43–47, 54, 55–56, 58–59, 61, 69–70, 71, 82, 100, 102, 109, 116–117, 121, 125–128, 129, 130, 171, 172–175
patrilineality, 43, 44–46, 47–48, 128
peacekeeping, peacekeepers, 56–57, 58, 59, 69, 70–71, 73–74, 125, 133–134, 167
Peel, Michael, 28–29, 31–32, 84–85
peer pressure, 75, 76, 77, 82, 86, 154–155
Peru, 21–22, 64–65, 160–161
Physicians for Human Rights, 135
pillaging, 18, 19–20, 32, 84–85, 113
poststructuralism, 5, 123–124
post-traumatic stress. *See* trauma
Price, Lisa S., 73, 83, 154
PRIO, 150–151

Quijano, Anibal, 55–56

race, racism, 18–19, 37, 39, 48–49, 53, 54–57, 58–59, 100, 124–125, 125–126, 127, 163, 164–165
rape:
gang rape, 19–20, 25–26, 31–32, 32–33, 34, 40, 41, 65–66, 81, 86–87, 154, 164;
weapon of war thesis, 2–3, 17, 18, 19–20, 21, 41–42, 124–125, 127, 149, 171, 172
Razack, Sherene, 54
reconciliation, 15, 92, 111–112, 112–113, 117
Refugee Law Project, 24–25, 109–110, 137–138, 139, 144–145, 164–166
refugees, 8–10, 11, 24–25, 29–30, 100, 106–107, 109–110, 121–122, 131–132, 134–135, 136, 137–138, 139, 161–162, 163, 172–173
religion:
religious group, 17, 26–27, 27–28, 29–30, 48–49, 50–51, 55–56, 71, 105, 148–149, 175;
religious identity, 1, 5–6, 30, 35–36, 55–56, 88, 104, 120–121, 136–137, 147, 164–165, 171, 174
reporting, 2–3, 15–16, 21–22, 25–26, 33–34, 65–66, 95, 97–98, 113, 118–119, 140–141, 142, 150–151, 156–157, 167–168
resilience, 8, 12–13, 52–53, 105, 110, 121–122, 171–172, 174
Ricardo, Christine, 65, 70–71, 73–74
Rome Statute of the International Criminal Court, 163–164, 164–165, 167–168
Ross, Marlon B., 48–49, 54–55, 124–125
Rumbold, Victoria, 141
Russell, Wynne, 144
Rwanda, 8–9, 12–13, 24–25, 29, 30, 32, 41, 68, 69–70, 72–73, 76–77, 86, 91–92, 105, 106, 114

Sabo, Don, 1–2
Scarry, Elaine, 125–126, 148
Schulte-Hillen, Catrin, 140
Serbia, 44
SERUKA, 120
Seto, Donna, 121–122
sexual minorities. *See* LGBTQI, sexual minorities
sexual slavery, 7, 17, 32–34, 41, 65–66, 101–102, 164–165
sexual torture, 1–2, 7, 8–9, 17, 21–22, 26–30, 31–32, 33–34, 40–42, 47–50, 53–56, 62–67, 68, 69, 73–74, 78–79, 80–81, 92–93, 104, 105, 106–107, 108, 110, 118, 122–123, 124–125, 129, 132–133, 136–137, 138–139, 155–156, 157, 159, 160–161, 163–166, 167, 172–173, 174
sexual violence in detention, 1–2, 8–9, 11, 14, 17, 22–23, 24, 25–34, 40–42, 47–49, 53–54, 55–56, 64–66, 66–67, 68, 69, 78–80, 84–85, 87, 88–89, 92–93, 99, 102, 104–105, 107, 118–119, 122–123, 124–125, 129–130, 132–133, 138–139, 148–149, 154, 161, 167, 172–173
sexual violence in wartime. *See* wartime sexual violence against boys; wartime sexual violence against women and girls
sexual violence, opportunistic, 18, 19, 21, 24–26, 29–30, 76, 171
sexual violence, prevention of, 15, 94, 108–109, 116, 120–121, 131–135, 140–141, 146, 148–151, 153–154, 172–173, 174
sexual violence, publicity of, 1–2, 31, 34, 40, 64–65, 86–87, 118–119
shame, 31, 77, 78, 81, 88, 95–98, 99, 101–102, 105, 106–107, 113–114, 119, 120, 129–130, 140–141, 144–145, 156–157
Sierra Leone, 17, 24–25, 33–34, 64–65, 66–67, 69–70, 153–154, 164–165, 168

Silberschmidt, Margrethe, 73
silence, 10–11, 11–12, 15, 25–26, 48, 102, 104, 107, 111, 113, 116–117, 120, 123–124, 127, 128, 129–130, 140–141, 156, 172, 175
Silent Scream (Nečujni Krik), 24
Sivakumaran, Sandesh, 22–23, 44–45, 122–123, 149–150
Skjelsbæk, Inger, 18–19, 75, 76, 82, 151
Sooka, Yasmin, 68, 85
South Africa, 54–55, 65, 111–112, 168
South Kivu, 8–9, 12–13, 25–26, 95–96, 101–102, 113
South Sudan, 24–25, 133–134
Special Court for Sierra Leone, 164–165, 165–166
Sri Lanka, 9–10, 24–27, 27–28, 28–29, 29–30, 31–32, 33–34, 53–54, 64–65, 68, 69–70, 75–76, 76–77, 85, 91–92, 105, 125–126, 150–151, 159
Stemple, Lara, 163
Stern, Maria, 19–20, 73, 84, 112–113
Stiglmayer, Alexandra, 19–20
stigma, 10–11, 49–50, 61–62, 71, 77, 100, 121–122, 132, 134–135, 140, 144–145, 156–157, 171–172
structuralism, 5, 18–19
Sudan, 9–10, 24–25, 132–133
suicide, suicidal thoughts, 96–97, 106, 119
survivors' groups, 15, 91–92, 109–110, 131–132, 134–135, 136, 137–139, 145
Syria, 8–10, 17, 24–25, 26–27, 27–28, 33–34, 132–133

taboo, 11, 12–13, 22–23, 32, 34, 40, 48, 49–50, 51, 52, 62–63, 65–66, 67, 73, 83, 84–85, 87, 97, 109–110, 113, 117, 129, 156
Tanzania, 65
Terrell, Carver, 52–53
Timor Leste, 168
Tokyo Trials, 153, 162, 164

Touquet, Heleen, 124
traditional tribunals, 12–13, 159
trauma, 3–4, 10–11, 11–12, 25–26, 75, 80–81, 96–97, 98, 99, 108, 114, 118, 130, 143, 147, 148–149
Trexler, Richard C., 32–33
Truth and Reconciliation Commission, South Africa, 168
Truth, Justice and Reconciliation Commission, Kenya, 168

Uganda, 9–10, 24–25, 26, 52, 109–110, 125–126, 137–139, 145, 161–162
Ukraine, 24–25
UNHCR, 132–133, 134–135, 136, 144–145, 145–146
United Kingdom, UK Army, 55–56, 64–65, 68
United Nations, 56–57, 58, 73–74, 125, 131, 132–135, 146, 164–165, 167
Universal Declaration of Human Rights, 162
United States, US Army, 54–56, 57, 58, 64–65, 69, 70–71, 99, 167
UNRWA, 136
UNSC Resolution 1325, 120–121, 121–122, 122–123
UNSC Resolution 1487, 167
UNSC Resolution 1820, 18, 121–123, 123–124
UNSC Resolution 1888, 121–122
UNSC Resolution 1889, 121–122
UNSC Resolution 1960, 121–122
UNSC Resolution 2106, 121–122
UNSC Resolution 2122, 121–122
UN Security Council, 18, 167
US Department of Defense, 22

Vaittinen, Tiina, 132, 143
Vietnam, 55–56, 99
violence. *See* forced actions; mutilation; *specific types*
Vojdik, Valorie K., 4, 36–37, 39
vulnerability, invulnerability, 3–6, 15, 44–45, 48, 87, 103, 106–107, 115–116, 116–117, 122–123, 125, 127–130, 134–135, 143, 144, 147, 148–149, 161, 163, 175

wartime sexual violence against boys, 1–2, 7, 22–23, 25–26, 30, 31, 32–33, 40, 53–54, 63–64, 69, 82, 106, 107, 120, 122–123, 124, 125, 132–133, 133–134, 165–166, 172
wartime sexual violence against women and girls, 1–3, 4, 5–6, 7, 8, 11, 14, 17, 18–19, 21–22, 25–26, 27, 29, 34, 36–39, 40, 41, 43, 44–45, 47, 50, 52, 57, 59, 61, 63–64, 67, 68, 69, 74–77, 80–81, 82, 84–85, 86–87, 93, 104, 108–109, 111–112, 112–113, 114, 115–116, 123, 124–126, 132–133, 134–135, 145–146, 148, 149–150, 153, 156–158, 164–166, 172–173, 174
Weishut, Daniel J. N., 55–56, 64–65
Wood, Elisabeth Jean, 18, 64–65, 150–151
World Health Organization, 7, 134–135

Zarkov, Dubravka, 2–3, 128
Zawati, Hilmi M, 22–23, 167

About the Author

Élise Féron is a docent and a university researcher at the Tampere Peace Research Institute (Finland). She is also a professor at the Université Lumière de Bujumbura (Burundi) where she co-convenes a Gender Studies Master Programme. She has extensive fieldwork experience in the Great Lakes region of Africa, but also in Northern Ireland and in the Caucasus. Her main research interests include sexual violence in conflict settings, gender and peace negotiations, as well as diasporas and conflicts. She is a member of the Feminist Peace Research Network, and she has been intervening as a gender and conflict expert for various institutions such as the European Commission, UNESCO, UN Women and the International Labour Organization.

Manufactured by Amazon.ca
Bolton, ON